TRAVEL VANS

Contents

Chapters

About the Author

JOHN SPEED was born in North Staffordshire in 1948 of parents from the Potteries and the Moorlands of Leek. From his earliest years he developed a taste for the excitement of travel through the 'epic' holiday journeys to Cornwall as a child in the days before motorways.

He gained a bachelor of science degree in mechanical engineering with economics and accountancy at University in Scotland.

After working 'on the road' as a rigger, electrician and lighting designer in the music business, John founded a company designing, developing and manufacturing a specialised range of computer controlled stage lighting systems, engineered to ensure that the touring stage extravaganzas would go on at a new venue every day in time and in style.

John's interests include writing and travelling, particularly in his motorcaravan, discovering new vistas and challenges and returning to old haunts. Now living high in the Pyrenees he is well placed for exploration of Europe and the not too distant lure of Africa. He enjoys both skiing and hiking in the mountains and scuba diving.

As an engineer, John says that the self-built motorcaravan is one of the best Mecano sets one could wish for, as it incorporates such a broad range of scientific disciplines. Best of all one can climb inside and drive it, eat and sleep in it too, and have a shower inside to boot. And one can take it away on holiday.

Cover picture
The author sitting on top of the cab of a Unimog expedition motorcaravan.

Acknowledgements

The Author would like to thank:
Aimee and Martin, for their dedicated proofreading, encouragement and invaluable input. Bob and Ray for their additional proofreading and helpful advice.
Christine, Stuart, Monique, Janet, Roger, Claire, and Josiah, whose enthusiasm helped to keep him on course.
Werner, without whose assistance, skill, commitment to quality, and search for perfection, the project may not have reached beyond a dream.
Mike and Maureen for spurring everyone on. Marcus, Maggie, Julian, and Norman for leading him 'off-piste'.
The staff at GeoPrisa.
Special thanks to Manel.
All the others who helped in many different ways.

A GEOPRISA BOOK

First published in 1996 by
GeoPrisa SL
BP31 La Massana, Andorra.

Designed and edited by GeoPrisa.

A CIP catalogue record for this book is available from the Andorran Library.

ISBN 99920-1-158-0
Dip. Legal 289-1996

Opposite: A superb, robust, expedition quality, motorcaravan which was built by 'Grand Erg' of Milan. It features a Man-Meccanica MM F99 4x4 chassis with a 3.2 metre wheelbase. The overall length is 6.4 metres, the height 3.26 metres, the width 2.3 metres and the maximum gross weight 7500 kg.

TRAVEL VANS

A BOOK ABOUT **CARAVANS**

MOTORCARAVANS

and their use

JOHN SPEED

GeoPrisa Publications

A delightful Dutch-owned Citroen 'H' van conversion waiting to board the Dover ferry at Calais. Vans with vertical flat sides make for easier internal conversion work.

PREFACE

The purpose of this book is to offer any keen caravanner a little indulgence in their favourite activity. It also goes much further, providing details of techniques that may be used, not only in the basic construction of a caravan and in the modification of ready built caravans, (from the raw components and accessories), but also in the building of sophisticated expedition vehicles. By way of example, these techniques are explained with reference to a continuous four month conversion of a panel van that I undertook towards the end of 1993. This conversion was to my design based on my specific requirements.

I enjoy camping in its several formats including in tents, particularly in the more remote environments in which I like to hike. When on the road my personal preference is to use a motor caravan but I recognise the clear advantages of a trailer caravan. Whilst the constructional detail and textual reference is mainly based on motor caravans, the cross over between trailer and motor caravans is so wide that in most cases the text is equally relevant to both and I trust that the reader will forgive me for not continually mentioning both. Much of the technology is equally relevant to boats.

There are different ways to build a caravan and many possibilities for the internal layout. Each no doubt has its merits and shortfalls. Ultimately however it is the user who must decide what is best for him or her and there is little doubt, after all, that the needs of a family of six are unlikely to coincide exactly with those of a hermit.

Given these clear variations in individual requirements I most certainly do not claim to offer the ultimate solution and I cannot for one moment hope to offer the best suggestions regarding the best base vehicle, van layout, or range of internal systems. After all my huge efforts my van certainly does not offer this for me, and so too, others are likely to be thwarted. The unavoidable, obliged compromise will always rear its head.

Nevertheless I have employed many techniques and systems in my van which have evolved over years of experiences and which subsequently have proved to meet the design criteria, and work as well as, or better than, planned or hoped. It is likely that some or even all of them will offer the reader details and information that may be adapted to their own ambitions, projects and applications, no matter how large or small.

Regarding the sections covering the details of everyday caravanning, I have tried to cover relevant aspects of the 'nitty-gritty' of actually being out there, dealing with the kinds of experiences which a traveller cannot avoid, and in many cases, with adequate forewarning, will not want to avoid because these experiences are the very spice of being on the road. I offer advance notice of some situations one most definitely will want to avoid, and which, with a little care and basic common sense, should have no difficulty in doing so.

Good luck and happy travelling! John Speed-Andorra 1995

An Aegean campsite, beside the sea, with very welcome raffia covered plots (though not ideal for caravans with solar panels on the roof which only work efficiently away from any shade!). The chairs provided here, whilst not the most photogenic, are useful provisions.

INTRODUCTION

Every journey is an adventure and sometimes more so than arriving at the destination. The extended trip can provide the most interesting experiences and what is more, with a conducive frame of mind and the opportunity not to rush, the developments and encounters along the way may prove to be the most rewarding. The tendency in our busy world, however, is to arrive as quickly as possible (indeed the journey is all too often totally discounted as the necessary evil we have no choice but to endure in order to reach our destination). In this process we not only deprive ourselves of interests along the way, but also expose ourselves to additional stress and the increased dangers associated with higher speed travelling.

The traveller often feels in a state of limbo, neither here nor there, so that the sooner he or she arrives the better.

I suspect that most caravanners know more which is perhaps one of the differences that sets them apart. With one's caravan and the right frame of mind, a simple philosophy, we need never be in limbo.

We are in fact always at home; we are the literal armchair travellers. We can be as in the thick of it as we want, with all our senses stimulated, or, when we have had enough, we can withdraw into our private, little world where we are able to recline in the comfort of our 'home', relax and revitalise until we are ready for the next adventure.

It is a little like changing channels on television but with full participation. We have 'Top Gear' at the front, the 'Soap' at the back and 'World About Us' outside to mention but three of the vast array of programs at our disposal.

Of course this type of viewing is not for everyone and luckily for the others they may never know what they are missing. This knowledge is what makes the difference. It is little wonder that the hobby of caravanning is gaining popularity and this is perhaps no more noticeable than out on the road where a trip along any highway is a good opportunity to observe many varieties and styles of travelling homes. For me at least, this provides a regular source of interest, to see how others turn out in their home on wheels and I often wonder what trip is in store for them. Where are they going? Where have they been?

Furthermore, motorcaravan owners seem to manage to locate the most interesting and remote places and it is unusual not to find a representation in the vicinity of beauty spots, however isolated. They have a habit of finding the pretty places. There is quite an art in knowing where to look and caravanners seem to have the knack.

I am sure that another reason for the increase in popularity of motor-caravanning in particular, is the wide range of luxuriously appointed vehicles now available at prices to suit almost everyone. The cost of a holiday in a van, particularly an extended holiday, can be significantly cheaper than the more traditional alternatives.

For me there was never any real doubt; it was just a question of time before I would have my own motorcaravan. The experience of time has shown, however, that the chances of acquiring the right vehicle at the first attempt are low. Only by trial and error is one going to discover what one is really looking for. Hence, for the uninitiated, I would recommend making efforts to gain as much experience as possible of using caravans and motorcaravans before taking the plunge and buying.

Furthermore, I hope that by the time you have read this book you will be better equipped to make your decision if you have not already done so.

I have to say that originally I rushed out and bought a van before I had really found out what I needed and it was an expensive mistake but perhaps really the best way to learn. Do consider renting a van though.

If, on the other hand, you already have your own rig, I hope you find enjoyment in this indulgence of mine in our mutually favourite world and also that you take an interest in some of the alternative technology which I have employed.

Even though you may already have experience of owning or using a caravan or motorcaravan and have developed your ideas of a preferred type of van and layout and its attributes, you may still have some unanswered questions or unsolved problems. It is my hope that some of the solutions may lie within these pages.

There is a vast array of fine vehicles now available 'off-the-shelf', some of which have evolved (often at great expense) through the years at the hands and minds of skilful developers. Many of them (inevitably not all) are available with conscientious after sales support. Consequently there is something for nearly everyone. Alas my requirements seemed rather different from every vehicle I investigated or owned.

Unfortunately almost the only way to approach acquiring exactly what you want is to build it yourself or pay someone else to do it for you. My decision was a combination of the two. I knew what I wanted but I was concerned that I had neither the skills nor the equipment to create the professional finish.

Technically I was reasonably sure that I was sufficiently skilled to install the electrics, plumbing and heating. With regard to carpentry, however, I was neither adequately trained nor in possession of enough specialised machinery although I had a good idea of the standards and finishes I was looking for.

The construction of a motorcaravan must be designed to cope satisfactorily with both vibrations from driving, and also varying rates of expansion and contraction of different construction materials. This differential movement results from the large temperature variations to which the van will surely be subjected, from the well below freezing temperatures of winter to the scorching heat from the sun's rays burning through clear skies in the summer, when the build up of heat inside a vehicle can be very significant. These additional demands require special consideration and experience.

I already had experience of several specialist companies' work on expedition vehicles used for professional applications in 'out of the way' places, and I had been impressed with their methods of dealing with an unusual set of problems.

When a multi-talented cabinet-maker with whom I had enjoyed working in one of these organisations, set up in business on his own in a well-equipped woodworking facility, my path seemed clearly marked. With our combined skills and his workshop, we should surely be able to create my ideal motorcaravan. The workshop had a bathroom, a shower and an out of the way room in which I could make my bed. Here, we planned, I could stay when necessary. We estimated that the project would take one complete month as well as a built-in contingency allowance of an extra month. The work ended up taking the best part of an accumulated five months!

Coming, as I had, from the manufacturing industry I might have expected to estimate more accurately, but sometimes, it seems, we just never learn! Nevertheless, the quality of the finished product surpassed my original hopes, not least as a result of the skills and unswerving attention to detail of Werner the cabinet maker. At times, when I wished for more detail but felt it was too much to ask, as if telepathically, he set about providing it. On occasions,.when I wanted to opt for less, his commitment to detail obliged me to do it right.

One may wonder what makes my van different from many others, and in a word the answer is '**autonomy**' - the facility to be able to survive in remote regions for extended periods without having to reconnect the umbilical cords, be it the water hose or the electrical '**hook-up**'.

The *water* issue is fairly easy to solve. I have included a four hundred litre fresh water tank that, when necessary and with care, is sufficient to keep thirst at bay for many days.

Electrically, an array of solar panels on my roof provides almost all the energy I have ever needed.

Another aspect of particular importance to me is **storage** and plenty of it. I wanted enough space **inside the van** to be able to carry lots of equipment: motor bike, bicycles, boat, engine, diving equipment, table, chairs and any of the paraphernalia caravanners like to have handy!

I have located this large storage capacity at the back of the van beneath the **permanent double bed**, (another essential part of my specification), with access from outside through the rear double doors.

Having searched for an 'off-the-shelf' model that offered me all the above and also in the way I wanted, it became quite clear that my motorcaravan specification was indeed different. To end up with just what I wanted there was no choice for me but to custom build my motorcaravan.

As it has subsequently turned out the final product has an air of having done it right. Like all things it is not perfect but it is a pleasure to use and the more often I am able to use it the better. ☺

Caravans waiting at Calais for late ferries to take them to Dover. Great savings can be made by catching night ferries.

CHAPTER 1

TYPES OF MOTORCARAVAN and the BASE VEHICLE

There are so many different types of motorcaravan, base vehicle and body combinations and such a wide array of internal layouts possible, not to mention the long list of facilities and features available, that the prospective buyer or builder might easily be confused and not know where to start. The easy answer may be to take the advice of the salesperson, who hopefully is conscientious and has sufficient wisdom and experience to offer the right answers. He will almost certainly be biased.

With careful consideration to the following pages, I am sure readers will find themselves rather better equipped both to understand the sales representatives' explanations and advice, and also to decide for themselves which features really are important to their needs.

Everyone has their ideas about what the word 'motorcaravan' means and the sort of facilities they expect to be incorporated. The purpose of this chapter is to explain some basics about the types of van available 'off-the-shelf'. (Although I have seen huge boat warehouses with rather large boats and yachts stored on shelves I have yet to see the motor caravan counterpart.)

TYPES OF MOTORCARAVAN

FIXED ROOF

A panel van conversion without standing height.

A 1965, 21 window, VW Samba with sunroof.

St. Michel by Island Plastics

FIXED HIGH ROOF

A panel van conversion
with standing height,
due to the commercial vehicle
manufacturer's high roof option,
either steel or glass fibre.

RISING ROOF

A panel van conversion with standing height,
due to the addition, by the converter,
of a roof that can be raised,
usually a combination of glass fibre top with
glass fibre or fabric sides.

Cockburn Holdsworth Villa

HIGH TOP

A panel van conversion with standing height, due to the addition, by the converter, of a permanent high roof, usually insulated glass fibre.

Swift Mondial

Compass Caravel on a Mercedes Sprinter chassis

COACHBUILT

A commercial chassis-cab base vehicle, with a coachbuilt caravan body or box, fixed to the chassis.

The driver's cab of this type, is the original commercial vehicle cab.

The rear cab wall is usually removed, and the caravan body joined to the cab, to create the desirable, clear 'walk-through' from the cab to the caravan body.

The caravan body is usually extended over the top of the cab to provide the popular 'luton' over-cab bed.

FFB Classic.

A-CLASS COACHBUILT or INTEGRATED or INTEGRAL

A commercial chassis-cowl base vehicle with a coachbuilt caravan body and integrated cab fixed to the base vehicle. The body of the driver's cab of the A-Class is coachbuilt and therefore unique to the coachbuilder.

DISMOUNTABLE

A commercial pick-up or flatbed truck base vehicle, with a coachbuilt caravan body or box, that may be removed, usually by legs lowered from the box to the ground.

The pick-up may then be driven away from under the box and used separately.

Margrove "Freeway" Demountable 9' x 6' x 6' luton coachbuilt bodyshell designed to fit most one ton pick-up trucks.

RECREATIONAL VEHICLE (RV)

RV is the generic term used in America for all the seven types of motorcaravan.

CAMPER, CAMPERVAN, CAMPING CAR or CAMPMOBILE

Generic terms for any of the seven types of motorcaravan.

Size and Price

These seven types should cover the whole range of motorcaravans. In size they can vary from 4 metres (13 ft) to over 12 metres (40 ft) in length, from 1.5 metres (5 ft) to over 2.5 metres (8 ft) wide and from 1.8 metres (6 ft) to over 3 metres (10 ft) high.

The price variation is equally wide, from a few thousand pounds to well over a hundred thousand pounds, with several hundred thousand pounds in some extreme cases. The more expensive versions often look similar to modern coaches.

Dual Purpose Facilities

Smaller vehicles usually have facilities with double functions, for example double beds may only be available by converting seats, work surfaces may have a sink or cooker beneath, and driver's cabs may turn into living rooms or bedrooms.

The larger the vehicle's interior, the less likely is the need to rearrange equipment to convert from one use to another.

Single Purpose Facilities

To have a motorcaravan with everything in its own permanent place, so that nothing needs to be converted, will require approximate minimum dimensions of 6.5 metres length, 2.2 metres width and a height of 2.7 metres, (the exception being with the use of a luton). This size would allow one permanent double bed, a permanent kitchen, bathroom, living room and driver's cab. It is a layout of this type which is described in detail in Chapter 7.

To incorporate these facilities in a smaller space usually requires a compromise. The most common is to combine the double bed with the living room or diner, so that going to bed requires conversion of the living room into a double bed. However, there is a way round this situation by the use of a 'luton' over-cab double bed. This is a common practice which has created the familiar appearance of the instantly recognisable 'coachbuilt' type of motorcaravan. The system works well, making full use of available space, and is probably the only way to have a permanent double bed as well as a kitchen, dining room and bathroom in a vehicle shorter than about six and a half metres (21 ft).

The A-Class Coachbuilt or Integrated motorcaravan refines this technique by integrating the cab with the body.

Standing Height

In the interests of comfort, an area which is high enough to stand in and also to step into from outside is desirable. This means a free height, above floor level, of 1830 mm (6 ft) for most people. As many extra inches of height as possible are required if we are to accommodate the taller person, without having to stoop. It is therefore a fact that, given a minimum likely wheel radius of 380 mm (15 inches), the motorhome with fixed internal standing height is unlikely to have an overall height of less than about two and a half metres (8 ft).

Width

Motorcaravan widths are as much as two and a half metres (8 ft) wide which can contribute to wonderful internal luxury, but may just pose a problem when it comes to manoeuvring through those narrow streets that we really do not want to miss. On the other hand, it is clear that tourist buses of such widths manage to reach most places. My preference is to try to find a compromise on width. As narrow as possible, without compromising comfort too much. My van is about 2.25 metres wide overall but it tapers at the top, which can be useful when avoiding overhanging balconies in narrow streets.

Weights

3.5 tonnes

At the time of writing, by far the largest group of motorcaravans weigh in under the maximum permissible weight category of 3.5 tonnes, and are indeed fairly manageable and easily driven vehicles.

The majority are based on panel vans and chassis cabs, modern versions of which are well designed for easy, comfortable driving and, like cars, are improving constantly.

Almost gone are the days of the production of very noisy, uncomfortable vans and trucks. The manufacturers now recognise that a comfortable driver will be safer and more productive, and subsequently therefore, a better customer.

These transporters, however, particularly the diesel engined versions, do not yet offer the same standard of comfort and driveability as the domestic car, not least concerning engine noise levels. It is not easy to overcome all the origins of the commercial vehicle, but the various options can help significantly to make driving these vehicles as effortless and enjoyable as possible.

3.5 tonnes to 7.5 tonnes

Regarding this larger class of vehicles it should be noted that, at present, the UK driving licence Group C1 allows the holder to drive vehicles up to 7.5 tonnes maximum mass. This is the category awarded, following successful negotiation of the car driving test, for the time being.

This is also the case in Germany. In France and Switzerland the weight limit awarded following a successful driving test is 3.5 tonnes.

However, under the United Nations Conference Treaty on Road Traffic 1968, (which France ratified in 1977), a licence issued in any member country is acceptable in the country of the signatories. (Similarly, if a car satisfies the construction and use regulations in its country, it is acceptable in the country of the signatories.)

Consequently a person with the older type licence with Category A entitlement, or the newer European Community format licence with Category C1 entitlement, is allowed, at the time of writing, to drive a vehicle of up to 7.5 tonnes maximum permissible weight throughout Europe.

According to The UK Department of Transport these drivers will also have continuing entitlement to drive these vehicles and they will not need to take a further test.

In the UK, an ordinary licence entitling the holder to drive a motor car with Category A entitlement, used to allow the holder to drive trucks of weights up to the old UK so-called '3 ton truck' which was a quite substantial vehicle with as big as twenty inch radius wheels. This vehicle was approximately the equivalent of the new classification of 7.49 tonnes maximum permissible weight. The former 3 ton classification referred to the load capacity and not the nowadays, more important, total permissible weight.

Second-Hand Vehicles

Whilst the price variations are great between the cheapest and most expensive models, as always it is possible to cheat the price barriers by buying second-hand. It should be possible to find a five year old A-Class Coachbuilt at the same price as a new High Top and you would, with luck, have better value for money. An A-Class however, is likely to be a rather larger vehicle than a High Top. With the extra size you have a vehicle which is in a much larger class than the average car or small panel van and so cannot be as manoeuvrable, but there will be a higher level of comfort inside the living area, and almost everyone eventually gets used to driving the larger size.

There is, however, always a risk when buying second-hand. It is unlikely that you are going to have any knowledge of the former owner's attitude towards his vehicles and their upkeep. The more miles the vehicle has covered the sooner parts start to wear out and large service bills begin to come in. Some people are good at buying second-hand, while others are just lucky. The opposite can also apply. Unless the buyer is an expert, (even then they cannot be sure), it is the unseen that can be the problem with a second-hand vehicle. If the price is right, and it is a low mileage vehicle which the owner cared for, there is a good chance that any little problems will have been sorted out and you might be lucky. If at all possible though, I would not recommend making a quick decision, at least try to sleep on it. Maybe enlist the help of a knowledgeable friend or professional organisation which specialises in advising second hand buyers, and if you decide that you like the vehicle enough to want to own it, perhaps it should be on the condition that the price is lowered and some sort of worthwhile guarantee is included. If a higher mileage vehicle is bought, it would be a wise precaution to join one of the automobile clubs to avoid recovery costs following a more probable breakdown.

The Base Vehicle

At the time of writing, the following table is an indication of most of the base vehicles which are available as panel van, chassis cab or chassis cowl. They offer a variation of payloads, wheelbases and options depending on models.

Clearly it will always be appropriate to check specifics with the manufacturers. It is quite usual for them to make different options available according to the country although the reasoning behind their decisions can be hard to fathom. However, any reader prepared to go to the considerable trouble of checking the markets in other countries may find not only variations in specifications but also considerable price differences. ☼

	Front/Rear Wheel Drive	Petrol (L=Litres)	Diesel (L=Litres)	Options
Citroen C15	FWD	4spd 1.1L	5spd 1.8L	
Fiat Ducato	FWD	5spd 2L	5spd 1.9L 5spd 2.5L	Turbo, Power Steering 4WD (2923 SWB only)
Fiat Talento	FWD		5spd 1.9L	
Ford Courier	FWD	5spd 1.3L	5spd 1.8L	Power Steering, Auto
Ford Transit	RWD	5spd 2L 5spd 2L FI 5spd 2.9L FI	5spd 2.5L	Turbo, Auto, ABS Power Steering Limited Slip Diff.
Iveco Ford	RWD		5spd 2.5L	Turbo, ABS
Mazda	FWD	5spd 2L	5spd 2.2L	Power Steering
Mercedes Benz 210, 214, 310, 510 208D, 308D, 508D 212D, 310D, 410D, 312D, 412D, 609D, 709D, 711D 809D, 811D, 814D	RWD	5spd 2.3L	5spd 2.3L 5spd 2.9L 5spd 4L 5spd 4L	Turbo, Power Steering ABS, 4WD Diff. Locks A.C., Auto (WB 3150,3700,4250)
Nissan Serena	FWD	5spd 1.6L 5spd 2L	5spd 2.3L	Power Steering
Nissan Urvan	RWD	5spd 2L	5spd 2.5L	
Nissan Vanette	RWD	5spd 1.5L	5spd 2L	
Peugeot Boxer	FWD	5spd 2L	5spd 1.9L 5spd 2.5L	Turbo, Power Steering
Talbot Express	FWD	5spd 2L	5spd 1.9L 5spd 2.5L	Turbo, Power Steering 4WD
Renault Extra	FWD	5spd 1.4L	5spd 1.6L	Power Steering
Renault Traffic	FWD	5spd 1.7L 5spd 2L	5spd 2.1L 5spd 2.5L	
Renault Master	FWD		5spd 2.5L	Turbo, Power Steering (WB 3200,3840)
Toyota Hi-Ace	RWD	5spd 2L	5spd 2.4L	
Toyota Lite-Ace	RWD	5spd 1.5L	5spd 2L	
Vauxhall Midi	RWD	5spd 2L	5spd 2.2L	
Volkswagen LT	RWD	5spd 2.4L	5spd 2.4L	Turbo, Power Steering
Volkswagen T4	FWD	5spd 2L 5spd 2.5L	5spd 1.9L 5spd 2.4L	Turbo, Power Steering Auto, 4WD

Base vehicle specification of the most commonly used types

A large coach-towed caravan, parked on hardstanding, at Ouarzazate campsite on the northern edge of the Sahara Desert in Morocco.

This is the astonishing sight of a Rotel Tours rig. The company, based in Passau Germany, take coaches full of tourists, with towed caravans, to remote locations. For more challenging excursions they are supported by an additional six wheel drive tow truck.

The caravan itself has, amongst other facilities, forty-two single bedrooms each with its own window. Do not select a pitch too close to one of these monsters as they strike camp at about 4 a.m., and no matter how hard they may or may not try, forty-two people cannot get up, wash, dress, and have breakfast quietly. Nor can the coach warm up its engine in silence. If I had known, I would not have parked my white jeep where you see it on the left!

An Elddis Highwayman on a Peugeot chassis

CHAPTER 2

PLACES TO GO

The obvious and first choice of destination should always be the campsite somewhere along, or at the end of, the road. It is our oasis, and the choice is often vast, with a reasonable likelihood that a welcome awaits at any of the many wonderful sites; what could be more comforting? But remember, now you are equipped with your shell, you can go almost anywhere along the millions of miles of highways and byways, and you have the means to stop in comfort, even without overnighting within the confines of a safe haven. The campsite is not the only safe place to stop for the night.

A wise camper will always give very careful consideration to where he is going to park up and be able to sleep without fear of unreasonable disturbance.

There are several philosophies from which one could approach the issue of safety whilst living in a camper van. Mine has been to err on the side of caution, as I think that there is no point in tempting providence.

There is no question that there are many people out on the road who earn their living by theft, and their compassion for the traveller is not a virtue on which we should rely. The multitude of horror stories we hear, quite clearly, should signal us to be on our guard.

We must find a routine, which is not a chore but a simple set of rules which we obey, in order that we may minimise the chances of our holiday being marred, if not ruined, by careless exposure to the opportunist thief. Later in the book, in the chapters on wild camping and security, I look more closely at some of the precautions we might consider taking.

How the world has opened up for us. Our cars offer us the opportunity to travel in comfort but the motorcaravan is different. We do not have to go home in the evening or to find a hotel, and what is more, whenever we want to stop for a cup of tea or a rest nothing could be simpler.

Any quiet or noisy spot, if you prefer, will do. You have your sanctuary with you and it is homely, warm, comfortable, and relaxing. Lie down if you like and rest, or make a snack or cook a favourite dish. You are now in a different world and you can start to explore the possibilities in a more earthy way.

I certainly do not advocate staying in the van and avoiding contact with the outside world but now you have the choice. You are no longer obliged to eat every meal out. Instead the restaurant can be the treat when you choose it rather than the necessity. You still have the choice to take a hotel for a night or two if you wish or are feeling flush.

The decision is yours. Chase your rainbows, look at the stars. Nestle amongst the peaks and brace the elements.

The first place for the British to explore just has to be Britain. England, Wales, Scotland and Ireland are so full of treasures that the traveller can find a vast array of beauty and history without leaving the shores of their own country. Britain offers lush green countryside, picturesque villages, hills and dales, moorlands, glens, lochs and forests, harbours and coastline, castles and grand houses, jewels and paintings, flora and fauna, cities, theatre, music and entertainment, to mention some.

The caravanner can roam through Britain, staying in the many campsites, either the custom-built with all facilities in popular areas, or the more select certified (certificated) locations, offering the most basic amenities in remote and secluded fields.

It may be that the lure of other countries and perhaps rumours of better weather will attract the traveller (and why not?). Crossing the English Channel to France, Belgium and Holland could not be easier or quicker, while longer distance ferries - for those who wish to take advantage of the benefits of spending one or more days and nights on board - sail to Spain, Norway or Denmark. These overnight ferries present a way of taking the caravan greater distances with less effort and can be an efficient means of travelling to more distant lands, when holidaying for relatively short durations.

The only restriction on driving is the time available. All the countries of Europe are readily accessible and have much to offer the caravanner. Both the standards and the quantity of the 'continental' campsites are legendary.

Of late, the countries of the former Eastern Bloc have opened their doors, are only too aware of the demands of tourism, and are welcoming visits from caravanners. Such countries can provide the tourist with a more challenging holiday and an opportunity to gain a first-hand insight into hitherto less visited lands.

Africa is a whole challenge unto itself and the more adventurous tourist need look no further. Morocco is a country where things are different from 'the norm' as most motorcaravanners know it. Some of the camping sites can leave much to be desired and the tourist can find it an intense and trying experience, but nevertheless, with the right frame of mind, it can be highly rewarding. The main roads are generally good.

To venture further into Africa requires careful planning and vehicle preparation, and in particular investigation into the current political climate and to specialised literature.

To travel beyond Europe with a motorcaravan is only for the few, but for those with both the time and the money, not to mention the stamina and will, it does appear that there are no limits to the possibilities. Indeed, from time to time, we hear of intrepid travellers who have ventured in their motorcaravans into the most distant lands, even as far as Australia. Clearly the farther one takes ones van the better equipped one ought to be. ❖

Driving down through the Todra Gorge in Morocco

The attractive palmed campsite at the southern end of the Todra Gorge in Morocco.

Putts Corner Caravan Club campsite near Honiton in Devon. This fine open site, one of many operated by The Caravan Club, is surrounded by trees which shelter it from all directions. Situated in an area known for its mild climate, this is one of the sites which the club has selected to restrict to members only.

CHAPTER 3

CAMPSITES

The campsite is the caravaner's oasis. For most, after a long drive, it is the home from home.
It is the pot of gold at the end of the rainbow.
It is the port in a storm.

Throughout the World there are innumerable campsites waiting to make us welcome with, at very least, a place to park our van for as long as we wish. Of course we have all grown accustomed to expecting rather more, and the array of comforts and facilities which are usually available all help to make the modern campsite a very viable alternative to hotel accommodation. In fact some people do not like sleeping in hotel beds, preferring the reliability of that in their caravan.

How to find them

The big four British camping, caravanning and motor caravanning clubs offer Camping Site Directories for Britain and Europe, listing many thousands of sites from the exclusive CLs, (Certified or Certificated Locations consisting of small sites usually in farmers' fields often, but by no means always, with limited facilities), up to the 'fully loaded', quality sites which can include, hardstandings (pitches with concrete surfaces), toilets, wash and shower rooms, razor points, hot and cold water, drinking water taps, laundry rooms, electrical hook ups, supermarkets, cafés, restaurants, swimming pools, telephones and more. The better travel bookshops also sell various campsite directories.

It has to be said however, that there are so many sites in existence, particularly in the vicinity of beauty spots, that it is not difficult to find one when the time of day has come to start looking, (please note that all-year-open sites are harder to find). Furthermore, there is usually a choice, although the better ones are often the first to fill up at the busiest times and places. The only way to guarantee a placing during busy holiday periods is to book in advance.

Sites are usually well signposted in advance and it is not unusual, when once on the track of one, to encounter others along the way. At such times there is no reason not to ask permission to look around each one before selecting the most suitable. This is particularly sensible if a few days' stay is contemplated and the facilities are to be best enjoyed.

Sometimes one is lucky enough to stumble on a particularly lovely site, one that has that extra special 'something', often resulting from a combination of caring owners and fine location. These are the ones that are remembered with affection and are those to which campers return. If you hear about one and intend to visit in August, the busiest month, then it would be wise to book in advance.

A good place to learn of some of these treasures is in the caravan and motorcaravan magazines; the excellent 'MMM', for example, often has articles contributed by readers describing sites worthy of recommendation to others.

Many campsites have their own free brochures, stickers and maps of both the site and the surrounding attractions. Apart from providing a useful insight into where you are and what is on offer, these can be useful for reminding you, when back home, just how enjoyable the site was.

Prices

The costs tend to vary with the time of the year. July and August, being the busiest, may cost the most. A basic CL site in a field is not going to be expensive and about three or four pounds in 1996 is likely.

Some countries can be more expensive than others and I paid the equivalent of fifteen pounds for one night for a couple and a motorcaravan at a scruffy site in Italy in 1993.

Currently, one might hope to pay less than the equivalent of about ten pounds for a van and a couple with electrical hook-up.

Camping Card International

Some of the camping and motorcaravanning clubs are able to issue this credit card sized document for a nominal charge (about two pounds sterling at the time of writing). Campsites normally hold a camper's passport during their stay at the campsite. Most however, will accept the CCI in lieu of the passport and often also give a ten per cent discount off the camping charges on presentation of the card. Clearly, no motorcaravanner should therefore be without a CCI as the savings they afford soon cover not only the cost of the card but also the cost of joining the club issuing it.

Dates of Opening

Most camp sites unfortunately have a rather short opening season, usually at best April to October, often May to September. It is not good news for those of us who like to use their vans in the colder months. This is where the Sites Directories are a boon, for the 'all year' open campsites are few and far between and much harder to find 'on spec'.

The Caravan Club Sites Directory & Handbook is very comprehensive in this respect. 'All year' site entries are marked in red. There is a single volume with seven hundred pages dedicated to the UK. The two volume Continental Sites Guide has about 1000 pages. Individual site information, (contributed by members), is helpfully detailed including location directions. These guides also contain much useful practical advice on caravanning in general and also when travelling overseas.

Horsley: one of the many sites of The Camping and Caravanning Club which welcomes non-members. It is in a tranquil setting amidst weeping willows and with grassy banks beside Lake Horsley. London is only 40 minutes away by train from East Horsley station - a mile from the site.

Of the club's 83 sites, 70 are open to non-members, and it is possible to join the club on arrival at any of the sites. Members enjoy reduced member rates and other benefits.

A well equipped home-built motorcaravan based on the excellent Saviem (Renault) TP3 4x4 light truck chassis.

CHAPTER 4

WILD CAMPING

If ever there were a topic that polarised the camping fraternity the most contentious surely has to be that of wild camping. In order to be sure what we are talking about it is perhaps best to define the two words, not least because a dictionary definition of wild is "not domesticated or cultivated, not civilised, barbarous, unrestrained, wayward, disorderly" all of which might just create the wrong impression.

There are some amongst us who may well feel that these definitions could not be more apt in describing that particular group of campers known as 'new age travellers' who in fact are well known for their wild camping and unfortunately rather better known for their all too frequent altercations with the police. It seems on this particular issue however, that 'harassment by' rather than 'altercations with' would probably be some peoples' opinion, but I could not possibly comment.

On the other hand, 'out in the wilds' could be defined as 'far from towns'. Another definition of wild is 'having conspicuously desolate appearance' which I think is bringing us a little closer to the meaning wild camping, but not exactly. For all practical purposes, when wild camping is referred to, what is actually implied is 'free camping' which usually suggests stopping overnight at any place not designated for such a purpose and very often a desolate location is also thought of. However, whilst this stopover may be out in the wilds, it may also be in a town centre car park.

As far as I am able to ascertain the lowest common denominator in all instances of wild camping is that there is no payment for the privilege of the overnight stop.

The other common factor usually associated with this thorny subject is that no permission is granted for the overnight stop, which in itself does not imply any authoritative objection.

I therefore put forward the following definition:-

wild camping: stopping overnight at a place not specifically designated for such purposes, without payment and without permission but not necessarily illegally.

It is well known that wild camping is frowned upon by many throughout Europe. Indeed several countries have laws that specifically forbid Wild Camping.

For example, Greece, which welcomes tourists, has the following cautionary notice printed at the beginning and end of its helpful, official publication 'Camping in Greece 1994', which details over three hundred organised camp sites:-

'WARNING Wild Camping, Parking, or use of Camping Accommodation outside licensed Areas is strictly FORBIDDEN, under very serious penalties (Law 2160/93)'

In spite of these strong words, however, there are plenty of tourist guides for Greece that include the suggestion that wild camping in Greece is de rigeur.

The Danish Tourist Board says that overnight stays in motor caravans parked outside camping sites are not permitted in Denmark without prior permission of the respective landowner. They add that camping in car parks and lay-bys is not permitted either, and that strong measures are taken against unauthorised parking in dunes and on beaches - offenders being fined on the spot.

It is fairly obvious that in most countries, local authorities responsible for tourist attractions have the task of ensuring that their areas of responsibility are kept clean, in good order and are as accessible to visitors as possible. It should therefore be no surprise that indiscriminate overnight parking, quite rightly would not readily be tolerated. The authorities usually take the view that camping will be organised by campsites and that is where all types of tents and caravans should be situated overnight.

All this does not mean that wild camping is never possible but it does lead to the formulation of some basic guidelines which should always be carefully considered before levelling the van for that unofficial stop.

A Guide to Wild Camping

1. Know the laws and local rules relating to overnight stops in the area, and do not break them.

2. Try to avoid a location if you have any reason for believing that your presence there will interfere with either the reasonable convenience or enjoyment of others.

3. Ask for permission to stop overnight, if possible.

4. Unless bins are available take away all your refuse.

5. Leave the site as clean or cleaner than you found it.

6. Use your self-contained chemical toilet and do not empty it until a proper facility or toilet is encountered.

   If necessary, in remote locations, waste can be buried 'off the beaten track', but ensure there is no likelihood of it draining into any watercourse.
   Remove a piece of turf about half a metre square and dig a hole about half a metre deep. Empty all the waste into the pit, back-fill the earth on top and replace the turf. Check the work and be sure that no one would ever know!
   (Compact army surplus type, folding, trenching tools are ideal for this purpose.)
   It is always better to take all waste away.

7. Be aware that as a wild camper you cannot be as private as you may wish, and you are exposed to intrusion even after midnight when soundly asleep.

   Nobody wants to be awoken at two o'clock in the morning by a knock on the door, but it can happen when wild camping. Dealing effectively with this possibility requires a positive state of mind.

   - Try to assess the visitor through the window before opening the door.
   - If the visitor is clearly official, a friendly (if sleepy) attitude and courteousness can help. (Most visitors after midnight are probably doing their job, at more civilised times they may be just plain inquisitive.)
   - Try to be polite and show respect.
   - Always be prepared to move on if necessary, no matter how late it may be.

Safety and Security:

There can be no guarantees that you will be safe and undisturbed during your overnight stop. (This even is the case if you stay at home.) With a little care and thought however, the chances of experiencing any problems can be significantly reduced.

- There is strength in numbers, so if you come across other campers obviously parked up for the night, park amongst them.
  Motorway services in most countries can be useful.
- It is sensible to park in such a way that an early, speedy, and clear departure is possible.
- In remote unknown towns, parking next to a police station (possibly with their approval) is a safe bet.
- If it is very late, park next to the village green or town centre, be ready for a very early departure.
- If you are in the wilds with no other campers in sight, look for a place to stop which is out of sight of through traffic, along a side road or up a track perhaps. Do not block it however deserted it looks, you can not be sure who may need it, perhaps a farmer for access early in the morning.
  If you are out of sight you are out of mind, particularly from passing opportunists.
- Always lock everything.
- Leave no loose equipment or clothing outside the vehicle.

I have tried to apply all of the above guidelines when parking overnight and the only uninvited visitors I have ever had have been police. I have always found them to be polite. On occasions they have asked me to move.

A Hanomag four wheel drive ex-military ambulance overnighting at a French Aire. These rugged vehicles are much-favoured for conversion by German expeditioners.

After arriving from a long journey one evening I parked in the grounds of the wonderful Alhambra Palace in Grenada, Spain. We went to bed almost immediately but it was not long before there was a loud knock on the van door. I must say that knock that wakens you out of your slumber in the middle of the night, especially after you have gone to bed uncertain of your right to be there, sends a shiver through me and sets my heart beating a little faster.

On investigation I discovered a police officer with a motorbike who told me I must move. I explained that I was in bed and could not possibly just drive off. He replied that he would come back in fifteen minutes to collect me and I must follow him. Unfortunately my lack of fluency in Spanish was such that his exact reason for wanting me to follow him was not immediately revealed but it seemed futile to do anything other than dress, batten down the hatches, await his return, and discover the meaning of this little mystery.

True to his word, he returned and bid me drive behind him. We motored up through the beautiful tree enshrouded cobbled road within the towering red stone walls of the Palace, alongside ancient water-channels and past watering statues at intersecting avenues. I kept a distance from my motorcycle escort as he proceeded through a vast car park sheltering several coaches, until he turned into a rather private tree lined enclosure and pulled up. I climbed down from the elevated position of my driver's cab and approached him. He went on to explain that we were free for the night to choose any place in this car park and that, provided we moved out and parked in the main car park during the day, we were welcome to stay as many nights as we wished. We were home!

Another trip into the Iberian peninsula took place in winter to experience a Christmas with a difference by spending it on a warm beach. We headed for one of the warmest parts of Spain at that time of year, a beach north of Cabo de Gata near Almeria, where we hoped for temperatures around twenty degrees Celsius.

We spent a cosy night in our motorcaravan in the Pyrenees at minus five degrees Celsius along a side road leading to the charming, remote village of Castellbo (Lleida), which offers a welcoming campsite, (Camping Castellbo, Juan Buchaca), surrounded by ancient buildings with many stories to tell. The following night, before reaching Madrid, we found a quiet stop in an olive grove and noted a temperature increase of fifteen degrees in twenty four hours - we knew then that we were heading in the right direction. We reached our secret cove early on Christmas eve to find that we were alone beside an unspoiled beach which in summer would be alive with holidaymakers.

We stayed for an idyllic week, seeing-in the New Year with two German chaps who arrived late one night to pitch their tent close by in a hidden valley. They came with similar ideas, mainly to see-in 1992 in a beautiful, remote, but warm, location.

Unlike the low profile tent of our German friends which could not easily be detected, our motorcaravan could not be missed, and after a few days we were visited one afternoon by park wardens back to work after their Christmas holidays. They explained that overnight stops were not normally allowed but they did not object to our seeing in the New Year beside their beach. It was clear that they checked us out very carefully, not least to make sure that we were tidy and respectful of our surroundings, but it is unlikely that we would be as welcome later in the year when the demand for such stops would be far greater.

After our New Year's festivities, the time came to move on and drive towards the Algarve. We continued our treck more or less following the coast as far as the most southwesterly tip of Portugal dominated by Fort Fortaleza at Sagres. The cliffs around Cabo de Sao Vicente are high indeed but does this deter the fishermen? Not a bit of it, we spent a day watching them earning their precarious living from the high cliffs just south of Carrapateira.

One intrepid fellow set about a climbing expedition down to the water's edge at which point, with his equipment strapped to his back, he plunged into the foaming brine and set about a half hour's swim to an adjacent island where he fished for the day up to the time that the island was about to disappear under the rising sea and this was not calm water, the sea was heaving. He then set about the slow but steady swim back to the mainland, managing to keep his sizeable back pack and fishing rod clear of the water. He then eased his way back up the near vertical rock face before attaining the track upon which he had left his bicycle. I was filled with admiration for the man and his toils. That night was spent on a very windy track on top of the cliffs. We saw a police patrol pass by but they appeared not to be interested in us.

Some days later, further north between Lisbon and Porto, we found a remote spot again beside the sea but by now the high cliffs had turned into sand dunes. We stopped amongst them for the day and night but were rather rudely disturbed from our sleep at two o'clock in the morning by a knock on our door.

Very cautiously I peered out through a window to be confronted by no less than seven police officers, three four-wheel drive vehicles with their dazzling headlights pointing towards us, and many torches. Having ascertained that they were in uniform and presumably 'on duty' I opened the door and climbed down amongst them.

At such times I consider it important, before opening the door, to be satisfied that the visitors are official, for one hears too many stories of intruders of the other kind, those that should be avoided at all costs. I am happy to say that I have no personal experience of such arrivals, but of their existence we should have no doubt, and consequently always be on our guard. I am never too sure how I would react under such circumstances and I suppose and hope that I will have to continue guessing, although I think the main requirement would be to try to start the engine and drive away as quickly as possible. This does not mean however, that one is condemned to leading a life of paranoia expecting to find the worst around every corner.

I think it should be more a matter of expecting the best around every corner but being prepared to cope with the worst in the very unlikely event that it will rear its ugly head. It seems, to me, pointless to be constantly worrying about the worst that statistically will not happen. With this more positive approach, one lives with a philosophy which should allow one to find life more relaxing and enjoyable.

On this occasion our visitors asked to see our passports but said little else. Having satisfied themselves that we were innocuous tourists they then informed us that there was no problem and their visit was routine. They bid us good night and left us in peace. They had been polite and most of them remained quietly in the background.

It was subsequently concluded that these visitors were not in fact police but customs officers and they were on the look out for drug smugglers arriving by sea, an occurrence which apparently is not unheard of along this coastline.

On another occasion, when travelling with my dog, I could not find a site prepared to accept dogs and so I took up residence on a clear patch of ground. It was overlooking the Straits of Gibraltar near Tarifa, which proudly claims to have three hundred and sixty five days of wind a year (which is fine if you are there to wind surf).

After three days I was visited by a couple of police officers who were very friendly but said that they had observed my presence at the same place for three days and wild camping was not allowed there. They then reluctantly handed me a card upon which was repeated, in several languages, information which stated that wild camping within the town boundaries was not allowed and having been seen to have wild camped within the boundaries I was obliged to drive across the borders of the town and must not be seen within the boundaries during the next twenty four hours. Of course I did as requested with apologies and pleasantries from both sides. ⌘

A wild stop in Portugal

'Some people are concerned about taking on something larger'...
This bus-size motorcaravan, of German origin, with its two motor scooters, was spotted occupying two pitches on this Catalonian campsite.

CHAPTER 5

DRIVING and PARKING

Most newcomers to the world of caravanning have little or no experience driving a vehicle of greater proportions than the average family saloon and they are, quite naturally, concerned about the prospects of taking on something larger, or towing. This may be one of the reasons why many choose the smallest vans possible.

One of the smaller vans.

Driving larger vehicles does take some learning (but then so did driving a car). Many drivers have had difficulties with low bridges or garage awnings and protruding balconies. Reversing a vehicle 6 or 7 metres long, with limited rear vision, calls for care and skill above that of the average car driver.

These skills can be learned however, and, like driving a car, experience, the most valuable asset to skilful driving, comes only with practice, but come it does.

Reversing Aids - Closed Circuit Video

Regarding driving backwards, the van driver has to learn to rely on his mirrors but there are several reversing aids currently available, which go a long way to making up for the obvious disadvantages of longer vehicles when it comes to manoeuvring. Perhaps the most sophisticated of these is a video system, consisting of a camera fixed outside at the top of the back of the van facing backwards, which is linked to a small monitor or TV screen mounted in place of the rear view mirror. The wide angle of the camera's lens presents a more informative view than a mirror ever could of the 'blind spot' at the back of the van, and certainly makes for safer reversing. With the use of such a facility properly installed, the chances of reversing over, or into, an otherwise unseen obstacle are virtually eliminated.

Whilst this type of equipment is not cheap, the cost of dealing with a single reversing accident could exceed its installed cost. It is hard to put a price on the peace of mind that these systems can provide.

Probably every motorist, and particularly those with experience of road accidents, may testify that safety should come first. Such systems, whilst perhaps usually associated with larger vehicles, are becoming a more common sight on motorcaravans.

The rear-view screen offers more information than a rear-view mirror.

The Sony system which I have installed on my van is surprisingly light-sensitive. At night, with illumination from normal rear lights, the picture is remarkably clear, and reversing into limited spaces becomes routine and simple. As a matter of course I drive with the system always switched on, day or night, as I find it useful not only for reversing but also generally to keep me informed of what is happening behind.

It has been designed with a connection for linking to the gear change, to switch on the monitor automatically when shifting to reverse, but since I use it for driving at all times I have overridden this option.

I have positioned the camera so that the view in the screen is from immediately behind the van to a point about fifteen metres behind. I find this the right compromise for slow speed and reversing work as well as providing vision of vehicles travelling closely behind on motorways. Any vehicles further back than these fifteen metres can be seen in the outside rear view mirrors.

Reversing Aids - Sensors

There is a system called PDM which uses sensors mounted at the rear of the vehicle. They detect the proximity of any objects behind. A display inside the cab gives warning as objects are approached. This type of equipment, whilst not as effective as rear-view closed circuit video, is much cheaper and should increase a driver's ability to reverse safely.

Power Steering and Power Brakes

Where available, power steering should never be left out even on light vehicles. It takes the strain out of low speed manoeuvring.

Power brakes reduce the strain on the right leg and foot, and are equally desirable, giving more stopping power for less effort.

Automatic Transmission

I am a great believer in automatic transmission if available and at an acceptable cost. A well-designed gearbox can be a pleasure to use (or more to the point 'not to use') particularly in town traffic. I appreciate any feature that allows the driver more time to concentrate on the road. Unfortunately, there is an additional price to pay above the initial cost of an automatic gear box. This is due to their lower efficiency, with reported fuel costs being about ten per cent higher than those of manual gearboxes.

If available, a 'lock-up' feature, by which the fluid coupling in the automatic transmission can be locked into direct drive in top gear, helps to reduce the extra fuel consumption.

Cruise Control

This is a feature which is more common in America than in Europe and so is something of an unknown to many on the European side of the Atlantic.

It is available, as a bolt-on addition, to fit most vehicles and offers an extra level of driving comfort, by allowing the driver to relax the accelerator foot.

Particularly during a long day's motorway driving, it can contribute to less fatigue and correspondingly safer driving. Also, there are claims it can improve fuel economy.

Merely by pressing a button on a stalk beside the steering wheel, the system allows the current speed to be set and maintained accurately by computer rather than by foot, with shutdown when the brake or clutch is depressed or the unit switched off. It is possible, at a touch of the button, to increase or decrease the set speed slightly. Successive touches (taps) multiply the effect. A driver may accelerate above the set speed, to overtake for example, by accelerating with the foot as normal, subsequent removal of the foot from the accelerator allows the cruise control to return the vehicle to the previously set speed.

After braking or declutching, pressing the 'Resume' switch automatically accelerates the vehicle back to the previously set speed.

I installed an 'Auto Pilot' from Ultimate Design on my van and am able to report that driving fatigue is significantly reduced as a result of a more relaxed accelerator leg. Most noticeably on motorways, the cruise control holds the van exactly at any set speed with no effort and far more accuracy than is possible manually. Furthermore, I find that driving with the system makes a journey rather more interesting than without it.

The installation, in my opinion, is complicated, but the instructions and kit of parts supplied, are sufficiently comprehensive to enable a satisfying job to be achieved. The work, including perhaps some modifications, customising, adjustments and fine tuning, could easily take a day.

PARKING

Whilst it may be thought that a large vehicle is harder to park than a car, both are similarly manoeuvrable. A large van with power steering might well require less effort to handle at slow speed than a car without it.

However, it is not only length and width which are relevant, but also height. There is a danger of forgetting just how high the van really is. The driver of a larger motorcaravan must always have it in mind that they are in control of a vehicle which is three metres high or more.

In practice this means looking out for that rock overhang or leaning tree, perhaps an awkwardly positioned road sign, or maybe the infamous height barrier. A time to be particularly vigilant is when having to reverse out of a tight spot, such as might happen in a remote village with narrow streets and overhanging balconies. One might be distracted by pedestrians or vehicles. This is an occasion when it may be all too easy to overlook that overhanging obstacle which is waiting to crunch into a reversing vehicle.

Entering and parking in towns is therefore an aspect of driving motorcaravans worthy of special consideration. Indeed, it is sometimes advisable to avoid a town centre completely. Unfortunately this is not always evident until too late, even in towns with roads which are simply too narrow to accommodate vehicles of motorcaravan dimensions. On occasions, the main road passes through the town centre, ***but is restricted***.

It is probably safer to avoid town centres with the larger rigs...This tough little Unimog motorcaravan, with its comprehensive gear ratios, will make slow but steady progress towing its long trailer, but to find parking space may not be so straightforward.

Many towns ban larger vehicles; some in fact ban all 'unauthorised' vehicles. It is clearly essential to keep a sharp lookout for all relevant signs at town boundaries. At the approach to unknown towns the driver should perhaps be looking for an opportunity to pull up, off the road if possible, to study the map and guide books (if he has not already done so), and all the signs on display.

Of course well prepared drivers, in particular those with very large vehicles, should know in advance of any road restrictions, exactly which routes to take, and where they will be able to park.

Siena

Let the reader beware that the exquisite town of Siena in Tuscany, which no traveller would wish to miss, is a good example of a difficult case. It is a medieval walled city with signs at the approaches to its imposing gates. Sadly, like many Italian tourist attractions, there are what may seem as many as a hundred signs fixed on a forest of poles near the entrance. The art is to learn to differentiate between the *'one'* which is important and the other 'ninety-nine'.

In Siena's case the ***really*** important *'one'* is the car with a red circle around it indicating ***'no'*** unauthorised vehicles. I missed it and drove through the imposing and verdant city gate into an enchanting narrow high-walled street. It very soon became apparent that the gauntlet was being run when a police officer threw his arms up in despair after I explained that I was heading for the centre. I had no choice but to press on and to a large extent felt that my presence in the city had been sanctioned by the officer. What looked like the centre came into sight surprisingly soon, but the road curved away from it and back on itself with no sign of any parking.

It was further along this still high-walled one-way street, with traffic following me, that I encountered a commercial flat bed truck which was parked so closely to one of the walls that it appeared to be touching it, but there was still insufficient room for my van to pass. I switched off my engine and decided to wait for something to happen.

I had foolishly got myself into this mess and there was no simple way out, but it did seem likely that the build up of traffic behind and their horn blowing might precipitate some sort of action! Surely enough it was not long before a small group of interested locals emerged from a door, in the wall, on my left.

One of them looked as if he might be a wrestler and it was he who took it on himself to stand squarely in front of my van facing me. He carefully looked at each side, and then with both hands beckoned me to proceed. I noticed the enormous size of his hands.

I did not leave the van but made an exaggerated point of looking with concern at the space available before shaking my head miming "no". He looked at each side again and then, displaying the back of his hands and curled fingers, exuberantly wafted air past his now angering face, once again requesting me to proceed.

Again I shook my head, at which point he started to yell:
"A-V-A-N-T-I...A-V-A-N-T-I", wildly gesticulating with his weapons for me to move forward.

As I shook my head a third time he suddenly rushed over to the truck, got in, and with a great flurry, and to my profound relief, shot off up the street and out of sight.
This was only the middle of the problem as I was to discover after driving around more narrow bends, holding my breath whilst squeezing past two or three more almost impassable obstacles. There was traffic (presumably authorised) parked all the way. At last I saw an opportunity to stop briefly and allow the traffic that had built up behind to pass me. I felt I owed them this.

It was at this moment that from nowhere another police officer appeared at my window demanding my "documenti". I handed them over and he then explained in Italian that I was to proceed about eighty metres to the piazza where I was to stop and wait for him. He vanished just as quickly as he had appeared. Suddenly feeling naked and vulnerable without my papers, and wondering what I could have done to stop him taking them, I reluctantly and without choice did as I was bidden. For those few metres driving without papers I felt guilty.

To my relief the piazza soon appeared as I hoped (bearing in mind my uncertain translation of the police officer's words) and it was not long before he sped to a halt in front of me. He came to my window and began to talk again in Italian of the town's restriction on all unauthorised vehicles. He then went to his car and set about an interminable process of filling in forms. It was at this stage that I became aware of an apparently identical process taking place with another traveller and police officer across the piazza (all the more noticeable by the coincidental fact that his vehicle registration was of the same rare origin as mine). Eventually he returned with the words "Mr. Speed, one hundred thousand lire now" in English, and asked me if I had anything to say. I humbly apologised whilst noticing his refusal to return any papers or my documents until I had given him the money (equivalent to about forty-five pounds). Luckily I had been to the bank earlier that morning.

The procedure was very formal and I was given a clear and official receipt. He then explained, all in English, that there were signs at the city gates banning unauthorised vehicles and he gave me directions to several car parks which were available, free of charge, just outside the city walls. It was not difficult to find one of these which was less than a five minute walk from a city entrance gate and an interesting fifteen minute's walk from the very heart of the city. Sometimes the best way to learn is the hard way and the lesson is clear.

Luckily for me, and miffed though I was, the incident did not put me off returning to the city and discovering some of its many treasures. ◆

One of the entrances to the Campo, the centre of Siena, which is dominated by the 320 ft bell tower of the Communal Palace.

A MAN 8.150 FAE (4x4) chassis with a caravan added, by the Austrian company Action Mobil. The company specialises in the construction of motorcaravans for more demanding applications including expeditions into Africa.

Whilst getting bogged down in this van may not be as likely as with one less well specified, getting unstuck could be more difficult than with a smaller, lighter vehicle.

Forays across difficult terrain should not be attempted by individual vans, rather by groups of at least two well equipped vehicles. There is strength in numbers.

CHAPTER 6

GETTING STUCK and UNSTUCK

Getting stuck is very easy to do. Getting unstuck tends to be rather more difficult. Wet and muddy fields can be the bane of the motorcaravanner's life. They can be the most challenging to deal with, often catching the van driver off his guard, particularly when the field was dry when he parked the van in the first place. Having then to drive off the muddy field is where wheel traction can be lacking and the wheels start to spin.

There is little doubt that the more tread, and also the more aggressive the tread on the tyres, the better the chance of dealing with slippery mud. A tyre such as the Michelin XCL is very effective, but few motorcaravanners would wish to put up with its limited road manners, not to mention the 'singing' as they whir along the road! The best compromise might be a less rugged 4x4 tyre.

Golden Rules

1. Be aware of the ever present possibility of getting stuck. Try to avoid situations likely to cause the problem in the first place.

2. Surfaces to be suspicious of:-
   - Wet grass.
   - Mud.
   - Any yielding surface such as soft soil, particularly freshly turned or ploughed.
   - Sand.
   - Slippery downhill slopes requiring uphill exits.
   - Hollows which may subsequently fill with water.
   - Deep ruts, with humps in between, upon which the differential case or other low slung parts can ground.
   - Snow and ice.
   - Combinations of the above.

3. Before driving onto any questionable surfaces, park the van and walk around the area, carefully inspecting the ground for potential wheel sinking, slip, spin or grounding.

4. Plan the least hazardous route onto and off the site and the place to park in between.

5. If there is any risk of getting stuck either do not drive in, or if you do, be sure that some helping hands to push or tow you out will be available.
It would be comforting to know, that as a last resort, a tow out from a local tractor or well-equipped off-road vehicle would be available.

6. Having chosen a parking spot on the site, stop with the wheels pointing ahead. When the time comes to leave, inspect the exit route again looking for potential problems. If there are any, give them careful consideration and work out how to deal with them. Be patient, positive and take your time.

7. Warm up the engine for a few minutes.

8. Engage any differential locks fitted to the vehicle.

9. Engage first gear and, if you have room in front, point the wheels straight ahead. Lean out of the window to watch the drive wheel as you very gently take up the drive.

10. If the wheel begins to slip, depress the clutch immediately.
This is very important before any wheel starts to spin and 'dig in'.

11. Be aware that if the drive wheel, that you cannot see, is on a slippier patch of ground, it may start to spin, while the one you can see remains stationary. This is normal and is due to the differential doing its job. (The only way to avoid this possibility of differential wheel spin is to use a lockable differential on the drive axle, if available.)

12. On no account allow either drive wheel to spin, as traction will be lost and the only direction the vehicle will go is down! Once any part of the axles or chassis is resting on the ground there is little hope of driving away. It is then necessary to jack up a wheel, sufficiently clear of the ground, to place perhaps stones under it so that when lowered the axle or chassis no longer rests on the ground. This is hard and mucky work.

13. Try to get some willing helpers to push you while again you go through stages 8, 9, and 10.

14. Try reducing all the tyre pressures as low as you dare, perhaps to 1.5 bar (22 psi) or lower, and again try stages 8, 9 and 10.
This pressure reduction will provide greater flotation and traction, due to the increased area of tyre in ground contact, and almost without doubt will produce heart warming results in soft sand providing the vehicle is not already grounded, (remember too that lowering pressures also lowers the vehicle).

For sand and mud conditions, Michelin recommend pressures as low as 0.7 bar (10psi) claiming that it is possible to use either tubed or tubeless tyres at low pressures, but for those of less than 1.5 bar, bead locks should be fitted to avoid 'rim slip'.

I have found that lowering pressures to 1.7 bar has allowed me to drive effortlessly out of soft sand, in which I had become bogged. (I normally run at about 4 bar, although for extended track work I lower pressures to about 2.9 bar (42 psi)).

15. Without a strong helping hand when stuck, the final resort, before going in search of a tow, is to dig the vehicle out, and then lay some form of temporary track in front of, and under, the wheels. This will depend on what is available but may be no more than sticks and stones which could prove ineffective. If 'sand ladders' are to hand it will almost certainly be necessary to jack the drive wheels clear of the ground to put the sand ladders underneath. It can be a messy business calling for great care to create a stable base for the jack. The job should not be rushed.

I carry on my roof four 'sand ladders' (a type often referred to as p.s.p. or perforated steel plates although mine are aluminium). They were originally created in 3 metre lengths (with interlocking tabs) for military construction of temporary tracked surfaces, but are now being recycled for off-road use. I have cut mine in half and cut off the tabs: they are now 1.5 metres long and 40 centimetres wide. Except during the very rare occasions that I have to remove them, they provide a strong, non-slip surface for walking on the van roof.

*A rear view.
Note the sand ladders (p.s.p.) mounted across the back.
Note also the rear view video camera, upper centre and the powerful auxiliary reversing lights.*

16. If getting 'bogged' in fields becomes a recurring problem, there may be a strong case for a set of 4x4 tyres. Michelin XC4 or XCM+S4 tyres, or perhaps the XM+S244, (depending on the wheel size and driver's preference), are first-class tyres of which I have experience, but no doubt other makes with similar treads can be as effective. They provide good off-road traction and a good level of comfort on the road, with the legendary Michelin mileage, although it is unlikely that an aggressive tread pattern can return such long life as a smoother tread.

    It may be appropriate to acquire a set of sand ladders of one form or another: maybe planks of wood, or the heavy rubber 'Trac Mats' which have additional grip provided by studs on both sides. Such accessories can prove useful not only when in difficulties but also as a temporary hard standing for the van.

Snow Chains

There are several makes of snow chains and all can provide improved traction in mud. In snow and ice they are excellent. In sand they offer no benefits, as only tyre floatation is likely to help.

Chains can be fiddly and messy to fit. Using gloves is desirable and almost essential in snow. It is important to attach them correctly with no loose ends to whip about and do damage. They should be fitted *before* traction is lost and then removed at the first opportunity, when clear of trouble. Clearly, speeds should be kept to a crawl with them fitted.

The various types of chains range significantly in price, the more expensive usually offering more chain due to more complex chain patterns and correspondingly better grip. For occasional use the simpler and cheaper ones should suffice and are certainly lighter!

The problem with fitting most chains is that the normal system requires driving forwards or backwards about half a metre during the fitting process, to join up the ends. If already stuck, this can prove an additional problem to overcome. It is therefore clear that one must fit them *before* traction is lost.

The owner of a set of chains would be well advised to practise fitting them on a sunny day and away from mud or snow, giving careful consideration to how different the process could be in adverse conditions.

To some, the technique required to fit normal chains is just too complicated and messy. There are however other systems of chains or 'grips' specifically designed for simpler and quicker fitting. Although some are more expensive, they can avoid the 'shunting' process and should be considered. 'Snow Grips' are an example of clamps offering simpler attachment.

Winches

The most usual point of attachment for a winch is at the front of the vehicle (hopefully to the chassis). Some specialised vehicles are able to drive a mechanical winch from the engine by way of a power take off (PTO) shaft or with a hydraulic installation. However most winches are electrically powered being driven at 12 Volts directly from the vehicle starter battery.

Under favourable circumstances the use of a front mounted winch in a vehicle recovery situation can be very rewarding but the following points should be considered before investing in such an installation:-

1. A strong anchoring point must be available, or created, to attach the winch cable. This may be a tree, or perhaps another vehicle, or maybe a solid ground anchor.
2. For a front-mounted winch the vehicle normally can be pulled only forwards.
3. If it is necessary to pull the vehicle backwards out of trouble, a front-mounted winch will probably be useless.
4. An electric winch, recovering a van, will put a very heavy current drain on the battery.
5. The winch and installation can be expensive.
6. The use of a portable, hand operated, puller or winch, such as a Tirfor or a Greifzug, will prove more flexible in use and cheaper to buy. The van can be pulled in which ever direction is required, provided that a suitable anchorage can be arranged.
7. A portable electric or petrol driven winch can offer similar flexibility.

Winching is a potentially dangerous process which ideally should be practised in 'friendly' circumstances, preferably under the guidance of an expert. Due to the very high tensions generated in the ropes and wires, associated accidents can have serious consequences.

There are some basic rules which apply to the rigging of tow ropes, wire ropes, hooks, shackles, and anchoring, which go beyond the scope of this book. Those who wish to investigate further would be best advised to contact an organisation, (possibly a four-wheel-drive enthusiasts club), specialising in such applied sciences. ☯

CHAPTER 7: --- CONSTRUCTION: OPTIONS, CHOICES and TECHNIQUES

The 814 hot off the factory floor. The work is about to begin,

CHAPTER 7

CONSTRUCTION: OPTIONS, CHOICES and TECHNIQUES

Whilst this chapter with its twenty sections and the subsequent chapters covering Water, Electrics, Gas, Heating, Cooling, Refrigeration and Cooking, might seem at times to go into complex detail, I hope that the salient points can be gleaned as required.

Some aspects and options may appear over complicated, but the main point is to offer ideas and techniques which could be employed to create an enjoyable and comfortable caravan environment, in which everything works as designed, with a minimum of user effort and worry. Several aspects of the systems covered are not typically used in caravan installations, but are more commonly (though by no means universally) found in nautical applications. Indeed, some of the equipment described may be more readily acquired from a yacht supplier or chandler than a caravan shop. A boat show can be a good place to track down specialist suppliers.

BODY TYPE

If the desire is to convert a panel van into a motorcaravan then the question of what type of external fabric to use is clear, it already exists and is likely to be the metal as supplied by the manufacturer. In several ways this provides the easiest answer not least because the external structure of the van is already quite clearly stated and obviously forms an integral part of a fully tested roadworthy vehicle. The other and rather more challenging option is to build some form of box structure which is then attached to a van or truck chassis. This second choice therefore requires four additional tasks: one of building the box structure or caravan itself, the second of fixing the box to the chassis, the third of making sure that it drives well, and the fourth of ensuring that the completed vehicle meets all legal requirements of roadworthiness.

The Van Conversion: Advantages:-

Ready made roadworthy integrated cab and body.

Manufacturers go to great lengths to ensure that their creations are shaped well for comfortable, legal and safe driving.

Disadvantages:-

1. They were not designed for motorcaravan conversions.

It becomes clear when the juggling has to be done with our layouts: the doors, the windows, the roof height, the step and so on, that the manufacturer of the van did not have the sketches of our layouts in front of him before making his blueprints. He designed his van for carrying boxes and not for conversion into a motorcaravan.

In other words, the van is never just the right size for the design you want to use, and the windows often can not be cut in the right place, the doors are not quite big or small enough and so it can go on. The design has to fit around the van and ends up something less than you want and more like the van dictates.

2. The walls are rarely flat and square

The consequence of non-square, non-flat walls, with structural members, is that building internal walls can take more time and effort involving the use of insulation materials and complicated wood shapes, particularly if internal width is to be optimised.

The transporter van. A ' Motorcaravan-To-Be'. The vertical and horizontal structrural members will hinder the conversion process.

Complex plywood wall profiles cut to match the irregular van walls.

The Custom-Built Box: Advantages:-

1. The box is built to the size of the layout.

When the final layout is chosen, the box can be designed and built exactly as required almost without compromise. The modern choice tends to be designed around the use of glass reinforced plastic sheets (GRP), of from one to three millimetres thickness, bonded on either side of a sheet of stiff cellular foam of between two and six centimetres thickness. The resulting sandwich sheets are light, have high structural rigidity and stability, and excellent insulating properties. The insulation qualities increase significantly with foam thickness. The sandwich sheets are glued together with special glue, as required, using GRP right-angle sections to form the box structure.

2. The internal walls are flat.

Apart from perhaps a paint or wall-covering, the flat walls are ready as the final surface. Fittings can be glued to the walls although it is sometimes necessary to reinforce with steel or hardwood inserts.

3. Insulation is built-in.

Due to the inherent good insulating properties of the plastic-foam sandwich construction there is no necessity for additional insulation to be added to the box. Cold bridges should not exist.

4. Door and window positions.

Openings for doors and windows can be cut precisely in accordance with the positions dictated by the design plan.

Disadvantages:-

1. Making the box

This specialised task results in a large item to be manoeuvred onto the truck chassis.

2. Fixing the box to the chassis

The box must be attached to the chassis by some means, often consisting of some form of steel (perhaps stainless) sub-chassis firmly attached to the underside of the box and bolted to the chassis. The precise nature of this device will depend on the fixing recommendations of the truck manufacturer and also on the wooden board which will be bonded to the floor section of the box.

3. Installation of driving lights

The combined chassis and box must be brought up to full roadworthiness, by the addition of driving lights, to the legal specification.

4. Suspension Considerations

Careful thought must be given to the ultimate loading of the chassis. Consultation with the manufacturers might result in a recommendation to stiffen the suspension.

5. Walk-Through Limitations

One of the very pleasant features of any motorcaravan is the facility to walk freely between the cab and the caravan. This is harder to achieve with the box option.

6. Cost

Additional materials are required, but this can be offset by simpler internal fitting work. Never forgetting however, that for the do-it-yourselfer time is free but materials are not.

A glass fibre reinforced plastic (GRP) box in the making.

The Final Decision

The prospective builder is faced with the hard decision of whether to take the van or add-on-box route. As above, it can be seen that there are strong points in favour of either option.

One way which might swing the choice towards the add-on box option is the compromise of having a specialist firm build a box onto your chosen chassis (perhaps supplied by you, perhaps second-hand), fitting as many or as few fixtures as you wish. This is bound to be a more expensive route, particularly so, if you are confident of the company's pedigree, and choose to have them supply a fully roadworthy vehicle, fit any doors and possibly the windows. Having gone this far it might also be wise for them to fit the waste water tank and any spare fuel tank to the chassis, as they will undoubtedly have developed their techniques over a long period of trial and error. This then leaves you to set about creating your internal dream.

INSULATION, CONDENSATION, COLD BRIDGES and VENTILATION

One of the major aspects of constructing a motorcaravan is avoidance of condensation. Wherever there exists a difference in temperatures, on either side of a partition such as the wall of a motorcaravan the problem of condensation will arise.

For example, if the outside temperature is zero degrees or freezing, whilst that inside the motorcaravan is say twenty degrees Celsius, any warm air containing moisture inside the van coming into contact with a surface cooled from the outside, will condense on the cold surface to form water.

This warm air containing moisture is exactly what is created by people breathing and cooking inside the van. Furthermore, an ideal cold surface on which the moisture can condense would be any conducting (probably metal) surface inside the van which is in direct contact with the external cold surface.

The way we can avoid this problem is to ensure that there are no metal surfaces inside the van (not even a screw head) which are in contact with the outside metal surface of the van. Metal is such a good conductor of heat that, if there is direct metal contact between the cold outer wall and the internal metal object, the latter will be at approximately the same temperature as the cold outside and any internal moisture will therefore form on it.

The name which has been given to a metal link between a cold outside and inside wall is a 'COLD BRIDGE'.

We must strive to ensure that our motorcaravan contains no 'cold bridges' and there are two techniques we can use:-

1. Judicious use of good INSULATION, and it is important not to skimp here.
2. Ensure that no internal metal surface, exposed to the internal air, is in metallic contact with any outside cold surface. (Not even a screw head used for fixing an internal wooden panel to a van body member. Any such screw must screw through the wooden panel into a piece of wood, which is itself fixed to the van body member, wood of course being an excellent insulator).

INSULATION

Of all the possibilities currently available, the material that I have chosen for insulation goes under the name "Xtrem" and is available from CMC Reimo.

It is a highly flexible closed cell polyethylene foam substance, containing innumerable tiny insulated air bubbles. It is very light and available in ten, fifteen, twenty and thirty millimetres thick sheets of one metre by two.

It can be compressed and quickly recovers, and can be cut very simply with a sharp knife. I have found sharp scissors give the cleanest cut. It is pliant, easily following any form, such as a curved metal panel, to which it can be readily glued with a contact adhesive. It is waterproof, does not absorb moisture, is resistant to high temperatures, and is also a good sound-insulator.

What is more, Xtrem forms an excellent sheet to lie on for that fiddly job under the van. I always travel with at least a half metre square piece for such a job. Even a small piece to kneel on is worth having handy. A square to sit on makes any cold, damp, or hard surface, comfortable.

I have used the material extensively, (in mainly fifteen millimetre thicknesses, sometimes doubled), throughout my motorcaravan conversion.

It is both pleasant to work with and, most importantly, effective as an insulation solution. I claim not to have a condensation problem in my van, although ventilation forms an essential part of the equation.

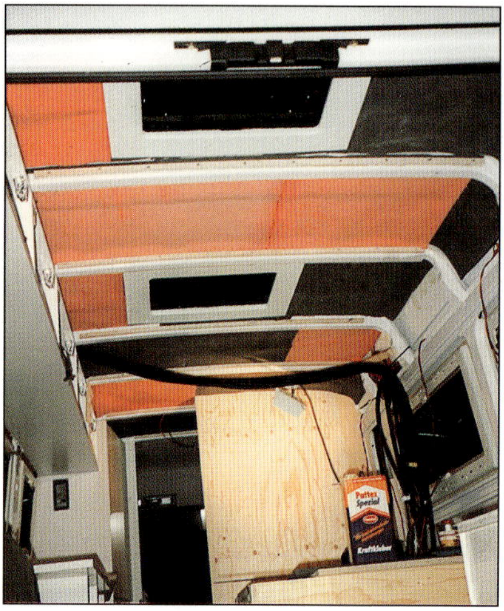

Red and black sheets of Xtrem glued to roof panels with contact adhesive. Oak battens can be seen screwed to roof cross-members. The roof panels will be screwed to the oak battens.

VENTILATION

Whilst good insulation and avoidance of 'cold bridges' are both required to avoid condensation inside the van, it is most important also to provide adequate internal ventilation. When the van is occupied, one or more windows and roof vents should be open, perhaps not much but enough to create an air flow. This is equally important when sleeping and cooking, if damp is to be avoided, (but do not sit or sleep in a draft, a stiff neck is worse than condensation!). One soon learns that leaving water boiling, without sufficient ventilation, will rapidly cover internal surfaces with a film of moisture.

LAYOUT

The earliest consideration for a basic motorhome design is its layout. Where do you want everything to go and why?

Probably the best way to start this process is by sketching a view of the floor plan. Many versions and variations are likely before a final plan is decided, which even then is inevitably going to be a compromise, because after all, we are trying to incorporate all the features of a house into what amounts to a few cubic metres in a box on wheels. We soon discover that every centimetre is important.

Areas and facilities to be included will consist of some or all of the following:-

- Entrances and exits
- Windows
- Sitting room(s)
- Dining room(s)
- Bedroom(s)
- Kitchen
- Bathroom
- Fresh water
- Waste water
- Hot water system
- W.C.
- Gas
- Electrical system
- Heating system
- Storage for clothes, food and essentials
- Storage for spare wheel.
- Storage for outdoor equipment
- Storage for extra petrol / diesel

The following questions will need to be answered:-

- How big should the bed be?
- Would you mind having to construct your bed every day?
- What size should the seats be?
- How much leg room will be required?
- What size should the table be?
- Is the van too high for the garage?
- Where can the van be parked?
- What size and type of windows are best, should they be sliding or top hinged?
- Should there be enough space and facilities to enable accommodation of friends travelling or staying with you in your van?
- Will the van be used in the winter?
- Is a hot water system necessary, or might heating water in a kettle on the stove suffice?
- How much fresh water should be carried?
- Should a fresh water tank be installed?
- Is there a need for a bathroom as well as a kitchen?
- Is a shower facility really necessary? Many owners think not, even though they have one.

Layout Views

I hope to help readers to find their own answers to these questions, and more, during the course of this book, all of which should lead to the essential stage, the finalised drawings of the internal layout of the motorhome. They need not be works of art, as long as they are legible, perhaps just freehand line drawings, roughly to scale, showing dimensions.

Many designers are quite happy to pencil their freehand sketches on small squares of paper. Others prefer to work on graph paper with a ruler, perhaps using a drawing board with parallel motion and a swivelling ninety-degree rule. The more widely equipped may wish to use a computer with a CAD program installed. The views shown here were created on a Power Mac running the comprehensive design program MiniCad.

An alternative approach is to start with, if available, a manufacturer's blue-print of the van in its various views. Some scaled cardboard cut-outs of all the components can then be juggled around to see how they might fit together.

The "plan" view, that from above, is the most useful initial sketch we can make of our ideas. It shows the respective positions of the sitting and dining area, the kitchen, the walkway, the wardrobe, the bed and the bathroom. What it does not show however, are their heights. To glean this additional information we need some front and back views.

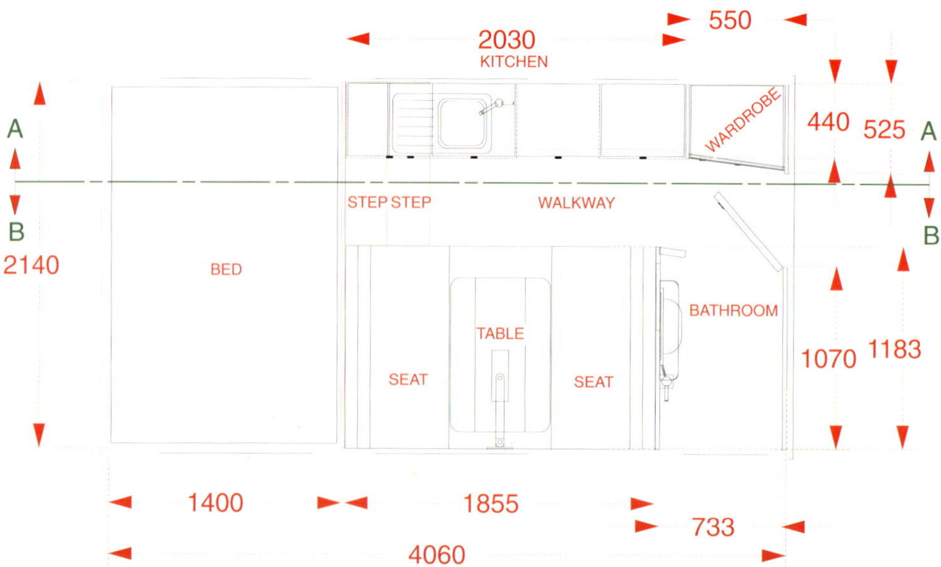

A plan view of the outlines of the main elements. Taken alone such a sketch can be confusing, but when combined with corresponding side views, the picture becomes more complete. This example, one of the plan views of my van, has been simplified by omitting the high-level cupboards.

The various side elevations can include front, rear, right and left views. After a few rough sketches it is a fairly simple task to create a set of drawings which together provide most of the information required to depict and understand the relative three dimensional positions of all the basic components of the van.

These improved drawings of my van are based on my original freehand sketches which provided me with positive solutions to most of the questions I had to answer.

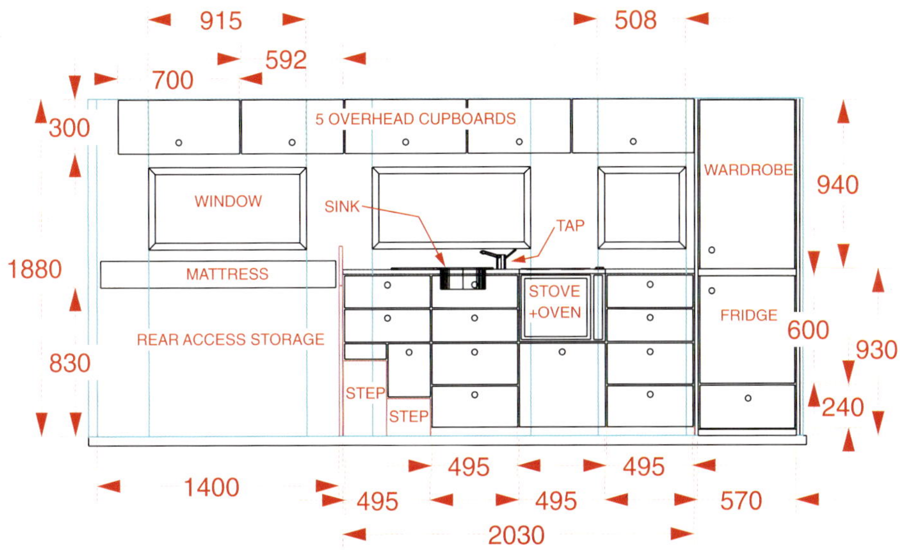

A front view of the kitchen. This is a front elevation of the section taken on AA from the previous plan view but with the overhead cupboards added.

The side or front view, looking towards the kitchen, which will be most useful to us, is that which would be seen from the green line in the direction of the two arrows A-A: this 'section' on A-A shows us the make-up of the front of the kitchen and the cupboard unit, it also shows us a section through the bed.

The equally important side or back view section on B-B, looking in the other direction, shows us more of the dining area, the bathroom, and the slice through the bed in the other direction.

We can choose the degree of complexity of each drawing according to where we take a section. The most interesting and visual views are the various rendered projections which can be created by either a draftsman or with a good design system.

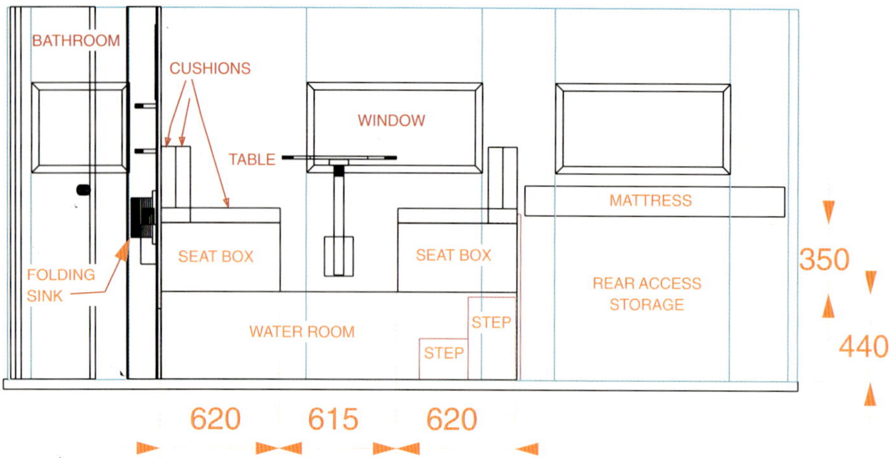

The back view towards the diner/sitting area, this time sectioned on BB (previous plan view) in order to leave out the kitchen and wardrobe.

A rendered perspective projection of the back view towards the diner/sitting area as above.

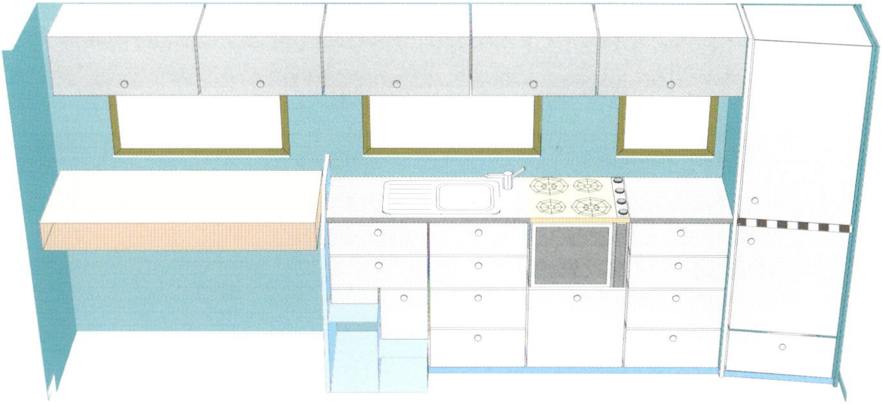

A rendered perspective projection of the front view of the Kitchen, wardrobe and fridge.

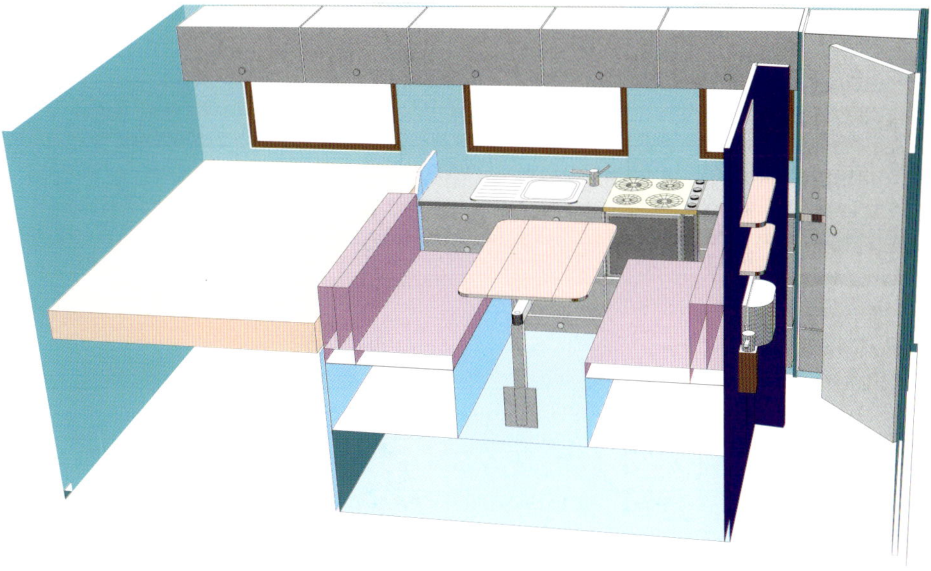

A rendered perspective projection. The perspective projection adds distortion to the drawing and the rendering adds solidity to the objects. This presents a view more closely related to how we see things in the real world with distant objects appearing smaller than those close to the viewer. This is perhaps the best way to obtain an overall impression of the layout, but not the exact dimensions.

ENTRANCES, ACCESS and WALK THROUGH

Some makes of panel van offer a choice of entrance, and clearly the final motorcaravan design will be influenced by the actual entrance position selected or available. Not only is the position of the entrance important, but also the size. It is essential that the entrance is wide enough to allow installation, and possible subsequent removal of the interior components, such as the fridge, and possibly any pre-constructed furniture.

If the base vehicle is a panel van the entrance will almost certainly be wide enough: it remains for the designer to ensure that his plans do not restrict access for installation of the fridge and other large items. If however, a custom-built box is the choice it must be remembered to allow a probable minimum access width of 50 cm for a fridge, as well as personal comfort. Fifty-five centimetres or sixty is better.

Here we see a distinct advantage of the custom-built box option; the door may be placed precisely as required, and the box based on the design rather than the other way round, as with a van conversion.

Side Entrance

Kerb access tends to be both more convenient and safer with a side entrance, which will normally be on the passenger side. If there is a choice of the door being on either side, (or even both sides as with some models), the scope of the interior design is broadened.

The side door on the right-hand side is technically the wrong side for pavement access with the vehicle parked on the left side of the road in the UK, and vice versa.

In practice, the parking of a left-hand-drive vehicle (which normally has its side entrance on the right) in right-hand-drive countries, (and vice versa), tends not to be too great a problem because the van may be parked to suit.

For sitting outside the van, a side entrance is likely to be rather more useful and convenient than a rear one as there is more room to set up table and chairs beside the van next to the entrance.

If parking is very close on each side, such as might be encountered in a supermarket car park, side entrance access can pose a problem.

Sliding or Hinged Side Door

Whilst most vans come with standard sliding side door, some of them offer the option of a hinged side door. Sliding side doors are designed by the manufacturers for cargo loading, so they are rather wider than is necessary purely for personnel access. This extra width can be a useful feature of a van conversion, but at a high price, this being the loss of internal space which might otherwise be used for internal facilities.

If there is a choice then the question has to be asked: Which is more important, the wide door, or bigger internal facilities such as cupboards, work surface, or dining area? On the other hand, some users speak highly of the airiness of the large opening when the sliding door is open.

A point to remember is that the sliding door may obstruct top-hinged side windows when open: sliding windows would therefore be more suitable.

If incidental large load carrying is envisaged, such loads might not fit through the hinged door, and it may be that the standard sliding door is the answer.

Rear Entrance and Doors

The most obvious advantage of a rear entrance is access into the van from the back when the van is so tightly parked that side doors could not be opened. Some motorcaravan designs make clever use of both side and rear entrances giving the best of both worlds. There are van manufacturers who offer various options for rear doors including:-

1. No rear door - if you do not need it why have it?

2. Doors which conveniently will hinge back through 270° and clip fully open to the side of the van.

3. Bus-type rear single door, hinged horizontally across the middle of the van, forming a boot lid. If this option can be incorporated in the design, it is an elegant solution for external storage.

Walk-Through

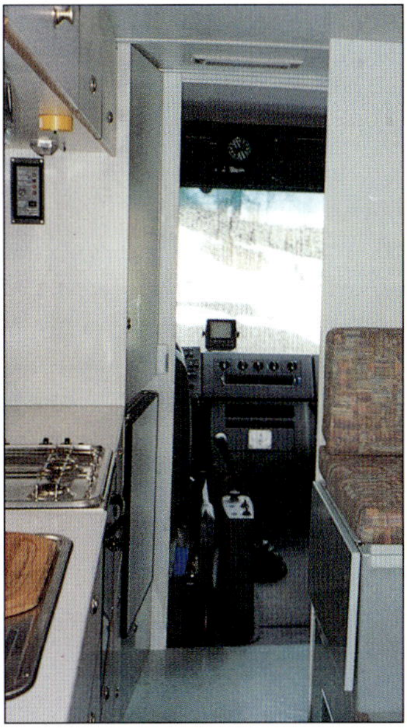

If a motorcaravan is bought off-the-shelf, almost certainly it will provide a clear walk through facility between the driver's cab and the caravan. Indeed the cab may be designed to become a part of the living quarters by rotating its seats. However, the desirability of this walk through facility may not immediately be clear and consequently may be designed out in the plans for a conversion.

Unless there are very specific reasons for taking this route I would suggest that the pleasure of living with a good clear walk through should not be underestimated.

Walk-Through Partition

It is also useful to have a means of closing the cab off from the living quarters, and whilst an insulated door is a desirable feature, a simpler solution need be no more complicated than the use of an opaque curtain. The reasons for this partition are twofold:-

1. Unless special attention is paid to the cab, it is particularly susceptible to outside temperatures and can become as cold as, or unbearably even hotter than outside due to its 'greenhouse' effect. This problem however, can be largely relieved by acquisition of a set of the windscreen insulation kits, or so called 'silver screens', as widely advertised.

2. Privacy. Clearly, without the partition, any passer-by can have a good view of the interior of the van through the cab windows. Again, insulation kits can provide a solution, but they are not the most convenient answer for a short stop when a quicker arrangement would more likely be made use of.

WINDOWS, ROOF WINDOWS and VENTS

The Openings

The size and position of windows, like many aspects of designing for the interior of a van, will be to a large extent controlled by the position of any structural members supporting the van walls. Main vertical structural sections should not be cut without the approval of the manufacturers, who might recommend the addition of steel strengthening. Ideally therefore, the windows should be located between these members to avoid cutting them. I selected the widest windows that could be fitted between the vertical members.

It was found essential to cut away one horizontal structural member for each opening, to be able to incorporate a window of reasonable size. It was considered that the strength put back into the van walls by both the windows and the frames, and ultimately by the internal wooden walls, more than compensated for any loss of strength resulting from the cutting.

Cutting Window Openings

A jig saw, or nibbler, is used to cut the openings in the wall panels, taking care not to damage the surrounding paintwork. The cut metal must be rustproofed. I used grey zinc-plate primer and a rustproof paint. This does not need to be a work of art since it will be covered.

The window openings are cut in the wall panels with a jig saw or nibbler. Here, one horizontal structural member has been cut away for each window.

The windows were designed for thicker walls, so wooden packing frames were fitted.

An inner window frame screwed to the outer and sandwiching the wooden packing frame and van wall.
This is a top-hinged window which opens outwards.

Choice of Window and Fitting

There are many options of window from which one can choose. The type I selected was that manufactured by the German company Seitz. These are integrated double glazed windows and frames with built-in cassettes (roller blinds and mosquito nets). They are constructed almost entirely from plastics, and most importantly, are totally cold bridge free. There appear to be other makes of similar construction.

They do not use glass but acrylics, so the view through them is not perfect but acceptable. They are warm to the touch however, with the great advantage of being double glazed and not attracting any condensation. This make is available in a multitude of sizes either sliding or opening outwards (top-hinged). I was able to use: four windows of one metre wide by forty-five centimetres high, and two square ones of the same height. Many prefer larger, picture-window sizes. It was my hope that the smaller, high set windows, might, in some way, deter thieves. The windows come in two parts:-

1. The black framed external part containing the window. This is offered up, from the outside, to the opening cut into the van wall.
2. The grey or beige internal part containing the roller cassette, which is offered up to the opening from the inside and screwed to the external part.

These windows are designed for a wall thickness of between twenty-two and fifty-three millimetres. Because my van walls are barely a millimetre or two thick, wooden frames of appropriate thickness were constructed and fixed to the inside of the van wall openings with Sikaflex glue. Later, these frames were also used for fixing the wooden wall panels.

Sikaflex Glue

Sikaflex glue sets flexibly. It can be used extensively by the caravan constructor. Things correctly stuck together with it do not come apart without wrecking something. Most importantly, its gap filling, setting, yet flexible, properties, allow for **differential expansion and contraction** between parts to be joined, which must be carefully cleaned.

The window may need future replacement and Sikaflex is too permanent for fixing it to the van wall. The external window frame has a rubber sealing strip which is compressed against the van wall. We applied a layer of non-setting window sealer to the rubber to improve watertightness. The gaps caused by the swaged strengthening grooves in the cut panel were also packed with the window sealer. It is called Scheibendicht supplied by the German company Würth.

Great care should be taken to ensure that the seals around the windows are 100% watertight. Before applying the sealer to the components, as with Sikaflex, the surfaces should be degreased thoroughly with either a proprietary cleaner recommended by the manufacturers of the sealer, or with a cleaning alcohol. The two parts of each window must be tightly screwed together. Periodically the windows and their surrounds should be inspected as thoroughly as possible for loose screws and any sign of leaks (which may be out of sight), ideally this should involve dismantling of any internal wall panels or other equipment sufficient to allow thorough checking.

Sliding Windows or Top-Hinged?

This may be a difficult choice to make, each type having its advantages. There is however one clear advantage to sliding windows in that they can be left open whilst driving. Windows that open outwards cannot.

Top-hinged windows (which open outwards) are less likely to let in rain when they are open, as the rain drips off the lower, outer edge of the opened window which is clear of the van, although this may depend on the make (Seitz work this way). My advice would be to have at least one of each type, perhaps half and half.

Roof Windows, Roof Lights and Hatches

Approximately the same considerations apply to fitting roof openings as side openings. With luck however, you will be able to find a section of the roof panel which can be removed without having to cut through any structural members or swaged grooves. Since it is much easier to fit a hatch or window on a completely flat panel, one must ascertain the dimensions of the flat panel sections, between structural members, before ordering an appropriate size of hatch or window.

The types of rooflights usually fitted to motor caravans provide light and ventilation but not access through to the roof, and my van requirements included easy access to the roof, preferably from inside. (Easy access from outside, such as up a fixed ladder, can be attractive to others who should not have access to the top of your van.) The way I achieved roof access from inside was by the installation of two boat roof hatches which require the same work to install as the more usually fitted roof lights.

One of the two roof hatches, fully opened through 180°. They allow unhindered access to the roof, ideal for cleaning the solar panels or removing the sand laddes which surround them. They also provide reassuring optional fire exits.

Previous experience of boat hatches had shown that not only are they strongly made to comply with the rigours at sea, but also in opening through one hundred and eighty degrees, apart from providing excellent access, they also form a very effective chimney which, with the side windows open, can create an extremely pleasant air flow through the inside of the van. The two I have fitted are over the bed and the dining / kitchen area. The precise positions were dictated by the swaged strengthening grooves in the roof panels.

The hatches, from a yacht chandler, are Canpa Low Line Hatches (59 x 46 cm). The frames are moulded from glass reinforced polyester. The panes are 10 mm thick tinted acrylic, with a lockable ventilation position as well as opening to four preset positions.

FLOOR

Cutting the window openings is probably the first task to undertake, but if you are waiting for the windows to arrive then why not press on with the floor?

A good thickness of wood is a practical floor material to walk on, to fix things to, and to provide a layer of insulation. In my case the van was supplied with a fitted floor of eighteen millimetre plywood which was glued with flexible silicone glue to the bodywork. We decided to add a layer of insulation and another of wood over this.

We sectioned the floor into four parts:-

1. The floor part which forms the walkway, kitchen and cupboard unit.

To this section we glued wooden battens of fourteen millimetres height between which were laid sheets of fifteen millimetres Xtrem.

On top of the battens we glued a twenty millimetres sheet of marine plywood (which is laminated at the factory with waterproof glue).

Xtrem sheets laid between the battens fixed to the floor. A sheet of 20 mm marine ply is standing above, ready to be glued down to the battens. The white section is 10 mm Forex.

2. The floor part which forms the 'dining area'.

The diner is built on a raised floor section forty four centimetres above the main van floor with the area beneath the dining area being used exclusively as a 'water room'. This area also includes a wheel arch.

The water room contains a custom made polyethylene water tank forward of which are mounted the hot water cylinder and all the water distribution equipment. The Porta Potti is also stored here. Following past experiences of water rooms sometimes getting wet, it was decided that this one should have a floor and sides made from a waterproof plastic material completely sealed from the rest of the floor, with Sikaflex polyurethane flexible adhesive. In this way any water leaks from the complex plumbing network would be totally contained within the water room (see chapter on water). The waterproof material used is available in sheets of ten millimetre thickness, consisting of a plastic foam with a smooth white surface. We also used this material for the walls of the bathroom.

It is called Forex and offers excellent thermal insulation properties. The sheet of Forex was glued directly to the van floor. Sides of Forex around this were also provided and all sealed again with Sikaflex to ensure the degree of waterproofness required. These sides were still not the full forty centimetre height planned but would be built up later with plywood.

3. The floor part which would become the bathroom.

This too was covered with Forex but it needed to be sloping to drain shower water away and was left until a much later stage (see The Bathroom, Shower Floor page 88).

4. The floor part which would become the garage with bed over it.

It was decided that insulation in the garage floor was less critical and the eighteen millimetre plywood floor supplied would suffice.

The floor sections: 20 mm pine plywood, left (Kitchen and walkway).
10 mm white Forex, right (Water-room).

The water boiler is standing just to the left of where it will finally be located.

The lower dark brown section is the original supplied floor (Garage section).

The two wheel arches are covered by the boxes left and right.

The wooden block on the garage floor is a mounting on which will stand an Eberspächer diesel fired air heater with exhausts and inlets passing through the hole to outside.

The other box next to the left wheel arch box will be part of the step structure at the end of the walkway up to the bed. It will contain the main battery switches and the electrical consumer unit .

The three 12 Volts batteries will be positioned in the garage section around the left wheel arch, a short wiring distance away from the consumer unit.

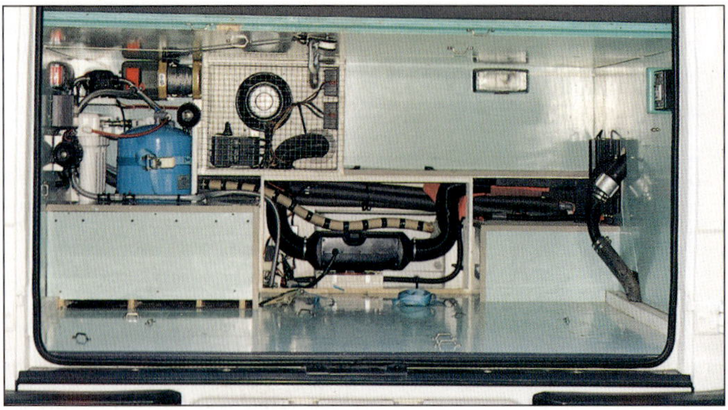

The garage section showing Eberspächer heater in centre. The blue box lower left houses the batteries. The water purification system is above left. The pipe runs can be seen crossing the van. Round sub-woofer and motorbike winch can also be seen.

WALLS, CEILINGS, and PARTITIONS

Electrical Cable Conduit.

Before the walls, ceilings and partitions are installed it is most important to have decided the routes of, and made provision for, the electrical cabling, the water pipes, and any heating pipes or tubes. In an ideal world these would all be contained in a totally accessible duct, thus allowing for any maintenance or modification that might be required at some time in the future.

In my case the electrical cables were drawn through flexible round plastic tubes which were routed around the van as necessary. They were installed alongside, and in some cases inside, structural body sections. In this way there was no obtrusive visible duct which, in the interests of serviceability, might have been preferable.

These tubes had to be installed before the installation of the overhead cupboards, the ceiling panels, and partitions. Mine is not a perfect system in that to add or remove cables from a tube would be difficult, but I compensated for this by including spare cables for any unforeseen future changes.

Water Pipes and Hot Air Ducting

Provision was made for the water pipes and hot air tube to run together around the van at lower level, but the plastic water pipes were well insulated from the hot air tubes and from outside cold with insulation jackets and Xtrem.

Wall Panels

Although all the wall and ceiling panels were made, fitted, and painted at an early stage, they were not finally installed until towards the end of the project. They were cut from 12 mm plywood, painted and screwed to wooden battens which were either screwed to structural van members or glued to van panels. In between the battens, as on the floor, were laid sheets of Xtrem.

Ceiling

A similar technique was employed. Due to the curved aspect of the van roof, the ceiling panels had to be pulled into shape. To achieve this, battens of oak were screwed to the roof cross members, and the ceiling panels (12 mm plywood) were then screwed into the immensely strong oak. Cold bridges were thus again avoided. Before fitting the panels, sheets of Xtrem were glued to the roof sections between the cross members as well as being glued to the back of the ceiling panels, so that there was a double layer of Xtrem insulation on the ceiling as well as an air gap. Thin wooden strips were then applied over the cross members so covering the panel joints.

Partitions

All the partitions were made from 18 or 20.5 mm plywood. They were fitted to the van sides with sufficient gaps for flexibly fixing into place with a thick layer of Sikaflex to allow for expansion and contraction. The sheets were laminated with light grey Formica.

DOORS, DRAWERS, CUPBOARDS and CATCHES

Storage in a motorcaravan must be extracted from every available square centimetre, as the space is so limited. My choice was to use as many drawers as possible in the kitchen area, for high density storage, and one large cupboard, as a wardrobe, with an eighty litre fridge beneath it. (See page 84)

The overhead cupboards provide important additional high level storage, preferably for lighter goods. (See page 84). Sliding doors can be used, or ones hinged along the top edge. My cabinet maker did not like sliding doors in mobile applications so that was that!

Drawer Slides

There was never any doubt about the use of slides for the drawers, they were just too nice not to be used and the latest models on offer not only supported the drawer firmly but also had a spring mechanism which held it closed without having to use the catch. Also available were attachments which allowed simple removal of the complete drawer.

Hinges

Stainless steel piano hinges and screws were selected for all hinge applications due to their appearance and resistance to corrosion.

Drawer Fronts and Doors

All the drawer fronts and cupboard doors were made from twelve millimetre birch ply covered with light grey laminate, back and front, and edged with cherry wood. This has created a strong, attractive product that is easy to clean.

Catches

For me there seemed to be only one choice of catch, having been dissatisfied with others in the past. The chosen version has a pop-out knob mechanism. In the locked position the knob is elegantly almost flush. On pressing the knob in slightly it pops out, this unlocks the door and allows the knob to be used as a handle to pull the door or draw open.

To lock a closed door simply push the knob in and it clicks into position almost flush with the door and locks it at the same time. The knobs and surrounds are available in grey, white, gold, silver and brown.

Drawers doors and knobs.

Knob

BEDROOMS

An overriding factor which dominated my design from the outset was the decision to incorporate a full size ready made double bed. Experience of the alternative, the need to convert one section of the motorcaravan into a bed each time there was a desire to lie down and then putting it all back again, had convinced me that in my next creation things were going to be different. It was my intention to spend periods of travel of several months in my new expedition vehicle and I did not want to have to put the bed away every morning.

Of course it is unlikely that one bed, be it big or small, is going to be sufficient for anyone contemplating the acquisition or construction of a motor caravan. In just about every case it will be necessary to ensure at very least that the dining area will be large enough to convert into a bed, preferably a double, albeit maybe a narrow one.

So it was with me and of all the variables at the start of the design stage, there were therefore four dimensions with their lower limits fixed:-

1. The permanent double bed had to be at least 6 feet (183 cm) long and 4 feet 6 in (137 cm) wide.

2. The diner had to be able to convert to a bed at least 6 feet long and more than 3 feet (100 cm) wide.

Rear permanent double bed also makes a comfortable lounge area.

My permanent bedroom ended up at the back of the van with the mattress positioned for sleeping across the full width of the van and the bed base board at 83 cm above the floor level. The space beneath the bed board, the 'garage', is totally sealed off from the living area with access gained through the rear loading doors.

Garage under rear bed with access from outside only.

The off-the-shelf mattress measures 190 x 140 x 15 cm (75 x 55 x 6 in) - it is not a King size (75 x 73 in) or even a Queen size (75 x 60 in) in American terms, but it is comfortable and most importantly the bed needs no daily construction.

Access to the bedroom is convenient, by two steps at the end of the walkway. Both of these steps have hinged lids and provide extra storage.

The head-room of 90 cm above the mattress is practical in use. It is high enough to allow good head-room when seated or lounging on the bed. The spaciousness is further enhanced by the fully opening roof hatch, above the middle of the bed, which has a blind and mosquito-net cassette let into the grained and wax painted pine roof panel.

Mould Growth under Mattress.

Sleeping generates moisture in a mattress: without adequate air flow there is a risk that mould will develop beneath it. Ideally therefore, any permanent bed should be provided with some means for the air to circulate around the mattress. There are various ways to achieve this.

The technique we employed was to span 20 wooden slats about 6 cm above the bed base board for the mattress to lie on. To assist the airing process, the edge of the mattress is propped up when convenient.

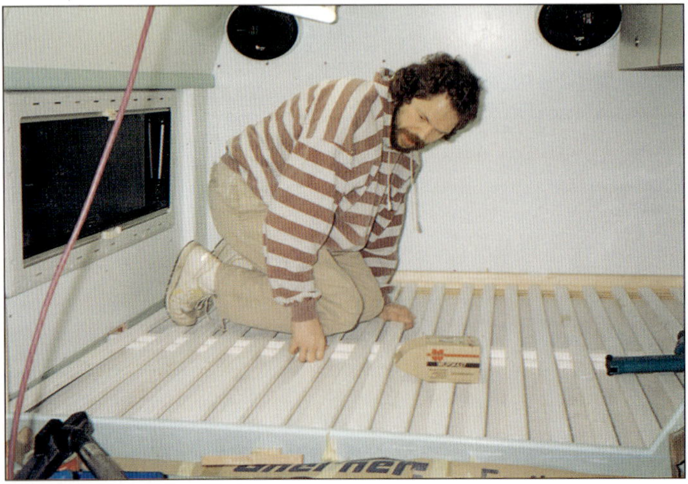

Bed slats in the making.

If there is insufficient room to incorporate such a large air gap, an alternative compromise solution is to make up a criss-cross matrix of thin wooden slats which is placed directly on the base board with the mattress laid on top of the matrix.

The Bedroom as a Lounge

At each end of the bed is a Seitz window with blind and mosquito-net cassette. Over the foot of the bed are two of the overhead cupboards with the cherry wood surrounded doors.

There is a 7 watt Resolux light at the head and one at the foot of the bed and two 5 Watts halogen reading lights at the head. The comprehensive lighting ensures that night time reading is possible in any position.

On one side of the bed, in the end wall, is a stereo pair of high fidelity Infinity loudspeakers.

The whole bedroom can be partitioned from the kitchen or dining area by drawing the double layered, double fullness (twice the width of material as the actual opening width) curtains.

The bed is an ideal place to lounge in comfort whilst still effectively being in the dining and kitchen area, unless privacy is obtained by drawing the curtains.

The Dining Area Bed

To convert the dining area to a bed it is necessary to remove the table and its leg. The central section between the two seats is then bridged with a separate table top, (normally stowed behind the passenger seat in the cab), which rests on a wooden support strip along the top front edge of each seat box.

This table top is then covered with one of the doubled back-rest cushions which folds out to exactly the right size. A good size single or a narrow double bed is thus formed.

The width can be increased by folding up a small table top on self locating brackets at the end of each seat box. The space in between is bridged by a further small piece of wood which merely rests between them on two aluminium angles attached to it. The other double cushion folds out lengthways to cover this additional bed extension creating a fully furnished bed of 185 x 125 cm (72 x 49 in).

Dining area bed layout.

THE DINING AREA or SITTING and DINING ROOM

This area must always be designed with its alternative role in mind, that of a bed. It will therefore need a minimum overall length of 183 cm (6 ft).

The desirability to have seats as wide, and hence as accommodating as possible, is also to the advantage of the bed's comfort. Each of the dining area seats should be able to seat two people which means not less than 80 cm width and preferably more.

My solution was a length of 185 cm which splits into three 60 cm sections for the two seats and the distance between occupied by a 60 cm wide table. The seat cushion foam thickness is 7.5 cm. The backrest cushions are also 7.5 cm but there are two per backrest, hinged together, and 30 cm high: thus they are able to fold out to cover the 60 cm centre section in bed mode.

The whole of the dining area has a floor level raised 44 cm above the van floor level, the space beneath, being the water room, contains 400 litres of fresh water, the hot water cylinder, all associated plumbing equipment and the Porta Potti compartment.

There is a Seitz window with cassette above the table. In the panel above are the controls for many of the electrical functions: a convenient position for access to the switches. On the panel also is a fixed 7 Watts Resolux lamp and three adjustable 5 Watts halogen reading lights, each plugged into a 12 Volts socket.

The Table Top

The main table is of Scandinavian origin and is designed as an auxiliary table for boats. It has a clever combination of leg and hinged top, which allow many degrees of freedom.

The leg is an upside down, two-part, 'L' shape and the vertical member slides into a grooved plate (allowing variable height) which is fixed to the van wall beneath the window. The table slots onto the end of the horizontal member and may be swung through an arc, rotated, and raised or lowered. The hinged teak top is in three equal sized sections, the outer leaves of which hinge over to allow the table to be half width, three quarter or full width.

The disadvantage of this flexibility is that the table is not suitable for the usual task of creating the central part of the converted dining area bed. The separate table top used for this is a piece of finished plywood which doubles as an outside table.

The 'Laguna' table, at its smallest, with its two leaves folded over, and swung against the side wall.

Heat Outlets

There is a hot air outlet in the foot-well beneath the table leg.

Thermometer and Map-Pockets

On the wall beside the front seat of the dining area are two A4 magazine or map pockets with restraining nets. Beside the upper one is a digital thermometer with two displays, one monitoring the interior temperature, the other the outside temperature by way of a probe under the van.

Seat Boxes

The two seat boxes each have a capacity of about two hundred litres. The forward one, being heated by warm air ducts and the hot water cylinder beneath, is well suited to storage of bedding. This one also contains two hinged lids inside, to provide upper access to the water equipment, (see picture on page 90).

The two seat boxes span the water room with the forward one resting on the wall beside the walkway and on a wooden support attached to the van side wall. The rear box rests on the walkway wall and the wheel arch.

The dining area floor is supported on wooden battens attached to the lower edge of each of the seat boxes and also on the walkway wall. It is readily removed to give access to two water tank cleaning holes.

THE KITCHEN and EQUIPMENT

The kitchen should provide primarily cooking and washing facilities, but also adequate storage facilities for all the usual kitchen equipment, including food. Furthermore the larger the area of work surface available the better.

There is a choice when it comes to selecting the fuel for cooking but the alternatives to gas are at present so rarely heard of, let alone seen, that it is unlikely that any option other than liquid petroleum gas (LPG), which is either butane or propane, will be selected. However for certain special applications, and in particular where gas cannot be used, there are alternatives.

Diesel Ceramic Cooker

Perhaps the most interesting alternative is a ceramic hotplate which runs on diesel fuel (or paraffin) with twelve Volts ignition. This particular piece of equipment is elegantly presented with two burners covered by the ceramic top and a stainless steel surround. It requires a small fuel reservoir, close by, with a capacity of a few litres.

What makes it so attractive is the fact that the actual combustion chamber and flame is sealed from the work top and therefore all the combustion gases, both the air for burning and the waste gases, are vented to the outside through the wall of the caravan. The ignition phase utilises about 6 Amps (12V) for three minutes thereafter dropping to a consumption of 0.65 Amps. The output is up to 1800 Watts at about 80 % efficiency. Of further interest is a blower attachment which converts the unit into a heater.

The obvious advantage of this cooker is not having to provide a gas installation. A disadvantage is the high cost of about seven hundred pounds at the time of writing.

Gas Cookers (See also page 173)

For sheer convenience of use, gas cooking is hard to better. (Page 158 provides information on the gas installation.)

A wide range of separate ovens, cookers, and grills is available, but the advantages of having all three cooking facilities in one unit in a caravan installation are at least threefold:-

1. The combination is smaller than three separate items.
2. The installation is easier, neater, and cheaper.
3. The gas connections are simpler with fewer junctions and components used.

I chose a combination of all three in one compact unit made by the Italian company SMEV. It is an elegant piece of stainless steel equipment with four burners, a grill, an oven with a mirrored glass door, an oven light, an oven thermometer, and full 12 Volts electronic ignition to light each flame, at the push of a button. (If at all possible do buy a gas burner with electronic ignition, as its ease of use is a pleasure.) A rotisserie attachment is also available. There are flame failure protection devices on each burner, which automatically switch off the gas supply, if a flame should go out.

When cooking with gas, there should always be a window open, and preferably some roof ventilation as well. The resulting air flow could blow out a flame, furthermore in sunlight it can be difficult to see if a flame is lit. It is therefore no small comfort to know that a flame failure safety feature is always working to protect you. I always recommend its incorporation.

Gas Cooker Installation

The nature of any cooker installation will depend on the maker's recommendations. The space which will need to be provided must therefore be built in accordingly.

It will also be desirable to ensure a clear minimum distance of 60 cm above the burners to avoid an excessive heat build up.

My oven and cooker combination was a close fit in the cabinet opening, with about two millimetres between the oven and each of the side walls. The actual space between either side of the top edge of the cooker and the work surface was almost nothing, which was good for the appearance.

When the oven was in exactly the right place, two holes were drilled through each cabinet side wall into the oven walls (prior to this process, clearly it was essential to remove the oven walls to check that the drilling of the holes through them would not do any internal damage). The oven was then removed and its four new holes enlarged to receive M5 hank bushes, or clinch nuts, which were firmly attached.

To maintain a space between the oven and cabinet walls, M8 spacing washers were glued with Araldite around the clinch nuts. Having countersunk the holes in the cabinet, the final assembly using four M5 countersunk screws has proved ideal, being a good fixing and as easy to disassemble as it was to put together.

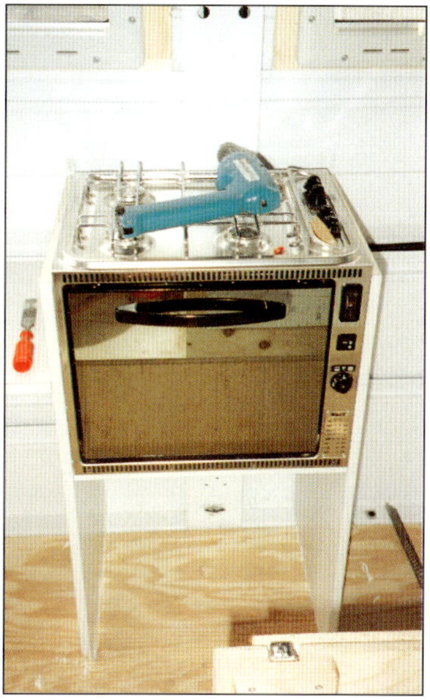

The comprehensive and compact SMEV integrated oven, hotplate and grill . Here it is being offered up to its slot in the kitchen area.

The gas pipe enters the van through a rubber grommeted hole in the van floor at the back of the cabinets, access being gained by removing the drawer beneath the oven. The pipe rises and makes a loop to the front of the cabinet, attached to the underside of the shelf on which the oven stands, where it joins a fixed gas tap, for isolation of the supply. This tap is immediately accessible by opening the drawer directly beneath the oven. The pipe leaves the tap, looping back to the lower, rear, right hand corner of the oven, where, along with the twelve Volts connection, (for electronic ignition and oven light), it is connected to the oven.

Microwave Ovens

Many people are now making more use of microwave ovens. Indeed some have completely forsaken the gas or electric oven for this alternative form of cooking, which is both very clean and efficient. These invisible, high frequency microwaves are directed to the food, actually passing through it and in the process causing the water molecules in the food to vibrate at great speed. This vibration causes friction which produces intense heat to cook the food.

Since the microwave energy generated during the cooking process is totally absorbed by the food, and since there is no direct application of heat, the oven casing remains cool. This cool running is a very attractive feature, particularly so in a caravan environment where, as always, space is at a premium.

There is no reason why a microwave oven can not be installed in a motor caravan kitchen, provided that any vents in the oven casing are not blocked. Condensation is a normal by-product of microwave cooking and the vents should be kept free.

There is however the problem of ensuring that a large enough electricity supply can be provided. Several possible ways of supplying this power are investigated in some detail in the chapter on electricity (see pages 144-146).

The Sink and Drainer

A sink is a must, and the drainer optional, but there is no doubt about the usefulness of the drainer. Apart from its obvious function of being a surface for wet dishes etcetera, it is also another useful surface, perhaps somewhere to place a hot pan. The simplest and most compact implementation of the drainer is in combination with and draining into the sink, hence requiring only one set of drain fittings and installation.

The logical conclusion to this compact format is a combination sink, drainer and gas hob. There are some lovely examples available and if space is strictly limited this may be the best solution.

Sink dimensions of about 30 cm square and 10 cm deep are comfortable to use and plastic bowls, if required, are available to fit in them.

Taps

Taps come in all shapes and sizes with various methods of operation. Whether a monobloc or separate units are used is of personal preference, mine being for a single lever monobloc which allows both hot and cold mixing and flow to be controlled with one movement. My monobloc taps are made from tough plastics by the German company Keller. Installation requires only one round 25 mm hole to be drilled (far simpler than other models I have encountered). It has fittings ideal for attachment to the usual flexible water hoses which are fixed to it with jubilee clips.

Normal domestic taps could certainly be installed, but they are large and it is worth noting here that the philosophy of water management in a caravan is rather different from that at home where we are accustomed to having an unlimited supply, and saving it is not normally uppermost in our minds.

Not so on the road: once we embark on our journey, water becomes a more precious commodity, which from time to time we need to go in search of, and we do not use it thoughtlessly like perhaps at home. Taps designed for the mobile market, (being smaller and with different fittings), have a lower flow rate and are better suited to this attitude of conservation of our vital water.

A Keller monobloc mixer tap and a filtered water tap.

Water Filters

Another system well worth considering installing, is some form of water filtration with its own separate tap at the sink. This can solve the problem that concerns many who worry about the uncertainty of the water quality they are having to take on board. Indeed, filtration equipment and purification chemicals that, together can make safe virtually any grade of water, are now available and well suited to caravan use. Such filters are considered in more detail in the chapter on water (see pages 114-116).

Kitchen Cabinets (See also page 74)

We formed the cabinets by cutting their walls to the shape of the van walls and gluing them in place with a thick layer of Sikaflex glue. The horizontal partitions were then fixed into place with the use of Lamello type biscuits and glued with wood glue. All the panels, the walls, and partitions are sheets of plywood covered on both sides with Formica.

Drawers, rather than cupboards were selected for the kitchen range. They were simply clipped onto their respective pair of telescopic drawer slides, which had been carefully positioned and firmly and painstakingly screwed into the walls.

The fitting of slides is precision work if they are to perform optimally, or even at all, and it is important for the draw opening (the space between the cabinet walls) not to be undersize or the draw will never fit. If oversize, spacers can always be inserted to move the slides closer to each other.

Xtrem is glued to the van walls behind the drawers.

Kitchen Work Surface

The work surface has many uses apart from food preparation and its surface area has been made as large as possible. The greater the area of work surface the better. A Formica surfaced kitchen top with post-formed edge can be had from do-it-yourself shops.

It will need to have its holes cut for the sink and taps. If the material is laminated chipboard it is wise to seal the chipboard thus exposed, and the back edge, with Sikaflex. This should significantly reduce the probability of water ingress, and subsequent rot so common with this type of wood once moisture has access. The worktop may then be located with dowels and fixed to the walls of the cabinets with brackets.

Water-Proofing

The layout of the kitchen area should make provision for water retention and avoidance of any spillages reaching the wrong places. A carefully thought-out splashback, and judicious use of appropriate kitchen sealers, will pay dividends when the inevitable happens and fluids are set flowing.

Wall Cupboards

The valuable space above the work surface may present the opportunity to install wall cupboards. These ought not to be as deep as the work surface or they will be obtrusive. For a 40 cm deep surface, a wall cupboard depth of 35 cm should be about the maximum. They can be glued in position with Sikaflex, can be partitioned, and shelved if tall enough, and have stays to hold their lids open. A method of retaining their contents when the lid is opened is required. Insulation material should be installed between them and the van walls.

Due to their height, heavy weights in these cupboards may adversely affect the driving characteristics of the van. Consequently, ideally only lighter goods, perhaps clothes, should be stored in them.

Kitchen Windows

If possible the sink and the work surface should be beneath an opening window to provide both natural light and also ventilation near to the gas stove.

Refrigerators

There are several options available and their relative merits are detailed in the Chapter on Refrigeration (page 167).

I chose to use a DC compressor refrigerator with an additional low profile fan module. The prime benefit of a compressor system is its relatively low current consumption. Its other advantages include quiet and cool running as well as very simple installation compared with an absorption refrigerator. Only a 12 or 24 Volts feed is necessary. No gas supply is used and no holes through to the outside required.

The Coolmatic RD80 is an 80 litre DC compressor refrigerator. It can be seen, installed beneath the wardrobe, behind the driver's seat.

THE BATHROOM or SHOWER ROOM

Even the most compact motor caravans, currently available, are likely to include a bathroom through one ingenious technique or another.

Some make use of the kitchen sink for this purpose but many provide a totally self-contained bathroom facility. For the large conversion the latter option is almost mandatory and was certainly my requirement, but try as I might to design an exclusive area for each facility, I could not quite manage to incorporate a permanent double bed and still have enough space available purely for a bathroom, within the 6.3 metres length of my chosen van. I opted for a compromise by which the bathroom doubled as a van entrance.

I would have preferred an even shorter vehicle, for easier manoeuvrability and less conspicuousness, but this would have obliged me to make more internal compromises than I wished. (I must reiterate though that one really does grow accustomed to driving a large vehicle and, as has often been said before, many of us now prefer it. I also particularly appreciate the height of the driving position which not only affords a better view of the road but also allows views over hedges which in a car would never be seen. I digress.)

The bathroom inner door closed in the forward position and the sink folded up, converts the bathroom area into an entrance hall, or lobby.

With the van side entrance door closed, and the sink folded down, the area can comfortably be used as a bathroom, and reasonably privately, still with its inner door in the forward position. For total privacy the inner door is closed in the rear position.

The compromise works well in practice not least because of the alternative van entrance, through the cab, which can be used at any time, including whenever the bathroom is in use whether it be for the usual ablutions, or drying laundry, or for storage or anything else.

The bathroom, with its inner door shut in the rear position for maximum privacy, and the sink folded down for use. The Porta Potti hatch, beneath the sink, can be hinged open to allow the Potti to be slid out.

Bathroom Door

As can be seen, the door between the bathroom and the walkway serves two purposes:

1. It can be shut in the rear position to close off the bathroom from the walkway and living quarters. In this case it keeps the bathroom private, and opens the walk-through between the driver's cab and the living quarters. There is a curtain across the walk-through to the cab which can be used if required or when the bathroom is in use.

2. When the door is closed in the forward position (as in the picture on the previous page) walk-through to the cab is blocked and there is a clear passage from outside, through the van side entrance into the bathroom, and round to the left into the living quarters.

The door itself is made from plywood, covered with 2 mm Forex, and fixed with a stainless steel piano hinge. It can be locked in either position, from either side, with draw bolts which do not rattle, due to their incorporated springs.

Bathroom Walls

Given the requirement to be able to shower in the bathroom, waterproof walls and floor are needed.

The forward wall is made from 20 mm plywood covered with 10 mm Forex. The back wall is made from 20 mm plywood covered with 2 mm Forex, and was curved to meet up with the side opening, due to the fact that the bathroom was not as wide as the side entrance door. (Forex, which is a plastic covered foam material, is waterproof with a matt surface pleasant and warm to the touch. It is ideal for the bathroom walls, and is easy to work.)

The reason for this width discrepancy was that the van was not long enough to be able to allocate the whole width of the side entrance door to bathroom space, although there is no doubt that if it had been, it would have made a more accommodating washing area.

Had the construction been arranged in such a manner, the rear bed would have been correspondingly less wide since the dining area could not sensibly have been shorter than the 1.83 m used, and required, for its second bed mode.

Side Entrance Door

A 10 mm sheet of Forex was fixed to the inside of the van side entrance door with stainless steel screws into hank bushes fastened to the door. This sheet surrounds a 45 cm square Seitz window, equipped as usual with blind and net cassette. This was fitted in just the same way as the other windows as outlined earlier in the section on Windows.

It was possible with slight modification to be able to attach the standard door opener and lock on top of the 10 mm Forex. Sheets of 15 mm Xtrem were glued to the inside walls of the door. This not only provided important heat and sound insulation but also contributed to a pleasing 'clunk' when closing the door.

Side Entrance Well

The entrance well, which forms the step into the side of the van and which is a common feature in most panel vans, was a complication requiring special attention. Were this to have been left unmodified, the hole in the floor, with the door closed, would have significantly reduced the size of the bathroom floor area.

A solution was required which retained the convenience of the step when entering the van but which covered the well when the door was closed.

This problem was solved by fixing to the door a storage box with a shelf on top. This box exactly filled the well with the door closed. The box had to be waterproof, and because the well received water during showering, a drain was required.

The shelf was made out of teak, a stable, attractive wood well known for its use in shipbuilding, with natural water-resistant characteristics. The box was both screwed and glued to the door with Sikaflex (as ever). (A problem with this wonderful adhesive is trying to break the joint should it ever be necessary in the future!).

Shower Drain

The standard entrance-well step cover is of a durable, flexible plastic and worthy of being retained and, of course, it fitted the well perfectly. Clearly it was designed to withstand the rigours of loading and unloading the van and under it there were standard drain holes, through the step floor, in much the same way that there are always drain holes provided along the lower edges of car's, and also this van's, doors.

A hole was drilled through the well step floor, large enough for a waste fitting with a siphon, for a 25 mm outlet pipe to be installed. A corresponding hole was drilled in the plastic well-surround which was sealed to the waste fitting with mastic.

The sides of the well were fitted with 10 mm Forex, glued in place, which overlapped the plastic surround in such a way that all shower water drained onto the plastic surround (and hence out through the waste) but still enabled removal of the surround for servicing.

Shower Floor

The barrier between the shower floor and the interior walkway was formed with a substantial stainless steel angle screwed down to the floor.

The floor of the shower was a sheet of 10 mm Forex glued in place but spaced upwards from the floor, at the inner end next to the stainless angle, with the use of a strip of closed-cell foam cut into a wedge. This creates a run-off for the water towards the entrance well and its waste outlet.

The Forex was also screwed down with stainless steel screws and carefully sealed all around with Sikaflex.

Finally in true nautical fashion, a teak wood grating was made to cover the floor, standing on small rubber feet. An aluminium angled edge strip has been added to provide suitable protection for the teak's leading edge.

Shower Curtain

Although all the elements of the bathroom compartment are waterproof, a shower curtain has been added which can be drawn across the bathroom door. This helps to ensure that all the water ends up in the right place, inside the shower room. It is suspended from a light-gauge curtain track fixed to the ceiling. The curtain can be held in place at strategic points by short strips of Velcro.

Shower Tap and Sink

The tap used in the bathroom is the same grey plastic single lever Keller model as used in the kitchen, except it has a plastic hose and adjustable shower head. It is fixed to the left of the sink, close to the side door (and also within reach when standing outside the van side door).

The shower head may be clipped in any of three positions:

1. Above the sink.
2. At high level for showering indoors.
3. To a fixing on the outside van wall for showering outside, immediately before entering the van.

Given the limited width of the bathroom, a normal fixed sink was too restrictive. The solution was to install a folding sink which drains out through its waste pipe when it is folded up.

Over the sink there are two teak shelves with a mirror above and an Aqua Signal electronic fluorescent light over.

Bathroom Storage

The front wall of the bathroom has a teak "cockpit box", a recessed compartment, let into it near the ceiling. Beneath this is a large towel rail. Above the entrance door is a shelf at forty-five degrees for wedging articles behind. Beneath this is another large towel rail.

Toilet

Beneath the sink is a door which hinges back to reveal a Porta-Potti that may be slid out of the 'water room' onto the teak grating and positioned for use.

Chemical Toilets

There are several versions of chemical toilet available. The Porta-Potti, which I use, is one of the better-known makes. In my opinion it is an excellent design. It has separate fresh water and waste water tanks. For emptying, the effectively sealed waste water tank is simply separated from the toilet and carried to the nearest wc to empty. It is hygienic, easy to clean, easy to empty and, provided it is used as instructed, with adequate use of chemical additive, has no unpleasant odour.

Entrance Handles

Entry into the van through the side entrance, up the step, is assisted by retention of the forward handle which screws directly into the van door pillar.

A double sized handle (which was rescued from the two that were removed from the rear van loading entrance) was attached to the rear bathroom wall.

Bathroom Heating

There is an air vent in the shower-room rear wall which provides hot air ducted from the combination of air heaters. This of course helps to make the bathroom a more comfortable space but furthermore it allows the bathroom to be used very effectively as an airing cabinet, when required.

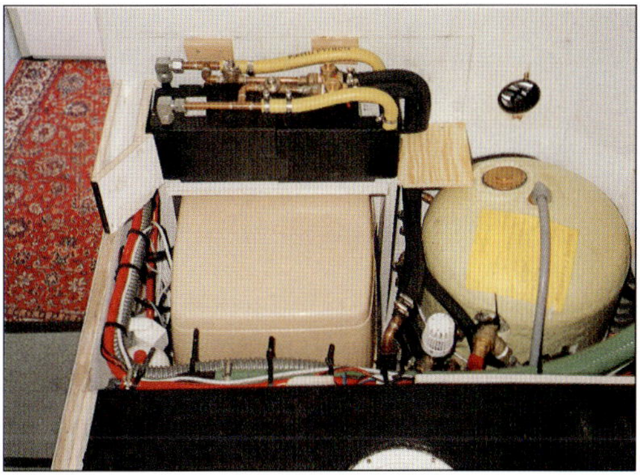

A view from behind the bathroom wall of the water room installation. The beige Porta-Potti can be seen with the auxiliary heater boxes over it. To the right is the green calorifier with the outlet vent for bathroom hot air above it.

STORAGE - Internal and External Access

It almost goes without saying that the camper can rarely have enough storage space. On our trips we like to take everything including the kitchen sink. Some items, such as outdoor table and chairs, and bicycles, need never come into the living area of the van whilst other things need never go out.

Storage with Internal Access

It is the cupboards, drawers and seat boxes that should provide what we want inside the van: as large a volume of storage space as possible, to accommodate items of clothing, washing things, food and associated equipment, and bedding. To this list we might add books, maps, documents, cameras, music and other essentials and conveniences.

Vital Volume

Storage space that has a heater, or perhaps a water tank, installed in it, is no longer an empty space and consequently not the storage that is really useful for our everyday essentials. All the equipment such as heaters and water tanks must go somewhere of course, but they should occupy no more space than necessary and preferably they will be carefully installed in their own close fitting compartments.

In this world of mobile equipment and motor caravans every cubic centimetre is important. Compact equipment and big empty spaces available for storage are beautiful. Carefully planned installations should ensure that none of these vital volumes are lost.

A seat box with hinged inspection covers which will give access to the water installation it will cover.

Good Access for Maintenance

All this is notwithstanding the access which should always be thoughtfully designed into any technical installation, to enable essential servicing or checking.

What is more, gaining access for checking, emptying, filling, cleaning, adjusting, modifying, or just admiring, should not be so complex a task that one puts it off.

Hopefully by design, we will avoid lost volumes which we cannot use due to lack of access, and we will not spoil a potentially good, clear cupboard space by installing a boiler or some other item in it.

We might take a leaf out of the motor car designers' book which keeps technical items out of sight in their own area but accessible when necessary, and manages to squeeze storage compartments out of otherwise wasted spaces.

Storage with External Access

Items that are not required inside the motor caravan are best stored in external compartments with outside access. The most obvious of these is the collection of comfy chairs and camping table which are the first items to be set up on arrival at our 'stop', whether for the night, week, or perhaps fortnight, or just for an impromptu meal stop on a fine day. Ideally these should be readily removable from their slot without too much juggling of other equipment.

Other things which are prime candidates for relegation to external storage are beach accessories, lilos, sun umbrellas, beach mats, diving gear, fishing tackle, boats and their engines, outdoor games, spare canisters, tools, and so on.

For security reasons, bicycles and motor bikes would ideally be stored inside compartments. It might be thought though, that it is unlikely that sufficient space would be available for enclosed storage of these larger items. The most likely method for taking them along is mounted on a proprietary rack which has been fixed to the back of the van. Several well thought out systems are available.

However, if the motorcaravan body type is a custom-built box, then it is a fairly straightforward matter to add external access doors for separate compartments, and indeed these may be designed very specifically with the future contents in mind.

If, on the other hand, it is a van conversion, additional, external doors may be added to the van walls, kits being available for this approach, but door sizes are limited. By far the simplest and cheapest method is to use the access doors already there.

This is the option that I took, I have used the whole of the area underneath the rear double bed for storage. The area is sealed off from the living quarters, and access to it is gained through the rear van loading doors.

This storage area contains, within their separate compartments, the auxiliary batteries and an Eberspächer air heater. There is the water filtration plant, the spare wheel, a battery charger, and various electronic 'black boxes'. The additional storage of about two cubic metres is sufficient to accommodate a Honda Dax 70 cc motorbike, an inflatable rubber boat and engine, and many other accessories, as well as the usual table and chairs.

Fixings

It is necessary to provide secure fixings for most of these. The technique which I have used to good effect is very simple: I searched through the racks of yacht chandlers until I found stainless steel screw down fixings which were appropriate for 25 mm wide ratchet straps to pass under.

Ratchet Straps

Nylon ratchet straps with tested ratings of 500 or 1000 kg can now be had for a couple of pounds, with judicious buying. The ratchet tensioner allows the most secure tying down, whereas the more simple spring clip type (which gives no mechanical advantage when tightening) is also useful. These straps are a load -fixer's dream as not only are they very strong but also the lever and ratchet enables high tensions to be obtained.

By careful positioning of the fixings, I have found the securing of my cargo, with the straps, to be quick and effective.

FLOOR COVERINGS

The qualities that we should be looking for in a floor covering are durability, water repellence, non-slipping, good appearance, comfort and easy cleaning.

There are many lino-type coverings made from various materials which are well suited to the application but personal taste has to be the final arbiter.

My choice was to fix rubber tiles to the wooden floor and lower walls, using contact adhesive. These tiles are 2 mm thick and not too difficult to apply, and keep their appearance well. They have all the qualities which I have listed with the possible exception of comfort, since, on a cold day, they are cold under a bare foot. I have introduced an extra element of comfort by cutting to size some off-cuts of a woollen carpet. These I have edged with 50 mm gaffer tape and they are located on the floor by short strips of double sided sticky tape which deter the carpets from 'walking'.

The carpets catch the dirt and grit, which is not foiled by the door mat, and can be brushed clean, or removed for cleaning from time to time.

Vacuum Cleaners

This is a machine the qualities of which we are all aware. It is probably the only one capable of collecting dust, sand, and little stones, which always manage to accumulate in inaccessible corners. We probably take it for granted at home, and it is only when it is not available that we realise how important it is. The problem with taking one on tour in the van is obvious: it is just too big.

There is however a spate of smaller vacs. now available which are compact enough to justify taking along. Beware though of the time a rechargeable unit will run on one charge. It does not run for many minutes before it needs recharging, a process which can take many hours. Furthermore the suction power leaves a lot to be desired.

Look out for the low powered units which run directly from the mains. I have found a compact one from Argos rated at 240 Volts and only 150 Watts. The cloth filter very quickly becomes clogged with dust but provided this is cleaned every few minutes the machine does a reasonably creditable job.

Gaffer Tape

This indispensable fabric backed tape is polyethylene or p.v.c. coated. It is strong, flexible, with a very sticky rubber adhesive on one side, and is highly conformable with good waterproofing qualities. It is available in black, white and silver usually in 50 mm widths but it may easily be sub-divided without cutting. It is used in the heating trade to seal air ducts. It is also used in the music industry by roadies to make their temporary stage installations safe by taping down cables and anything needing fixing. The army know it well and make good use of it. Probably it acquired its name from the 'gaffer' or senior lighting electrician on film or TV sets who has long put its qualities to good use in similar applications to the roadie. It is expensive but one roll used sparingly can last a caravanner a long time and prove worth its weight in gold.

SOFT FURNISHINGS

The soft furnishings are amongst the last considerations of the construction process, because it is only when all the furniture is finally in place that cushion dimensions are able to be determined accurately. They are certainly not least, because the seat cushions, scatter cushions, and curtains, add the soft touch to the caravan. They can provide an opportunity to add a feeling of luxury and comfort to what might otherwise appear to be a fairly austere environment. It is therefore worth making an effort to identify an attractive, quality, durable fabric, which blends in with the furniture, and which will stand the test of time in a situation which will come in for much hard use and possibly, dare I say, abuse.

Upholstery is not a skill that everyone will want to tackle themselves. A professional may be able to make better covered cushions, to size, and at very competitive prices, compared with the alternative of you buying foam, fabric, zips, and accessories, and then sitting down at the sewing machine.

If his price includes discussing the project, offering samples, measuring up, manufacture, and finally fitting, then so much the better. This is the option I took. The upholsterer I went to was familiar with this type of work, and showed an interest in the project. Equally importantly, he was able to incorporate my own specific requirements. He offered various grades and thicknesses of foam. The samples he supplied, combined with his invaluable experience in this type of work enabled me, with his guidance, to make appropriate decisions.

Seat Cushions

Quilting on the seat cushions can contribute to the feeling of luxury but it also creates innumerable dust and dirt traps which are not easy to clean, so a plain covering might prove more suitable.

Almost certainly the seat boxes in the caravan will be required to fulfil two roles, each of which ideally would require different degrees of cushion firmness.

As seats, the cushions should not 'bottom out' when in use, so the foam should therefore be stiff or deep enough to avoid being completely compressed. At all costs one must not feel the hardness of the seat box lid through the cushion.

As a bed on the other hand, the body's weight is distributed over a greater area, and a softer foam is more comfortable.

Naturally enough this issue is complicated further by the wide variation in people's weights and sizes, so clearly some level of compromise is required.

Practically every motorcaravan has storage under the seat-banks and in nearly every case, to maximise storage, entry is gained by lifting the usually hinged lid. This lid is of course covered by the seat cushion, and a consequence is that gaining access to the seat box can be hampered by the pressure exerted by the seat and backrest cushions. Alternatively both the cushions can be removed to give full access for lid opening. Either way does not help to make a happy camper.

The way I circumnavigated this particular little pet annoyance was by cutting the lid lengthways and hinging the two parts together with a (stainless steel) piano hinge so that the rear section is fixed to the seat box, with only the front section hinging open. It was then necessary to hinge the seat cushion in such a way, and by careful positioning of the Velcro cushion retention strips, that it allowed the lid (now smaller) to open vertically quite unhindered. The lid is held both open and closed with the use of a sprung lid stay.

The upholsterer fitted a layer of expanded, polyester felt between the foam and the fabric cover which primarily is designed to prevent the fabric from working its way around the foam and also to provide additional padding.

Each of the cushion covers is fitted with a full length zip enabling removal for cleaning.

To the back of each of the seat and backrest cushion covers, is sewn a strip of Velcro which correspond with their counterparts glued to both the seat lids and back rests. Although self-adhesive Velcro is used, the use of an impact adhesive is essential on the lids and back rests to prevent the Velcro tearing away from the woodwork.

The backrests are 30 cm high, consist of two separate layers of the same 7.5 cm foam as the seats, and are hinged so that they may be folded out to complete the bed option.

Curtains

There can be little doubt that curtains on the windows add a finishing touch to a caravan, particularly when they are colour matched to the seat cushions. Given their small scale, it is possible to use the smallest size curtain track available, but the curtains must be kept well clear of the cooking process. During the daytime, open, bunched curtains must be at the end of the track most distant from the stove.

I do not have any curtains on my windows and rely on the roller blind cassettes which do an excellent job as far as privacy is concerned, being opaque when closed, but leave something to be desired in the prettiness stakes. So far I have not added curtains to my 'to do' list.

I do however have curtains which may be drawn to close off the bedroom from the kitchen and dining area, which have a softening or prettying effect even when open.

The track is a small variety which is simply screwed to a roof panel. The curtains have a weight chain along the lower edge. At least 50 % fullness (one and a half times as much fabric as the span) helps to make them more elegant. (100 % is better).

The other place I have installed curtains is between the driver's cab and the caravan. Clearly it makes sense to have all the curtains made from the same fabric, and for warmth, comfort, and opaqueness, a thick or doubled fabric is better.

Scatter Cushions

It is always handy to have a few cushions around and in my case I have them covered in the curtain fabric and filled with a mixture of feathers and loose foam. They are fine for comfortable lounging on the bed.

INTERNAL FINISHES

The internal appearance of any caravan is to a large extent going to be controlled by the type of internal finish selected, and there are several options available for the various surfaces to be covered.

Of course internal decor is a very personal matter and everyone will have their ideas of what they like. The great advantage of home construction is that the finishes can all be personalised. Conversely, the disadvantage is that the ultimate effect is not going to be seen until it is too late to change it so any means of having some sort of preview may not go amiss. One possible way of having a glimpse of how things may end up looking is to do some line drawings of the layout and then colour them, or create some three dimensional colour rendered projections with a suitable CAD system.

Ceiling and Wall Panels and Finishes

These are likely to be some form of wood base which may be unfinished, pre-finished, or perhaps covered with a plastic coating. Clearly the pre-finished sheets will require least effort and some of the surfaces available can be durable.

There are several good, tough versions of wood finish obtainable. They can be clear or in various wood-like colours, and some have coloured tints through which the grain of the wood remains visible, offering much scope for colour co-ordination.

Fond though I am of natural wood finishes, I thought that the confined nature of the inside of a motorcaravan was such that the darker the finish the smaller and more oppressive the space might feel. Consequently a light pine plywood for the walls and ceilings was selected which although less hard and tough than for example a birch plywood, is only about half the weight. A particular aspect of the pine is the pronounced sweeping curves of grain.

Given the closeness of both the walls and the ceiling, a paint was selected based on natural plant oils and waxes through which the grain remains visible. Not wanting the starkness of pure white walls, a slight cyan tint in a white paint for all the plain wood surfaces was used, with some long narrow strips of wood finished in a darker cyan. The paint is waterproof and readily 'touched-up'.

The kitchen work surface, doors, and drawer fronts are covered with a light grey Formica, the doors and fronts being surrounded with American cherry wood. All the surfaces are flat, smooth, practical, and easy to clean.

The combination of the paintwork, the curtains and scatter cushions in the same green and mauve material, the complementary-coloured seat fabric, and the turquoise floor and wall tiles, creates a reasonably coordinated overall appearance which is light, airy, and distinctive, and all the more interesting when the sun reflects in differing hues.

LIGHTING

Lighting can be put into two distinct categories, functional and effect lighting.

Functional Lighting

This ensures that there is sufficient light in the right place to enable the occupant clearly to see what he needs or wants to see.

Effect Lighting

The purpose of effect lighting is to make the environment more attractive, interesting, and pleasant. It is best achieved by focusing light on a specific feature or area.

At its most exotic it can involve the use of coloured light. It may not in itself provide sufficient light for detailed activities such as reading or sewing.

Inside the motor caravan the prime requirement is to concentrate on functional lighting and probably only white light. There are simple ways to provide functional lighting which can double as effect lighting when required.

Power Consumption of Lamps

Whilst it is always possible to take along a mains powered lamp, there is the problem that unless the van is plugged into an external supply the lamp is useless. The exception is by the use of an inverter to convert the battery power to 220 or 240 Volts but this is not the most efficient use of the energy available.

Again it is important enough to be repeated that, to the motorcaravanner, electrical power is precious and wherever possible electrical consumer items should be carefully selected for their efficiency and lower power consumption.

This applies to lighting fittings where good advantage can be taken of highly efficient, low Voltage products, which with a nominal 12 Volts input, are very suitable for use in motorcaravans.

Fluorescent Lamps and Compact Fluorescent Lamps

As an example, there is now available a range of compact fluorescent lamps from Osram and Philips which can be run from a 12 Volts supply. They last on average eight times longer using only 20 to 25 % of the energy of corresponding tungsten GLS filament lamps (the light bulbs we typically use at home).

What is more, they have a good colour rendering with a warm appearance similar to our domestic light bulbs. The older 'transistorised' fluorescent strip lights for 12 Volts, typically have a colder or harsher colour temperature, providing a less homely feeling than the newer compact fluorescents, with their efficiency being about half that of the compacts.

The disadvantage with both the 'transistor' and the newer, compact fluorescents, is that they require electronic control gear to run them, hence the word "transistorised" often used to describe them. In itself this is not a problem, as the light fittings contain all the electronics to convert the 12 Volts supply into the high frequency power necessary to run the tubes: the problem is that the complete assembly with bulb is fairly expensive. But the compact fluorescent can be superb, and worth the investment.

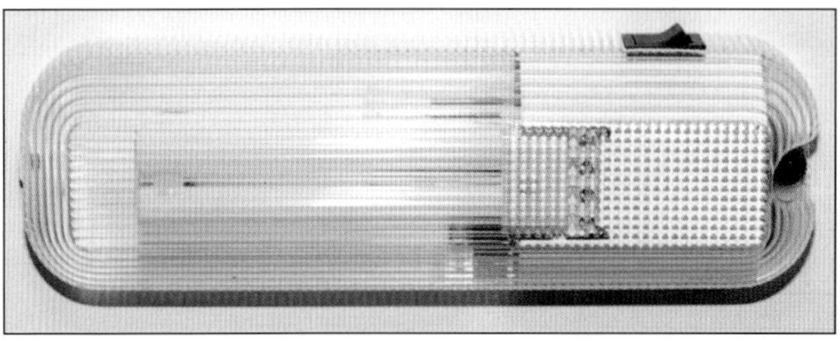

A 7 Watts compact fluorescent lamp by Resolux.
The electronic control gear is housed in the section on the right. The switch is top right.
All light fittings should have a switch incorporated.

Filament Bulbs

An alternative to the fluorescent range is the bulb similar to those found in torches but typically more powerful. That found in many motorcaravan and boat fittings is the miniature bayonet cap or MBC type also known as Ba9s.

The most suitable, efficient, and commonly specified is the 5 Watts tungsten halogen bulb, which has a far greater light output than its vacuum, krypton, or xenon counterpart available in both 4 and 5 Watts. Both of the latter alternatives are relatively quite dim.

The brightest MBC bulb suitable for this type of 12 Volts application is the 10 Watts tungsten halogen. It can be substituted for the 5 Watts version, but it may burn too hot for some fittings which specify the 5 Watts type.

An advantage of some lights using filament bulbs is their swivel base which allows them to be pointed in any direction.

There is also available the version on a stalk much like a 'map-reading' light. With a tungsten halogen bulb this is good for pointing light of reasonably high intensity exactly where required.

A 5 Watts halogen lamp by Aqua Signal.
It slots into a bracket and plugs into a 12 Volts socket.
The swivel base allows the beam to be pointed in most directions.
The red lever adjusts polarisation filters which dim the light.

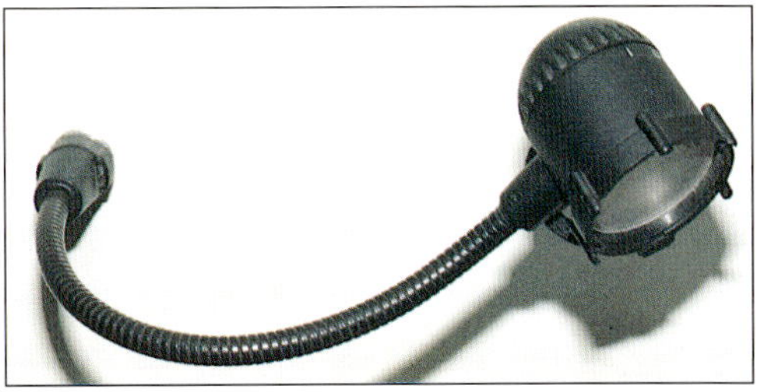

A flexible stalk, 5 Watts halogen lamp by Osram.
It plugs into a 12 Volts socket.

Another bulb type in common use is the festoon, as often found in car interior roof lights. These are available in 5 and 10 Watts ratings.

A higher power bulb sometimes encountered in caravan type fittings is the 21 Watts car stop light bulb. Whilst this bulb provides good light, it burns hot and, like all non-halogen filament bulbs, is not very efficient. The best application for a lamp of this power is via an auxiliary power hook-up when power consumption is less critical.

Light Fitting Applications

As suggested earlier, there is little point having a light installed in a motorcaravan which will only work if there is a mains hook-up. This may be fine, or indeed normal, for a caravan in which mains hook-ups are generally accepted as standard, but where the trend is towards a higher degree of self-sufficiency it would be less so. To this end I harp back to the sense in striving for electrical efficiency and the search for low-power consumers. This tends to narrow down the field significantly as far as lamps are concerned.

There is little doubt that in terms of maximum lumen output for minimum power input, fluorescent tubes cannot be matched, and the compact version is the best. Furthermore, both these types of tube last far longer than any of the alternatives.

For general ambient lighting the fluorescents, because of this higher light output, are the most effective. A 7 Watts compact fluorescent bulb can provide sufficient light for pleasant, warm coloured, general motorcaravan illumination. The 8 Watts single tube fluorescent will also do this job, but not so well as it is less bright and harsher (or colder) in appearance.

A single 7 Watts compact unit is ideal for providing adequate lighting for detailed activities such as reading, providing it is reasonably close to the work.

For a chatty or relaxed atmosphere, where a lower level of light is sometimes appropriate, the glare from direct view of the light source can be a strain on the eyes. On such an occasion it is useful to be able either to cover the lamp with a shade, or if possible to re-focus it.

This is where adjustable lights with filament bulbs come into their own as they can be directed exactly as required. To provide a low level ambient illumination, this type of fitting can, for example, be pointed towards a light coloured wall from which the light will be reflected around the van thus avoiding any glare. Also, in this way, otherwise dark corners can be brightened up, to help create a more spacious feel.

These adjustable lamps can also be used for detailed work by focusing the light directly onto the job in hand.

My technical and stage lighting background obliged me to overkill the lighting which I installed in my van. Consequently, I have placed a lamp wherever detailed work or reading was likely to be done as well as in areas just for effect. As might be guessed from my enthusiasm for compact fluorescents I have made wide use of them and find their warm colour temperature pleasant. A number of 7 Watts units, each of which provides a comfortable light level for the relatively close locations in the van layout, have been used. These levels are good for reading and other detailed work.

An advantage of the 7 Watts fitting is that it runs satisfactorily with a 5 Watts tube installed should the light from the larger source prove too high.

This type of lamp is also available with two tubes installed and the option to switch on either or both. However, more flexibility can be gained by installing two separate single-tubed units which together cost about the same as the double-tubed version.

12 Volts Ring

To add to my lighting possibilities I have installed a 12 Volts ring around the van at high level to which are connected at regular, short intervals, twelve 12 Volts 2 pole sockets. The version of plug and socket selected is not the usual cigarette lighter type but the smaller 2 pole version, which is more solid in construction and connection.

In use are two types of 5 Watts tungsten halogen bulbed lamps, and stalk lamps, which may be plugged directly into any of these sockets on the ring, thus allowing a high degree of lighting flexibility.

An added bonus of the ring sockets, is the ability to plug in any other 12 Volts accessory such as travelling iron, soldering iron, portable radio power supply, razor, fan, or nicad battery charger.

Spurs off this ring feed all the fixed compact fluorescents as well as the cassette radio and disc player installation.

Radio and TV Interference

A word of warning about fluorescent lamps for those who enjoy listening to short-wave radio, the BBC World Service for example (that excellent British institution which for the overseas traveller, offers an unparalleled opportunity to listen to not only the nine o'clock news, but also many other interesting broadcasts); unfiltered fluorescent lamps radiate an intolerable amount of short-wave radio and TV interference. Unless adequate filters are used, filament bulbs are the best choice during AM radio and TV reception.

Colour Temperatures

The light emitted by any 'white' bulb will have a colour hue and it will vary with type. Bulbs do not normally have any direct reference to their colour temperature printed on them, and it is unlikely that their appearance will give an indication of their colour-rendering properties. The only way to be sure of the so-called 'colour temperature' of a bulb will be by referring to the manufacturers' publications. Generally speaking, a warmer temperature will have a more comfortable 'feel' to it.

- Colour temperature of domestic type bulb = 2700°K (Warm)
- Colour temperature of Compact Fluorescent = 2700°K (Warm)
- Colour temperature of regular Fluorescent Tube = 3500° - 4200°K (Cool)

THE ROOF and FIXINGS

There are various fixtures and fittings that can be attached to a motorcaravan roof, and one should create a short-list of those most likely to be required during the van's life.

The nature of roof fittings is that once in place they might not easily, if at all, be moveable, so it is critical to be right first time. It may not be easy to make future, unplanned for, additions.

Here is a list of most of the possibilities likely to be considered for roof fitment:-

1. Roof rack
2. Top boxes
3. Spare wheels
4. Roof vents
5. Air conditioners
6. Radio aerials
7. TV aerials
8. TV satellite dish
9. Navigation aerials
10. Roof hatches
11. Elevating roof
12. Roof fixing rings (for fixing luggage)
13. Solar panels
14. Wind generator
15. Marker or spot lights
16. Bicycle racks
17. Sand ladders
18. Awnings

Roof Layout

Once the shortlist is complete it is a straightforward matter to decide the best way to lay out the options, not forgetting to make allowance for the items one may wish to add later. As always, the available space is finite and rarely big enough so be prepared yet again to compromise. This means that the list must be prioritised.

In my case this was not too difficult because above all else I needed two roof hatches,

five solar panels (with provision for possible additions), and four sand ladders, which did not leave room for much else. I made some scaled cut-outs of the roof and the chosen components, and arranged them for a preferred fit. (If you want to use opening hatches like mine, do remember to allow twice the hatch size to ensure that they will open fully.)

Roof Fixings

In fixing any of the options to the roof it is best, wherever possible, to avoid making holes in the roof. The fewer potential sources of leaks the better.

It may seem that the best method of fixing is always with the use of bolts passing straight through the body, but this is not necessarily the case thanks to the wonderful range of glues at our disposal. Again it is Sikaflex 221 or Sikaflex 252 to our rescue. They are both, gap-filling flexible adhesive sealants, and either is appropriate for bonding plastics, metal, ceramics, wood, and other materials. Type 252 is quicker setting with a harder consistency. Whatever type of body we are working with be it a panel van or a GFP (glass fibre reinforced polyester) box, these glues may be used for fixing many if not all our options to the roof.

It can be seen from the following examples that with the use of whatever brackets may be appropriate, which in turn may be glued to the roof, most options may be fixed.

Hatch Fixing

Clearly a hatch is going to require a hole through the roof (and a rather large one at that). The frame is glued with Sikaflex. There can be no room for mistakes here and it is imperative that all recommendations of the glue manufacturer are strictly followed. In particular the surfaces to be bonded must be cleaned scrupulously.

Solar Panel Fixing

To fix the solar panels four hard aluminium right angles were bolted to the panels and then glued to the roof. Having used clinch nuts or hank rivet bushes fixed to the panels, the panels may subsequently be unscrewed from the angles, if necessary, leaving the angles securely glued to the roof. To pass the electrical cables through the roof required waterproof cable glands which were enclosed in a waterproof plastic junction box,

Sand Ladder Fixing

The sand ladders were fixed to the roof in the following way: for each pair of ladders (which nestle together) a pair of fixing brackets were made. Each fixing bracket consists of a thick strip of oak with two long (M14) bolts fixed through it with the head carefully fitted flush so that the bolt will not turn. These wooden brackets are glued to the roof with the bolts standing vertically to locate and fix the ladders with nuts and large washers.

This job could perhaps have been done better with the M14 bolts welded to steel brackets, but a problem of raising the ladders adequately to clear the curve in the van roof had to be overcome. Furthermore, the oak forms a suitable (and quiet) surface on which the ladders bear.

Roof Height and Air Flow

In spite of the inevitability that one or several items will be fixed to the roof, it is also equally certain that the taller this makes the vehicle the less manoeuvrable it will be.

• Greater height means restricted access. In the interest of general access it is best to keep the overall height as low as possible. It may therefore be better to fit bicycles for example at the back of the van.

• Protrusions on top of the front of the roof are more likely to increase fuel consumption. The airflow over a vehicle moving forward tends to lift over the front top edge of the vehicle. Ideally this airflow should not then come into contact with, or be broken by, any subsequent part of the vehicle. If it is, turbulence (disturbed and irregular airflows) will be created which will result in greater air drag with a corresponding increase in fuel consumption.

This is the reason for trucks and caravan rigs having spoilers fitted to the top front edge of their cabs: they lift the smooth airflow completely over the rig. The cost of the spoiler is soon recovered in fuel savings.

It is therefore good design to set back from the front edge any additions to a roof in the hope that the airflow will pass above them unbroken (the airflow may not lift very much so tall additions, without a spoiler, are likely to break the flow and increase fuel costs). Unfortunately without testing in a wind-tunnel it is difficult to know quite how the air will flow around the van. Checks around the van after a long journey at steady higher speeds in bad weather might give some indication of any turbulence which may have been present. The telltale signs are usually to be spotted as ruffled patterns of dirt on the body work.

BULL BARS and SPOTLIGHTS

Bullbars

Bullbars seem to raise quite a lot of controversy and not a small amount of indignation. This may be due to a misunderstanding arising from their use to create a macho appearance, assuming that is a reason for their popularity. Other reasons may be the possibility that they can save expensive damage to the vehicle in an accident. As well as the additional safety protection that they might be able to offer the occupant of a vehicle so adorned.

At present I am not aware of any statistics which might indicate that they are able to do either, although logically it seems likely that they would do both assuming solid attachment to the vehicle. However I do have personal experience of an accident, not involving third parties, in which I am convinced that the presence of a bull bar on the vehicle in which I had the accident contributed to my life being saved.

The vehicle, with me at the wheel, totally lost traction on an inclined field due to ice concealed just beneath the surface. We gathered speed at an alarming rate and nose dived over a three metre high bank into a track below, the bull bar taking much of the impact.

Incredibly I stepped out unscathed. There was considerable damage, not least to the bull bar but surely it had helped to save my life.

I think the salient point here is that the vehicle had a chassis to which the bullbar was attached. In such a case there seems to be every likelihood that, if there is a front collision, significant frontal damage can be avoided.

I have not yet fitted one to my van because it was conceived as a low profile motorcaravan. However I am aware of the safety attributes which I think a bullbar engenders.

Spotlights

Spotlights and driving lights can usually be nestled amidst a bull bar and are capable of offering considerably improved night vision.

I have fitted spotlights onto my bumper and find they offer safer night driving. Spotlights usually use H3 bulbs with a power rating of 55 Watts. Two of these are 110 Watts and a pair therefore will draw an additional 9 Amps from the alternator. Before installing this type of equipment it is important to be sure that the alternator is strong enough to power them as well as everything else whilst still maintaining an adequate charge rate. Usually a spotlight comes with a choice of suggested installation circuits: the one I prefer wires the new lamps through their own on/off switch (and relay) but so that when they are switched on, they come on only with headlight 'Full Beam'- They go off automatically when the headlights are 'Dipped'.

Spot or Driving Beams? And Fog lamps

In my opinion the medium range 'driving' lamp (with its wider, shorter range beam) offers more useful light than the narrow beam long-range spot. For those who want the best and have the alternator to cope, a pair of each could present the best of both worlds.

Fog lamps are also advantageous, particularly for drivers who cover large distances and hence are likely to encounter fog more often, but they should be mounted as low as possible (in or below the bumper) to reduce light throw-back, and provide more relaxed driving in fog. ☺

BASE VEHICLE SPECIFICATION (Including Factory Fitted Options)

Model:	MERCEDES-BENZ 814 DA/3700 Van.
Wheelbase:	3700 mm.
Engine:	OM 364 LA 4 stroke, 4 cylinder diesel, 3972 cc direct injection, turbocharged with intercooler.
Output:	102 kW (139 HP) at 2600 rpm.
Max. Torque:	428 Nm at 1300 - 1800 rpm.
Top speed:	100 kph (62 mph.) approx.
Compression Ratio:	16.5:1.
Consumer System:	24 Volts.
Alternator:	28 V / 55 A (3 phase).
Batteries:	2 x 12 V / 88 Ah each.
Gearbox:	Manual 5 speed all synchromesh.
Transfer Case:	Road gear 1.037 Cross country gear 1.670 Central differential lock.
Four wheel drive:	Permanent.
Torque distribution:	1:2.62 front:rear axle. Differential lock at rear axle.
Frame:	Ladder type frame, bending and torsion resistant U-profile side members and tube type cross-members, front cross-member with incorporated pintle hook.
Suspension:	Front live axle (3 ton capacity) parabolic springs with shock absorbers and stabiliser bar. Rear axle (5.8 ton capacity) parabolic springs with shock absorbers and stabiliser bar.
Steering:	Recirculating ball power-steering with ratio 1:19.
Brakes:	Front disc rear drum dual circuit hydraulic with compressed air assistance, automatic load dependent, anti-lock braking system (ABS), compressed air activated exhaust brake (disengageable) connected to service brake.
Tyres fitted:	8.5R17.5 Michelin XZY.
Diesel Tank:	70 litre.
Instruments:	Speedometer, fuel, water temperature, oil pressure, revolution counter, duplex air pressure gauge.
Indicator lamps:	Direction indicators, high beam, charging current, oil pressure, brake fluid, parking brake and brake wear indicator for front break linings, brake pressure warning light, indicator for air filter cartridge exchange, front and rear differential locks engaged, flame starting system, fuel reserve, ABS indicator, garage light indicator.
Combination Switch:	Stalk, low/high beam, headlight flasher, turn signals, horn, windscreen wiper, 2-speed, intermittent, windscreen washers.

Heater:	Fine adjustable water heating system with five rotating knobs: 3-speed blower, upper/lower distribution, temperature selector, fresh/recirculated air, air conditioner.
Air Conditioning:	System in front cowl. Temperature selector, separate vents for heads.
Water heater:	Warm water auxiliary heater (diesel) type Eberspächer D5W with automatic controls and digital clock timer.
Other:	High roof, no internal partition, hinged side door, 270° rear door hinges, sun roller visor, heated outside rear view mirrors, ramp mirror, four outside van upper corner marker lights, visco-coupled radiator fan. RDS Radio and tape player with front/rear speakers, battery 'controller' to monitor voltage, net current flow and state of charge of batteries, fluxgate compass display, precision level gauges, side/side, front/rear, rear view video display, air horns.

DIMENSIONS

Overall length:	6330 mm / 20 ft 9 in
Overall width:	2240 mm / 7 ft 4 in (excluding mirrors)
Overall height:	3000 mm / 9 ft 10 in
Turning circle:	13.4 m / 44 ft
Step up height to caravan:	450 + 200 + 250 mm / 18 + 8 + 10 in.
Door aperture:	780 x 1835 mm / 2 ft 3 in x 6 ft 2 in
Interior length from dash:	4990 mm / 16 ft 4 in
Interior length behind cab:	4020 mm / 13 ft 2 in
Interior width at waist level:	1920 mm / 6 ft 4 in
Interior height:	1900 mm / 6 ft 3 in
Work surface height:	915 mm / 3 ft
Work surface length:	2020 mm / 6 ft 8 in
Table dimensions (LxBxH):	900 x 600 x 680-780 mm / 35x24x27-31in. Folded B: 300mm
Bed dimensions (LxBxD):	
1) Permanent double bed:	1900 x 1400 x 150 mm / 6 ft 3 in x 4 ft 7 in x 6 in
Available headroom:	900 mm / 35 in
2) Diner bed conversion:	1850 x 1250 x 75 mm / 6 ft 1 in x 4 ft 1 in x 3 in
Available headroom:	1040 mm / 41 in
Bathroom dimensions (LxBxH):	730 x 720 - 870 x 1900 mm / 29 in x 28-34 in x 6 ft 3 in.
Wardrobe (HxWxD):	940 x 550 x 400 mm / 37 x 22 x 16 in
Rear storage (WxDxH,V):	1935 x 1280 x 830 mm, 2 m^3 / 6ft 4in x 4ft 2in x 33in, 70 cuft
Gross vehicle weight:	7490 kg
Unladen weight:	5570 kg
Load capacity:	1920 kg

CARAVAN SPECIFICATION

Body type:	Panel van conversion with factory fitted high roof option.
Insulation:	Closed cell polyurethane foam 10 mm, 15 mm and 20 mm sheets, doubled as necessary. 12 mm, 18 mm and 20 mm plywood sheets.
Windows:	Six double glazed polyurethane top hinged in hard foam frames with roller blinds/screens.
Roof lights:	Two boat hatches with 10 mm smoke grey transparent acrylic panes mounted in glass fibre reinforced frames. Acrylic panes may be fully opened 180° on hinges, roller blinds/screens.
Consumer system:	Dual voltage, 12 V and 24 V system.
Batteries:	3 x 12 V / 115 Ah each. Lead calcium, sealed, maintenance free solar batteries.
12 Volts Charging:	1) Up to 3 A from 1 x 48 W Siemens solar panel and regulator. 2) Up to 17 A available from 24 V system via voltage and charging converter.
24 Volts Charging:	1) Up to 7 A from 4 x 55 W BP solar panels and regulator. 2) Up to 10 A available from engine alternator via charge splitter relay. 3) Up to 15 A available from switch mode constant voltage compact mains charger.
Control Panels:	1) Master isolation switches on 12 V and 24 V batteries. 2) 14 circuit consumer unit with thermal magnetic breakers supplying main circuits. 3) Main control panel with illuminated switches for 2 x rear heat exchangers, main water pump, water filter pump, diesel transfer pump, gas regulator de-icer, diesel pre-heater, waste tank emptier. 4) Rear Air heater control panels. 5) Refrigerator indicator and temperature control.
Battery Monitors:	2 x 'Controllers' to monitor voltage, net current flow and state of charge of 12 V + 24 V battery circuits.
Gauges:	1) Water: 10 led. fresh water and waste water tank levels, switchable. 2) Diesel: 10 led. auxiliary diesel tank level. 3) Gas: analogue dial LPG tank level.
Mains Power inlet:	External inlet via RCBO to battery charger.
Mains Power outlet:	1 x 16 A outlet from 200 W (peak 400) Inverter.
Lighting:	5 x 7 W compact fluorescents, 2 x double 8 W fluorescents, 2 x halogen 5 W stalk lights, 2 x halogen 5 W reading lights, 2 x 20 W halogen general floods in boot area.
Refrigerator:	Coolmatic RA-80, 80 litre (2.83 cu ft) capacity with electronic program control and cold accumulator, 24 V operation.

Cooking:	SMEV gas hob with four burners, grill and oven, all with piezo ignition and flame failure gas cut-outs.
Cooker Ventilation:	Opening windows behind hob, low level from cab vent, roof hatches.
Sink and Drainer:	SMEV stainless steel combination unit.
Water system:	400 litre food quality plastic fresh water tank under seating/dining area supplies hot/cold mixer taps in bathroom and kitchen and filtered water tap in kitchen.
Hot water:	28 litre marine calorifier heated by engine cooling water and auxiliary diesel powered water heater, supplies hot/cold mixer taps in bathroom and kitchen.
Water filtration:	Reverse osmosis and carbon water filtration plant in boot area with separate tap outlet in kitchen.
Water pumps:	2 x Flojet quad diaphragm automatic self-priming 12 V to pressurise main and filtered water systems.
Waste water:	65 litre tank externally underfloor receives all waste water and emptied remotely via electrically operated gate valve.
Heating:	1) Eberspächer diesel 3 kW warm air heater full/half setting. 2) 2 x 1 kW heat exchanger warm air blowers heated by engine cooling water and auxiliary diesel water heater (Eberspächer D5W). Both with ducted blown air to sitting area and bathroom.
Gas Tank:	60 litre LPG tank and regulator system mounted externally underfloor. 28/35 mbar regulator and aux. outlet. Icex defroster.
Bathroom:	Single lever hot/cold mixer tap on hose supplies folding sink with shower spray setting for internal and outside shower. Shower curtain, mirror, shaver socket, double fluorescent light, opening window with roller blind/screen, teak shower grating, shelves, storage, towel rails, Porta Potti in concealed compartment.
Seating/Dining:	Forward facing and rear facing double seats with adjustable table in between. Converts to double bed. 2 x magazine racks. Under seat storage. Internal/external max.min thermometer.
Bedroom:	Permanent double bed at rear of van with 15 cm latex and wool covered mattress.
Wardrobe:	Front to back extending rail. Large mirror on door.
Flooring:	Rubber covered throughout, carpets over.
Other:	Thirteen drawers on slides in kitchen area, one deep to take bottles, five overhead cupboards, fire extinguisher, RDS radio, tape, disc player, CO detector. Door to cab and bathroom. 2 m^3 storage under bed with access through rear doors only. Auxiliary 250 litre diesel tank under van. 4 x 1.5 m sand ladders mounted on roof.

FABRICATION MATERIALS

Floor:	Board of French pine plywood (Pine des Landes) 20 mm, 7 plies. Face and inner plies rotary cut veneers, the same throughout. Gluing AW 100 (W.B.P.).
Walls:	Board of Finnish Spruce plywood 18 and 20.5 mm, 9 plies. Same type of production and waterproof gluing as 'Floor'.
Wall Panels:	Board of Finnish Pine plywood 12 mm, 9 plies. Production as 'Floor'.
Furniture:	As 'Walls' and also board of Finnish Birch plywood 18 and 21 mm, 13 and 15 plies. Production as 'Floor'. Laminated both sides with HPL (Formica).
Furniture Fronts:	Board of Finnish Birch plywood 15 mm, 11 plies. Production as 'Floor'. Laminated both sides with HPL (Formica).
Shower Walls:	Covered with Forex 2 mm or 10 mm.
Drawers:	German Beach plywood 12 mm, 7 plies. Production as 'Floor'.
Drawer Fronts, Doors:	Surrounded with American cherry wood 5 mm.
Bathroom:- Shelves, Grating:	Teak.
Small Parts:	Oak, Alder and Maplewood.
Paint:	Osmo Color Dekor Wachs Deckend:- Internal wall panels. Osmo Color Holz Deck Farbe:-Storage areas. (Ostermann & Scheiwe GmbH & Co., D-4400 Münster)
Floor Covering:	Mondo Natural Rubber Flooring 2mm. (Mondo S.p.A. 12060 Gallo D'Alba (CN) Italy.)

The end of the road at the remote Spanish village of Gosol in the pre-Pyrenees. To proceed North into the beautiful Cadi nature park involves driving over rough tracks.

The old and the new, both doing the same job at a campsite in central Spain.

CHAPTER 8

WATER, PLUMBING and WINTERISATION

Today's motorcaravan would not be complete without hot and cold running water in the kitchen and bathroom. A hot and cold shower facility also is normal. There are at least two water tanks; one, the fresh water tank, stores the water for drinking, cooking, and washing, while the other, the 'grey' water tank, holds the waste water thus generated which drains into it.

Some vans have a third tank installed, a 'black' water holding tank, which retains the soiled water from a marine type toilet. More commonly this third tank forms the lower part of a self-contained portable chemical toilet.

Water Sources

When on the move the frequency with which the motorcaravanner is obliged to fill up the fresh water tank will depend on two factors: the size of the tank and the rate at which the water is consumed. Also, the hotter the weather becomes the more water will be needed.

Campers who do not want to have their lives dominated by the daily search for water soon learn to conserve this precious commodity. The motorcaravan builder with similar intent wisely looks to designing into his creation as large a tank as he reasonably can find room for. It makes further sense to incorporate this fresh water tank within the insulated part of the van to avoid the problems of the water freezing in colder weather.

The places where fresh water may be taken on vary from country to country and depend on circumstances but are most likely to include the following:-

1. Campsites:
   All should be able to provide unlimited supplies of fresh, potable (drinkable) water.
2. Petrol and service stations:
   Many allow customers taking on petrol or diesel to fill up with fresh water.

3. Hotels and or restaurants:
   Customers might, with permission, be able to fill up with water at either of these, provided they have eaten or even stayed overnight.
4. Wells:
   In remote regions the local well may be the only source of water, and a polite request where necessary can be productive.

The Hose

Typical garden hoses, as might unwittingly be selected for transferring water from the source to the van, are not of food grade quality. In normal garden use they do not need to be. Such a hose might impart a taste to the water if not worse.

Ideally, a hose selected for refilling the fresh water tank should have the food grade stamp, (a glass and fork motif), marked at intervals along its length.

A length of twenty or more metres should be considered.

Garden hose quick release adaptors (which also might not be food grade) are very convenient for connecting to the various taps that will be encountered.

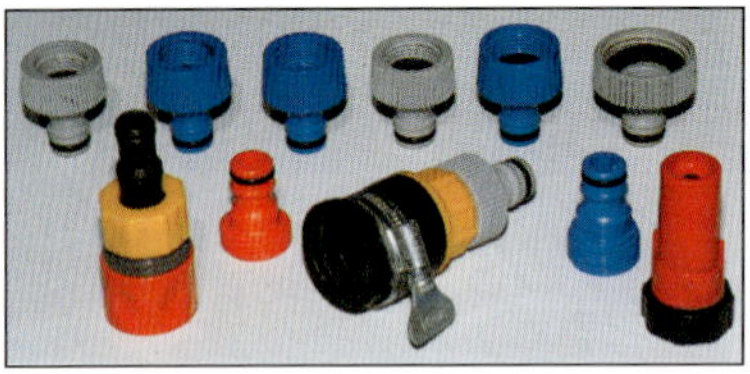

A selection with different threads for screwing to threaded taps and plugging into the hose will prove invaluable, as will an adaptor with rubber fitting and clamp for easing onto the spout of a threadless tap.

Water Purification

Whilst many water sources are likely to be safe enough to drink, the camper is always faced with uncertainty regarding the quality of any water on offer. It is therefore a comforting precaution to adopt some means of purifying the water taken on board.

1. There are several proprietary chemicals which can be added to the water at the time of filling up.
2. There are various types of filters which can be fitted in the van's cold water line immediately before the drinking tap. (These are in addition to the simple mesh filters which should always be fitted before the water pump to hold back larger particulate contamination and thus protect the pump.)
3. An almost certain way to be sure is to boil the water.

Purifying chemicals and carbon filters may both be used together. There are a number of in-line filter systems, available for domestic water purification, which have replaceable carbon filters. One could fairly easily be installed in the van to good effect.

Regarding chemicals, my preference is to add 'Micropur' powder to the tank each time I fill it. This disinfects the water, the tank and the water pipes. It is tasteless and, it is claimed, preserves the water for up to six months.

Also I have installed a water treatment system which uses a particulate filter, carbon filters, and a reverse osmosis membrane. It has its own ten litre holding tank and a separate pure water tap at the sink.

Reverse Osmosis and Carbon Filter Water Treatment System

The filter bank consists of four elements: a sediment pre-filter, a carbon pre-filter, a membrane filter and a carbon post-filter. This combination comprehensively removes, amongst others, organic water pollutants such as pesticides and herbicides, toxic metals (e.g. lead and mercury), and biological pollution (including bacteria and viruses).

Due to the pressure (2.5 bar-6.0 bar) required to force the water through these four filters I found it necessary to add a separate pump to the filter bank input. I had an old pump which I was able to regulate to its maximum possible pressure of about 2.5 bar which I find is sufficient to generate purified water at a rate of about one litre per hour although the rate depends on the temperature and the quality of the water. (A pump capable of 5 bar pressure would double this rate and be more suitable.)

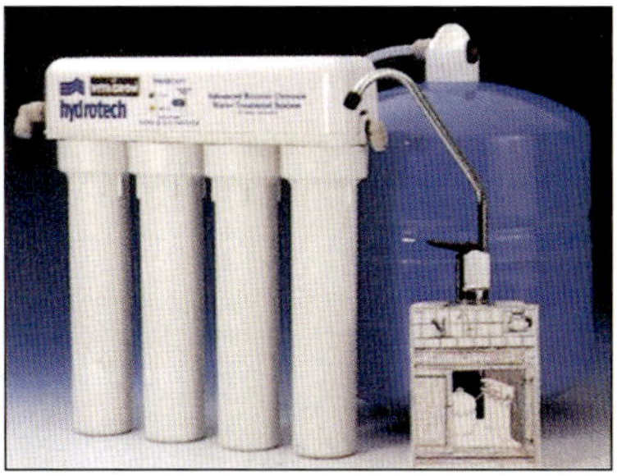

The treated water accumulates inside a pressurised membrane within its ten litre tank, and it may all be drawn off from the system's tap completely without switching on any pump.

In practice, when the system is treating the water, the pump runs for about three seconds every twenty or thirty seconds, (a pressure accumulator tank of a litre capacity, connected to the pump, convincingly increases this 'off-time' from a mere two or three seconds without it, to the twenty or thirty seconds). Generation stops when the tank is full after approximately ten hours, starting again only if any water is drawn off and has therefore to be replenished. Because this ten litre reserve is usually sufficient to last a day or two, (depending of course on the rate of consumption), the filter pump can be switched on to make more pure water when it is convenient such as during driving or when the van is empty, or other times when the noise of the pump does not disturb.

This combination of chemicals and filtering ensures that the purest drinking water is 'on-tap', obviating the need to buy any bottled water.

Katadyn and Safari Filters

Both Katadyn and Safari systems have been used for many years extensively in situations where water supplies are untreated. They are available in various formats to suit differing applications and consumption rates. The smallest Katadyn filter is a hand-held device weighing about half a kilogram.

It has a built-in hand-pump and is suitable for pumping and filtering water directly from a sink full of water of dubious quality, or even a dirty pond, into a drinking glass.

All models are based on the mechanical principle of ultra-filtration through a microporous ceramic filter element, which can be brushed clean time and again. In a van it would be appropriate to install an 'in-line' model with its own separate drinking water tap. The rate of flow depends on the pressure from the pump. Very approximately, at 2.5 bar it takes about half a minute to fill a cup (dependent on water temperature and quality). The quality of generated water is high, being clear and free of bacteria.

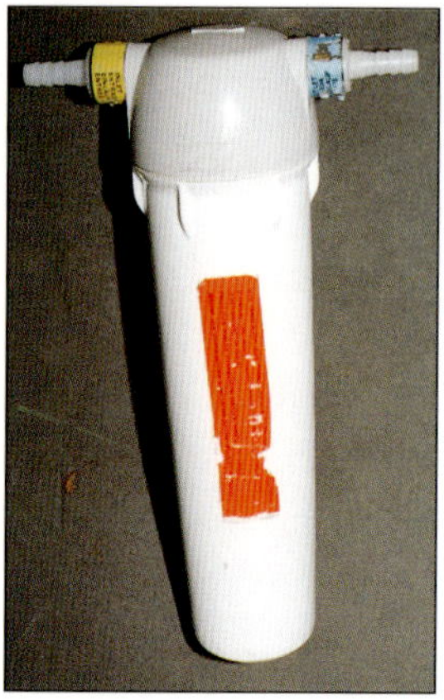

An 'in-line' Katadyn filter.

Fresh Water Tanks

Fresh water storage tanks should be made from a material which has a neutral effect on the water. Clearly they should not taint the taste of the water. Plastics are the best medium for mobile applications and if of sufficient thickness can be very strong and durable and most importantly watertight! Black is the colour of preference because the dark interior hinders the growth of bacteria. Food grade plastic is a material from which a tank can be moulded to fit exactly the space available.

I took this option. We supplied the tank-maker with a diagram of a fresh water tank designed to fit beneath the raised dining area (with a cut-out for the wheel arch). The exact positions of all the pipe attachments and other critical details were specified. It was constructed from 8 mm black polyethylene, has a capacity of about four hundred litres, and includes:-

1. Internal baffles to prevent the water from surging about.
2. The inlet, the outlet and breather pipes.
3. Three inspection and cleaning openings with lids.

However, if one of the many off-the-shelf tanks can be incorporated then so much the better. I was able to locate an appropriately sized unit for my waste water tank because I was not as concerned about the highest capacity for every last litre of waste water storage.

Frost-Protecting Tanks

Water freezing in a polyethylene tank will not be fast and bulbous, and it will hardly harm the tank, but such a situation will do nothing for the 'vanner who wants to use his van in the cold. It's a fiercely frustrating matter to find the fluid will not flow, following frost. This, like a squid eating dough, must be avoided at all cost.

The safest and simplest way to frost-protect a water tank is to situate it within the heated and insulated van. If this is not possible the alternatives are less satisfactory and more complicated:-

1. Provide an external heated compartment.
2. Electrically heat the tank with a small low power immersion heater.
3. Heat the tank with a warm air pipe passing through it.

Items **2.** and **3.** are both available from caravan suppliers.

Waste (Holding) Tanks

All the fresh water tank's aspects apply to waste tanks.

The waste water which empties into the waste or holding tank is 'grey' water consisting of washing water from the kitchen and bathroom and perhaps food particles. As such it is not so offensive or contaminating that it cannot easily be discarded. Nevertheless, there are laws pertaining to the discharge of any waste water, and it is therefore important that careful consideration is paid to where it is deposited.

In spite of these laws, a consequence of the relative ease with which the grey water may be discharged is that the tank does not have to be particularly large. In fact it makes sense not to be carrying around excessive quantities of waste water.

Notwithstanding this latter point, there is a requirement for commercially produced caravans to have a waste tank capacity of at least half that of the fresh water tank.

Waste Tank Location and Emptying

The waste tank can successfully be situated unprotected under the van. It is a pragmatic solution that avoids excessive paraphernalia.

This is the technique I have employed having spent long periods lying on a piece of Xtrem under the van puzzling over where it could best be located. Eventually the light dawned and I found an area between the main chassis members where I would be able to locate a 60 litre polyethylene off-the-shelf tank. It was necessary to have made up a pair of 'L' shaped steel brackets which cantilever off one chassis member with the tank sitting on them and fixed to them with two ratchet straps.

There is no frost protection for this tank although I made sure that there are no low-points (sumps) in the flexible pipes delivering the waste from the sinks to the tank: were there to be any, in freezing conditions a plug of ice could quickly form in the low-point and block the pipe. This would prevent subsequent waste tank emptying and a corresponding inability to use the sinks. When the temperature drops below freezing I must leave the emptying valve open to allow the water to pass straight through. It may be collected in a bucket which can be emptied regularly (the contents may be a block of ice!).

A word about the waste tank emptying valve: having lived in the past with the usual type of manually operated valve, I am well aware of their inherent problems: often they are slightly, to very, inaccessible, requiring crouching and reaching to operate. If you do not choose to use your waste hose to lead the waste away, you had better be quick off the mark to avoid being splashed as the waste starts to flow!

Electric Gate Valve

I had, from time to time seen advertised, and thought how useful would be, an electric gate valve. When the time came, and my new project was underway, I took the plunge and bought one.

It consists of a fairly standard sliding gate valve with an eight centimetre (three inch) diameter opening. It mounts flat on the bottom of the tank with four bolts. A sealing mastic should be used to avoid leaks.

There is a motorised opening attachment and a switch. The motor is bolted to any fixture such as the chassis, and is connected to the valve by a worm driven flexible drive cable. It is wired up to both the battery and a supplied rocker switch, which is mounted inside the van where required.

There is an l.e.d. indicator which should be positioned beside the switch. This lights when the valve is open. Emptying the tank has now become a treat to which I, in my simple way, look forward!

THE PLUMBING SYSTEM

The design and location of the plumbing system has to take into account many factors, most of which are common sense, but some of which can easily be forgotten, and all of which must work and fit well together:-

1. Tanks

To fill a tank quickly from a fast running hose, a large inlet pipe, perhaps 40 mm diameter is required. The outlet pipe and breather pipe can both be 12 mm.
Internal baffles will limit water surge effects.
Look for at least one large, watertight access hole to allow for inspection and cleaning.

2. Watertightness

This almost goes without saying, but it should never be taken for granted and every joint should be regularly inspected for leaks or drips, particularly in the early days after commissioning. Fittings bed in, and can loosen.

3. Tubes

The most common are flexible food grade plastic tubes connected to the fittings with stainless tube clamps. There are some excellent push-fit piping systems which use semi-rigid tubing and a wide range of push-fit fittings. These can offer ease of assembly and alteration, no leaks and an elegant solution.

4. Frost Protection

To enable the whole plumbing system to function normally, without freezing, when external temperatures fall below the freezing point of water, careful consideration should be given to rigorous insulation.

No part of the system, including any part of a pipe run, should be allowed to freeze, with the possible exception of an external waste tank as already discussed. It is a wise precaution to enclose all pipe runs in insulating jackets and pay particular attention to any part of the water system which may be unheated, possibly diverting a warm air flow towards vulnerable areas.

Heat rises, and pipes embedded in floors can still freeze in a warm van if they are not near a heat source. Care should also be taken not to overheat any pipes which might melt if directly adjacent to hot air pipes for example.

5. Strainers

Mesh in-line strainer-filters should be used between the tank outlet and pump inlet to protect the pump and its valves from particulate contamination.

6. Pressure Bottles

Pressure bottles are also called accumulator or expansion tanks. They may be mounted anywhere in the system after the outlet side of the pump.

An essential part of any pressurised water system, they smooth the flow and stop the pump from cycling, extending time between pump start-ups, and thus, reducing pump heating, saving battery power, and increasing pump life.

If pipe banging occurs, the installation of an additional pressure bottle or accumulator tank, close to the problem, should eliminate it.

Regular pressure bottles, without membranes, must be mounted vertically.

Pre-pressurised accumulator tanks, with membranes, can be mounted in any position and are self-draining when winterising.

7. Pumps

There are many types. It helps to use an automatic pump, with a pressure switch that switches off the pump when the pump pre-set pressure is reached. An automatic pump can be left switched on. A pump capable of running dry, without damage, is a safe bet. A self-priming pump capable of lifting the water at least as high as the distance between the tank and the pump is necessary.

8. Isolation Taps

When planning the system, thought should be given to incorporating as many strategically placed isolation taps in the pipe runs as will enable system maintenance without having to drain the tank, and to enable draining the various system components for winterisation.

9. Draining Pipes with Taps

To facilitate draining the system, at least one pipe with an in-line tap, connected to the lowest part, should pass through the floor (if necessary) to drain the fresh water under gravity directly to the ground.

10. Filler Pipes

Should be of sufficient diameter to avoid a fast flowing hose overflowing at the filler. 40 mm should suffice.

11. Filler Cap

Should be placed high enough to avoid the chance of water flowing out from the tank when the van is not level, on a steep hill for example. A lockable cap will reduce the risk of anybody tampering with the water or the cap.

12. Breather Pipes

As with filler caps, these should be placed high enough to avoid overflow. To avoid blow back when filling the tank there should not be a low-point in the breather pipe in which water can accumulate, if unavoidable any such residual water should be cleared by blowing down the tube before filling.

13. Compactness

In the interests of efficiency of the system and conservation of space it is good practice to keep the whole of the water system compact, and also, if possible, confined to an area designated as the 'water room' which can withstand becoming wet and prevent stray water reaching the wrong places. If the 'water room' has a drain plug to liberate any escaped water, so much the better.

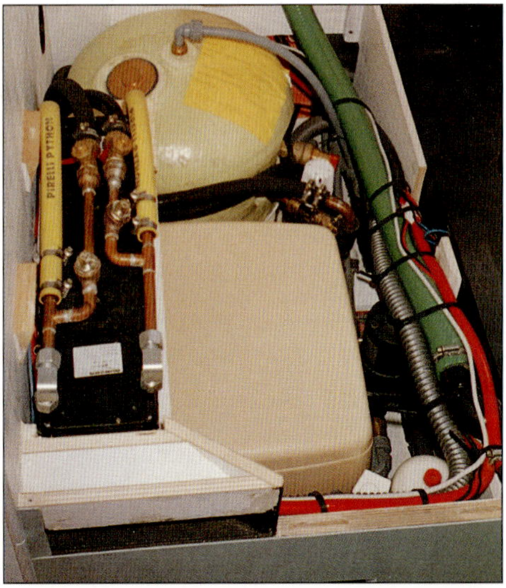

A compact 'water room' containing the light green calorifier and its thermostat, beige Porta Potti, extra heater boxes (black boxes with yellow hose and copper water pipes on the left), pump, pressure bottle, strainer, water tank (right), taps, filler, breather, fresh water pipes, waste pipe, and connections.

Pressurised fresh water system

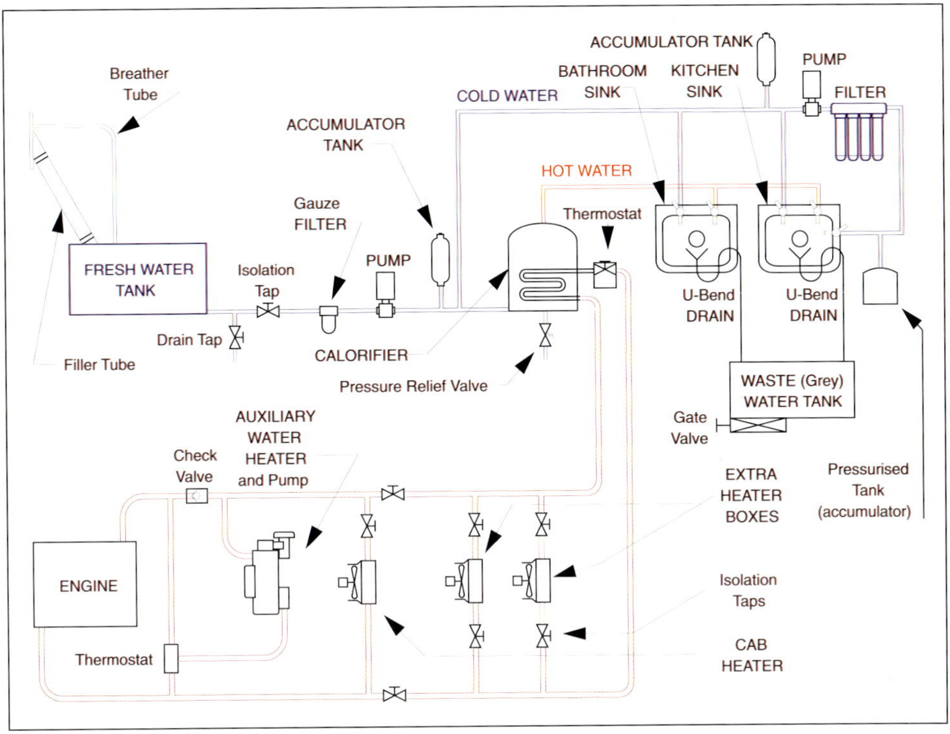

An example of a pressurised fresh water system. The individual layout will depend on, personal preferences, manufacturers' recommendations, relative component positions and any other specific influencing factors.

The calorifier and the extra heater box levels are critical in that their highest points should be lower than the vehicle water filler to avoid air locks.

The fresh water tank filler cap should be high enough to avoid any chance of the tank emptying through it (on steep hills for example). To avoid water sumps, the breather should be routed without low points .

Auxiliary water heaters must be installed in compliance with the corresponding manufacturers recommendations and always in compliance with any vehicle manufacturer requirements. Associated thermostats, check valves and other components are available from the water heater manufacturers.

Accumulator tanks can be installed wherever required. The pre-pressurised version with internal membrane offers several advantages including universal orientation and self draining.

For clarity, individual hot and cold taps are shown: monobloc mixers can be used instead. A gas water heater would more typically replace the calorifier and engine link.

U-bends or traps on the sink and shower wastes prevent rising drain smells.

WATER SYSTEM DESIGN

Probably the first consideration will be the location of the fresh water tank. My desire to incorporate a larger than usual tank (accommodation for 400 litres was created) inside the van where it would remain protected from frost (as long as the van was heated) certainly influenced the overall interior van design.

The choice of water heater is also significantly going to affect the design and layout. I was tempted to opt for a gas fired constant flow water heater. The advantage of this style of heater is the simple fact that it only heats the water 'on demand', that is when a hot tap is switched on. There is no wasted energy as there is no stored hot water to cool down, or continually be reheated, and there is little delay as the water is heated almost instantly.

WATER HEATERS

1. Storage Water Heater

Gas fired water heaters, with a tank to store the hot water, are available as either a wall mounting unit or concealed. Optional mains powered immersion heaters can be added. The heaters require a fresh water and a gas feed. Controllers and a thermostat allow automatic operation to maintain the water in the insulated tank at a preset temperature. Their balanced flues will pass through the caravan wall. (See also page 161)

2. Constant Flow Water Heater

A wall mounted gas fired water heater, without a storage tank, which heats cold water instantly, can provide hot water on demand. Again, they have a balanced flue.

3. Calorifier

Insulated water storage tanks, heated indirectly by the vehicle engine cooling water, and or an auxiliary water heater, can provide domestic hot water. These calorifier tanks are heat exchangers with a secondary heating coil, and resemble a small domestic hot water cylinder. An optional mains powered immersion heater can be added.

4. Heat Exchanger

This alternative is a flash, instant water heater, without storage tank, similar to the constant flow water heater above, but heated by the engine cooling water (and or an auxiliary water heater) which flows through a secondary heater coil. These marine devices tend to be too large for caravan applications.

EXTRA HEATER BOXES

I chose to install a calorifier to heat the domestic water. Along with extra heater boxes, it would be plumbed into the engine cooling water circuit.

The heater boxes (like a normal cab heater, consisting of a water pipe matrix or radiator with a low voltage fan blowing through it) blow warm air, heated by the engine cooling water when driving, or by using the auxiliary water heater.

Radiators

It is noteworthy that when the engine cooling water circuit has been extended for calorifier or heater boxes, it is a fairly simple matter to add additional equipment such as radiators or more heater boxes as in coaches.

AUXILIARY WATER HEATER

A diesel fired water heater can pre-heat the engine cooling water. This auxiliary heater can also independently heat the calorifier and air heaters. Normally, the prime use of this type of heater is for heating the cab and keeping the engine warm in cold conditions. Truck drivers use them frequently when overnighting in their cabs.

To plumb these small furnaces into the engine requires two water pipes to be connected into the engine cooling water circuit, in parallel with the vehicle cab heater pipes. They can be petrol or diesel fired, drawing their fuel directly from a standpipe fixed into the vehicle main fuel or auxiliary tank.

A compact, five kilowatt, diesel fired, auxiliary water heater, installed in the engine compartment.

It is plumbed into the engine cooling water system with an additional water pump.

In view is one of the two water pipe tee connections which link to an extra engine cooling water loop from the calorifier and extra heater boxes in the caravan section. This loop can be isolated by two green tapped valves one of which can be seen.

• When driving, either or both one-kilowatt heater box fans can be run to provide heat to keep the living quarters warm. Simultaneously, the calorifier heats the domestic water, requiring about twenty minutes to bring the tank of water to full temperature. The insulated calorifier holds its heat overnight.
• When stationary, (or in extreme cold when driving), at the push of a button the auxiliary heater can be activated to heat and circulate hot water for each of the following functions as required:-

1. The calorifier's domestic hot water.
2. The extra heater boxes.
3. The engine.
4. The cab.

The system presents an elegant solution that works most satisfactorily. Significantly, whilst driving, no fuel is used to generate domestic hot water and cabin heat (except for 25 Watts for each of the fan blowers), as it operates on excess engine heat. When stationary the auxiliary water heater is used, consuming little diesel oil which, being the vehicle fuel, is normally in plentiful supply.

NB. The water heater operates fully automatically. At switch on, and during the ignition phase, the combustion air blower, the water pump, and the glow plug, all come on. After about a minute the fuel metering pump starts and combustion should then take place correctly. During this starting process for perhaps two minutes, the battery consumption will be not less than 20 Amps. After, when the heater is running at full capacity, this current will fall to about 2.5 Amps. The heater maintains the water between 70°C and 80°C by switching between full and quarter heat, with a corresponding drop in battery drain.

A digital countdown timer is used to control the heater: one button-push switches the unit on for thirty minutes. The period can be extended or reduced. Alternatively it can be programmed to come on at a preset time.

Diesel or petrol fired air heaters are ignited in a similar way with similar current consumption, varying with make and capacity.

WINTERISATION, FROST DAMAGE and PREVENTION

If the van and water system are to be allowed to fall below the temperature at which water will freeze, (0° C or 32° F), the van must be 'winterised'. It is imperative to prepare the van *in advance* of such weather by being sure to empty water from all vulnerable parts of the water system, and minimise the water content of all the other parts. The expansion, as it freezes, of any water remaining, can easily cause component fractures.

Whilst the water tanks and the whole of the water system should be seen to be drained, the following should be considered particularly vulnerable and very conscientiously drained in accordance with the corresponding makers' instructions:-

1. **The pump**: diaphragms and other parts are susceptible to frost damage and must be emptied thoroughly.
2. **Accumulator tank**:
   - Non-membrane types should have the top screw or valve opened to allow draining from the outlet tap.
   - Pressurised membrane types should empty under their own pressure when the outlet tap is opened.
3. **Water Heater**.
4. **Calorifier** main tank to be emptied (not the coil which is filled with engine coolant and antifreeze).
5. **Water Filters** should be taken apart and drained, and preferably completely removed for storage indoors.

The maker's instructions should always be carefully implemented. Care should be taken that all the water is seen to drain from the various components; sometimes air locks can prevent it. Before opening the drain taps all the sink taps should be opened and left open during the draining process. It may help to blow back down taps to empty pipes.

Any frost damage can be both expensive and time consuming, not to mention possibly putting our home from home out of action until spares have been acquired and fitted. Sometimes the damage is not discovered until the van is required for a trip which may result in having to delay or worse, cancel the trip.

It is therefore wise practice to incorporate, at the design stage of the water system, adequate draining facilities to make the winterising process quick, easy and effective. The incorporation of an extra drain tap or two may take a little longer to install but the cost of components will be low, and certainly far less than a replacement pump for example. To add drain taps as an afterthought is harder.

If the draining process is fiddly, difficult or complicated then we might just put it off. That could spell disaster. Only one night of frost can do the damage, so the first hint of pending frost must not be ignored.

It should therefore be clear that not only must adequate draining facilities be designed into the water system, but also satisfactory access to the respective components in order to ensure ease of operation.

The winterisation process should be simple enough for us not to think twice about doing it. Furthermore, it should not put us off refilling the system in winter to prepare the van for even just a day out; to be comfortable doing so we must feel confident that the heating arrangements will subsequently keep the frost at bay. ❖

A motorcaravan containing a balanced electrical energy system.

CHAPTER 9

ELECTRICS

All caravans will use some 12 Volts electrical equipment, in addition to the normal vehicle electrics. The very least that a van will have will be additional lighting. Other low voltage consumers may include, refrigerator, water pump, radio, water gauge, and 12 Volts accessories such as an anti-mosquito machine. There are many possibilities, and to run any of these off the van's main starter battery can be risky.

Vehicle Main Battery

The vehicle's main battery is designed primarily to provide sufficient power to crank and start the engine. This requires a large current, surging in the order of a hundred Amps. The corresponding battery discharge is then replenished by the vehicle alternator.

When the engine is running, the battery should not deliver any net energy. The 12 Volts power required for the vehicle's electrical systems comes from the alternator. The battery acts as a reservoir of power. It is recharged quickly and then held there by a trickle charge, a small net flow of current into it. This process of ensuring that the battery is soon recharged prolongs its life.

Automotive electrical systems are designed to avoid leaving the battery in a discharged state, and do not require the battery to power any equipment without the engine running. Both situations would be detrimental to the life of a standard starter battery.

Caravan Application

The job of providing power for auxiliary caravan loads is best taken care of by one or more separate batteries exclusively selected and installed for the purpose.

This may seem to be extravagant, but I hope to demonstrate that it is a sound investment. A well designed balanced energy caravan system should provide all the power needed in a caravan with a minimum of user involvement or concern.

Gassing and Enclosures

All the batteries used are of the lead-acid type, and are subject to 'gassing' when they are charged. This causes loss of electrolyte, and the consequent requirement to add distilled water from time to time. Gassing also releases the explosive gas hydrogen, and corrosive electrolyte. Therefore lead-acid batteries must not be situated within an unventilated enclosure, nor must any open flame be allowed near them.

TYPES OF LEAD ACID BATTERY

- **Starter Batteries**

Vehicle main batteries for cranking the engine must be capable of supplying high currents for short times. After the engine starts they are recharged, initially at a high charge rate and thereafter maintained topped up with a trickle charge.

Normal starter batteries are not designed for deep cycling, which means that they are not intended to be steadily discharged over a long period before being recharged. They are therefore not the best choice for auxiliary caravan power.

- **Traction Batteries**

Full-traction batteries are deep cycling. They are ruggedly designed for steadily discharging a significant proportion of their capacity before requiring recharging. They are designed for many such cycles with high discharge and charge currents.

Typical applications are electric powered milk floats, fork lift trucks and electric cars. The batteries are discharged as they provide power to run the vehicle, and are then recharged, usually overnight, when the vehicle is out of use.

- **Leisure Batteries**

A leisure battery is a semi-traction battery which is built less substantially than the full-traction type. It is therefore cheaper. It is designed with a deep cycle capability but with a lower steady discharge and charge current capability than a full-traction battery.

Whilst a full traction battery is ideal for a caravan type application, it is perhaps over-specified due to the caravan's lower current demand. A leisure battery is therefore the more economical choice for the caravan application.

- **Maintenance Free Batteries**

This type, including gel batteries, are sealed, and need no topping up with electrolyte, and no periodic maintenance or servicing. They can be installed and forgotten, provided always that they are not placed within an unventilated enclosure. Although gassing from a sealed battery should be minimal in normal service, an automatically re-sealing safety vent is provided to relieve pressure, should overcharging occur.

- **Gel Batteries**

Some lead-acid batteries use a thixotropic gel of acid electrolyte, instead of the more common liquid electrolyte. Such units are maintenance free and even able to be used safely upside down! Some of these gel type batteries have superb deep cycling capabilities as well as being able to supply high starting currents, and they may be discharged by 100 % of their capacity. They can be recharged quickly with a high current. They are a good choice if high discharges are inevitable before any recharge is possible. They offer the best of all battery worlds, but their initial cost is high.

BATTERY SPECIFICATIONS

The so called 'solar' batteries I use are maintenance free and specified as follows:

- **Capacity**

115 Amp hours / 100 hours.
This 115 Ah capacity rating means that the steady continuous current the battery is able to supply for 100 hours, is 1.15 Amps (115 / 100),
For shorter periods and correspondingly higher discharge currents, the effective capacity of the battery is lower. The 10 hour capacity may be only 90 Amp hours.

- **Charge Cycles and Discharge Intensity**

Two sets of figures are specified:
1. 400 charge cycles at a discharge intensity of 40 %.
This means that if the battery is discharged by 40 % (40 % of 115 Ah = 46 Amp hours), and it is then recharged, it is able to provide 400 such cycles before it begins to lose capacity, becomes unable to hold its charge, and generally deteriorates.
2. 2000 charge cycles at a discharge intensity of 10 %.
If the battery is discharged by 10 % (10 % of 115 Ah = 11.5 Amp hours), and it is then recharged, it is able to provide 2000 such cycles before it begins to lose capacity and generally deteriorate.

Both the above specs are based on the 100 hour rate. For higher currents, the capacity will be lower.

As a further example, the cyclic life of a **Dryfit Gel Battery** is quoted as:
300 charge cycles at 100 % capacity withdrawn, 400 cycles at 50 %, 2000 cycles at 10 %, and 20,000 cycles at 1 %.

BATTERY SELECTION

Capacity and Discharge and Charge Currents

When it comes to selecting a suitable battery capacity, for a given set of battery loads, there is a useful rule of thumb. **Both the discharge and charge currents should not exceed about 10 % of the battery's capacity.** The capacity of the solar battery example is 115 AH at the 100 hour rate, and about 90 AH at the 10 hour rate. The rule of thumb indicates that the **net current flow** into or out of this battery should be limited to about 9 Amps. Ideally, any higher net current flow should be short term. Observing this rule will increase the battery's life.

Battery Discharge Limit

No battery can be expected to perform satisfactorily if it is regularly discharged to below its recommended discharge limit. Whilst some industrial or traction batteries are able to be discharged by 80 % of their capacity and some gel batteries by 100 %, we have seen that, even so, deeper discharges reduce a battery's life.

There is another useful rule of thumb. **Do not discharge a battery by more than about 50 % of its rated capacity.** To discharge some batteries much beyond this level could seriously damage them. To discharge some by 100 % could destroy them, particularly if left in a totally discharged state. A discharged battery should be charged as soon as possible.

Battery Efficiency

Lead-acid batteries are not 100 % efficient. The exact efficiency is impossible to know, and it will vary with circumstances such as, battery age, quality, cycle depth, temperature, state of charge, and size of current. For a battery in good condition, 80 % efficiency is a rough figure to work with, in other words, to assume that it will be necessary to put in 100 Amp hours to get 80 out.

This should be remembered when computing the power required to recharge batteries, by solar panels for example, where a balanced energy system is dependent on a limited source of energy.

Conclusion

Batteries are complex reservoirs of power with varying characteristics. None of them is completely efficient, and all of them must be treated with care. Even the best can be easily ruined by mistreatment.

Some maintenance free or gel type batteries, installed in a well planned, **balanced energy system**, can be a sound investment giving many years of trouble free use.

The way to optimise a battery's performance is to ensure that its capacity is adequate for the loads it will supply, (and use more batteries if necessary), and to install an appropriate, effective, charging and monitoring facility, and keep a watchful eye on its condition.

Inter Battery Connection

If a battery capacity is not adequate for the loads to be supplied, it is a simple matter to link two or three, to double or triple the capacity. Ideally, only batteries with similar characteristics should be linked.

Connections linking them should be made with 6 mm², 10 mm², 16 mm² cable, or more, if high currents are likely.

If the zero and positive connections of the load circuit are both connected to the first battery, (instead of ideally across the first and last batteries), the first battery will supply a greater current than the second, and the second more than the third. Similarly when charging the batteries, the first battery receives more charge than the second and so on. As a consequence, the first battery suffers the heaviest load and deteriorates more quickly than subsequent ones.

Since batteries connected to each other in series or parallel tend to adjust their condition to that of the worst battery, eventually all the batteries will have the same bad condition rather more quickly than need be the case.

This tendency can be avoided by connecting the batteries as below, which should result in an equal net current flow into or out of each, and a corresponding optimal life expectancy of all the batteries whether there are two, three, four or more.

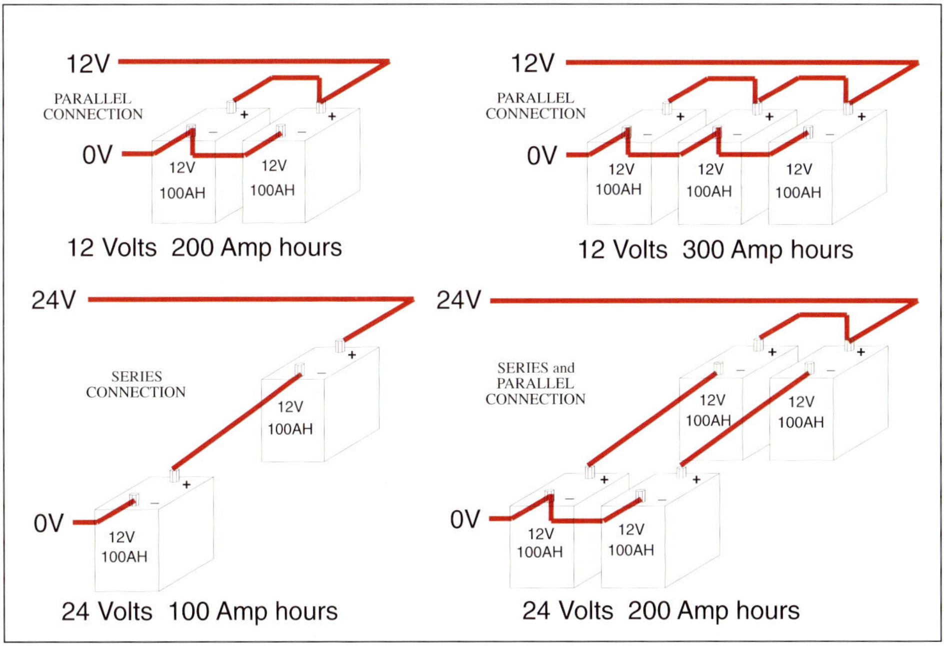

When linking batteries in parallel, and series, the main connection should be made with the zero Volts (negative) to the first battery and the twelve or twenty four Volts connection to the second, third or fourth.

BATTERY MONITORING

Voltage Measurement

To ensure that a battery is being operated within its limitations, it is essential to install specialised monitoring equipment. The issue is complicated by the fact that the Voltage of a battery can only indicate its state of charge if the battery is at rest and has not been charged or discharged for 24 hours, otherwise readings can be misleading.

A fully charged battery has a voltage of about 12.8 Volts, whilst at its rule of thumb safe discharge limit of 50 %, the voltage will have dropped to about 12.2 Volts. (Both measured after 24 hours of rest, and varying between manufacturers).

A standard voltmeter is simply not accurate enough to measure these small differences and is therefore of limited value in providing useful information about battery condition, particularly during normal service with the battery not at rest.

Amp-hours Extracted

The information needed is the display of Amp-hours extracted from the battery. This can be computed from accurate voltage measured at the battery terminals and flow of current into and out of the battery. Ideally Amp hours remaining should also be displayed.

With such knowledge one is able to know with greater certainty the state of charge of the battery at any time and thus be able to avoid dangerously low states of discharge.

Amp-hour Meters

There are digital meters available which measure and display the power extracted from the battery. They also measure and display the battery terminal voltage, and the net flow of current into and out of the battery.

To do this they require their shunt to be inserted into one of the main battery connections (preferably negative), a pair of wires to be attached to either side of the shunt as well as another pair to be attached to the battery terminals. The two pairs of small gauge wires are the only connections to the display unit which may be mounted wherever most convenient.

Such a unit goes a long way to keeping the user informed of the on-going battery condition.

The left hand lcd display of this battery monitor is showing a 0.3 Amp net charge rate. A net discharge rate would have a negative sign. If the red button beneath the display is pressed, the battery Voltage is shown.

The capacity display on the right shows a 0.1 Amp hour battery discharge. The red button beneath, zeros the capacity read out.

BATTERY CHARGING

The charging circuits form an essential aspect of the electrical system, and their quality will determine its effectiveness. There are several possibilities offering varying degrees of speed of recharge, battery preservation, and convenience of use. More than one of the charging methods, or even all of them, may be employed.

MAINS POWERED BATTERY CHARGER

This is the most common type of charging in use. It is available in several guises and degrees of sophistication.

The caravanner should avoid the type of battery charger which is based on old-technology. The newer, pure DC regulated devices, whilst costing more, will save on battery costs and worry from poor performance.

1. Resistance Method (WA DIN)

The typical charger found in an auto shop uses the resistance charge method perhaps with automatic switch-off. They provide pulses of DC power, not restful for the battery.

The charge time is long and the battery will not be charged completely. Such chargers may be adequate for typical automotive applications but the caravanner, using them daily, may find them leaving something to be desired.

These devices, even apparently higher powered ones, are often unable to charge the batteries at the same time that loads (consumers) are switched on. The consequence is that a caravan equipped with such a unit, could leave a site with an empty battery unable to supply power for a night without a hook-up, even though its charger had been connected during the stay on site. They cannot maximise the battery's life.

2. Constant Voltage (Pure Direct Current) with Reducing Current Method (IU DIN)

All consumers connected to a battery being charged by an automatic, pure DC, IU charger, are powered by the charger, (provided its rated current is not exceeded), whilst the battery, having been brought up to capacity, is held virtually at rest absorbing only sufficient current to maintain its capacity. The battery's life is thus extended. Such a charger may remain connected to the battery for reasonable periods without risk of overcharging.

A switched-mode, constant voltage charger, (as depicted over the page), with an output of say 15 Amps, can be surprisingly compact and weigh only about two kilos. For this type of unit, fan cooling is recommended, preferably built-in.

In its simplest form, the constant voltage charger applies a smooth voltage, usually about 13.8 Volts, to the discharged battery, and initially a high current (the rated current of the charger) flows. As the battery charges, the current gradually reduces until it settles at a low level sufficient to maintain the battery's charge.

This method is a good compromise based on the lowest fixed voltage required to charge fully a hot battery. It cannot ensure either a full charge, or the most rapid charge, in all temperatures.

Also it is possible in very hot weather, that connection over an extended period could lead to overheating and overcharge. The problem is overcome by adding temperature sensing.

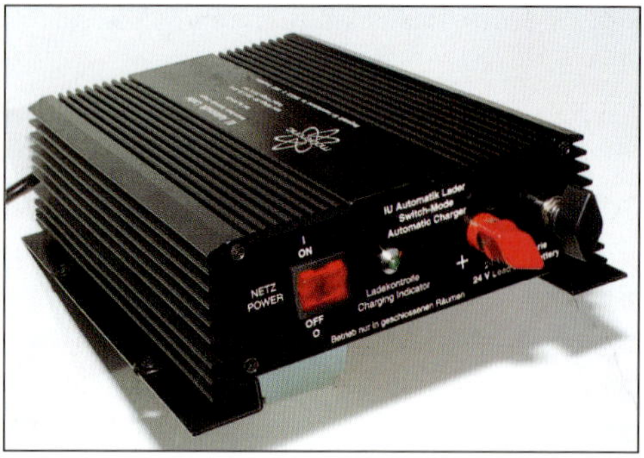

A switched mode constant voltage battery charger, with an ouput of 15 Amps. There is a cooling fan built into this unit.

3. Multi-Step Constant Voltage (Pure DC) Charging with Temperature Sensing: The Safest and Best Option

The complexity of batteries is such that charging them ideally, requires different smooth Voltages at different temperatures. Higher temperatures require lower voltages.

Furthermore, since it takes a higher voltage to charge a battery fully, and a lower voltage to maintain it at full charge, the ideal charger has to be one of the regulated multi-step variety which sense battery temperature and compensate their output accordingly. This is the only sure way to charge fully a battery and hold it at full charge safely, irrespective of temperature and duration of charger connection.

Such chargers usually base their charging on at least three separate steps:-

1. The first 'bulk' stage gives the maximum amount of current at a high voltage (about 14.2 Volts at 20° C) and brings the battery up to about 80 % charge.
2. The second 'absorption', or 'equalise', stage holds the high voltage but slowly reduces the current to bring the battery up to 100 % charge.
3. The third 'float' stage drops the voltage to a trickle charge level.

After a time the voltage may be lowered further to allow slight discharge before the whole cycle repeats.

The applied voltages are temperature compensated by monitoring the actual battery temperature and modifying the voltages correspondingly. The battery is thus maintained in optimum condition and not allowed to overheat. Its life is maximised.

The disadvantage of all mains powered battery chargers is that they must be plugged in to a separate mains supply which is not always available.

AUXILIARY BATTERY CHARGING RELAY

This is a device with two protection diodes which connects the auxiliary battery(ies) to the vehicle alternator. The purpose is to charge the auxiliary battery by the alternator, whilst driving, without fear of any interaction or feed back between the auxiliary and starter battery.

The auxiliary battery charge rate (like the starter battery charge rate) is controlled by the alternator regulator.

Vehicle Power Regulators - A New Generation

The vehicle alternator charges the starter battery under the control of the regulator, an electronic device which regulates the current flowing from the alternator into the battery. Immediately after starting, the current may typically be 30 to 40 Amps but as the starting drain is replenished the charge steadily reduces to a low level, just sufficient to keep the battery charged. The nature of standard vehicle regulators is such that starter batteries are brought up to only 60 to 70 % of their maximum capacity.

There is now a new generation of Power Regulators on the market which control the alternator to charge batteries up to 100 % of their maximum capacity. They do this typically in a stepped fashion similar to multi-step IU chargers with battery temperature sensing and compensation.

The combination of this device, along with an auxiliary battery charging relay, should allow both the starter and auxiliary batteries to be charged closer, and more quickly, to their maximum capacities by the vehicle alternator.

There are several such power regulators available from marine suppliers. Perhaps the most interesting for caravan use is the range recently launched by 'Hella' the German auto-part specialist. They offer several compact models to suit most car, truck, and boat alternators and supply each with the appropriate cable loom and fitting instructions.

SOLAR PANELS

The energy of the Sun can readily be converted into low voltage power suitable for boating or caravanning. Solar panels, in the form of low profile rectangular frames, contain photo-voltaic silicon cells to convert light into electricity. The cells are laminated to tempered glass forming a tough structure, in some cases strong enough to stand on.

A single panel of about one metre by half a metre and weighing about five kilos, is capable of charging a 12 Volts battery at a rate of up to 3 Amps. In daylight with some light cloud cover this might reduce to perhaps half an Amp.

To optimise the maximum charge rate available, the panels should face the sun at a right angle, which in effect means moving the panels as the sun moves across the sky. I have found however, that by far the easiest solution for caravan applications is to fix the panels flat on the van roof, preferably with a small air gap beneath to enable a cooling air flow, and forget them.

An array of several panels may be mounted flat on a van roof to provide all the free energy for which a caravanner could reasonably wish. Of course the number of panels required will depend on both the power consumed by the electrical equipment in the van, and the weather. The only sure way to find out is by trial and error which is easier said than done. Consequently, a practical approach is to do a very rough calculation based on estimates of expected power consumption and equate this to a guess of the power that might be available per panel per day. The final decision would be best to err on the safe side and install even twice as many panels as might at first be thought necessary. Any extra power generated is dissipated by the regulator.

Given the high cost of the panels but also the simplicity with which they can be installed, one approach would be to design the system with expansion in mind. Allocate space for perhaps four or even six panels, but install only one or two, adding more if necessary, and as funds become available.

I have five panels on my roof, four of which are rated at 55 Watts maximum, and one at 48 Watts maximum. There is a lot of low voltage electrical equipment installed in the van, (including a 24 Volts compressor fridge which runs only on electricity and which is always on), and to date the mains battery charger has rarely been used.

When stationary, the solar panels usually provide all the power required to charge the auxiliary batteries fully by midday. With this solar panel installation, I find that mains hook-ups are virtually a thing of the past, but parking in the shade, even partial tree cover on a campsite, must be avoided if the maximum possible charge rate is required. Irregular shade can significantly reduce output.

Connection of the panels is quite straightforward although it is essential to use a charge regulator to prevent the possibility of damaging the batteries by overcharging.

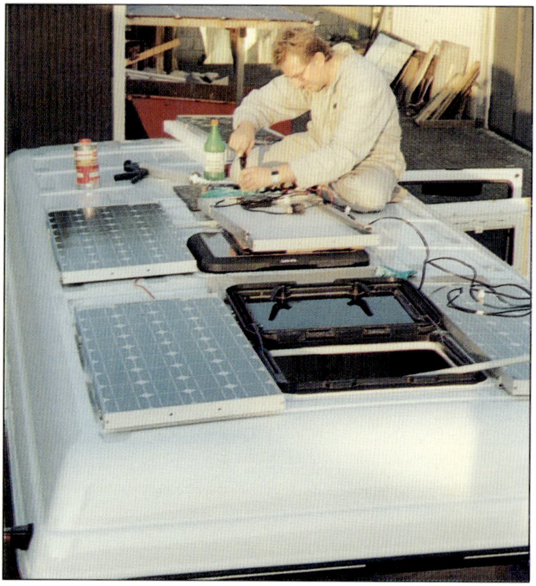

The panels are wired up before gluing them to the roof.
(See page 103)

WIND GENERATORS

Another means of harnessing natural, free energy, for use in a caravan, is the wind generator. It is a device perhaps more common in the boating world where it is more practical to leave the rotating blade fully rigged.

Nevertheless for those with a leaning in this direction, the wind generator is a very viable alternative energy source, which may be simply rigged onto the van when stationary. A compact unit with up to several Amps output can be quickly mounted on the van roof with appropriate fitted brackets. Whilst it is possible to be mounted beside the caravan, the wind is likely to be less advantageous at the lower elevation, and of course the turning blades pose something of a hazard.

Its advantage is that, providing there is adequate wind, it will generate power, night or day. If there is no wind then it is useless.

A disadvantage is the inconvenience of having to set it up on arrival and then dismantle it before departure. It must also be stored during travel.

Connection is much the same as with a solar panel except that a waterproof plug and socket will be required rather than permanent wiring. A suitable charge regulator should be used, if available. Alternatively a close watch must be kept on both the battery charge state, and the wind strength: the generator must be regulated (disconnected) manually, and the blade not allowed to race in high winds.

GENERATORS

Petrol, diesel or LPG powered generators are the surest means of charging a battery when a mains hook-up is not available. This can be achieved in two ways.

As most small generators have a battery charging output, delivering about 8 Amps at 12 Volts this can be connected directly to the battery.

Alternatively the generator can be treated as a mains electrical supply, and the van hook-up plugged straight into it. The advantage of this option is twofold: the caravan's internal mains battery charger can be switched on to charge the battery(ies), and the van's internal mains sockets can be used. If the van's charger is a high current constant voltage type, this will be a far more efficient way to charge the batteries than using the generator built-in charger.

A 15 Amp charger will draw up to 1.5 Amps at mains voltage (depending on the efficiency and power factor of the charger) leaving any extra generator capacity for the van sockets.

Generator Power

If a generator is to be bought, then care must be taken to buy a powerful enough unit. It is all too easy to buy an underpowered one.

It is important to differentiate between the numbers emblazoned on the sides of generators, and the actual continuous output they are capable of delivering. The important continuous rating may only be found in the small print on the unit's specification plate.

Anyone could be forgiven for thinking that a Kawasaki 1400 was a generator giving a 1400 Watts output, and of course they would be right. However, the following figures are to be found on the actual specification plate:

220 Volt	220 Volt
50 Hz	60 Hz
4.8 A 1050 VA (Watts)	5.45 A 1200 VA
D.C. Volts 12 D.C. Current 8.5 A	

A specification plate on a so-called '1400' generator. It shows that the normal continuous rating is only 1050 Watts.

As can be seen from the figures, the output at 50 Hertz, (the frequency at which most European appliances are designed to operate), is only 1050 Watts, which we might call its real or continuous rating. It is necessary to read the manual to discover that, when switched to 60 Hertz the generator can supply 1400 Watts for a fifteen minute period only. Therein is a clue to extracting the most from some generators: the generator above can be switched to 60 Hz for a 14 % increase in output. (Many 50 Hz appliances can be run at 60 Hz, and in the example above it can be seen that at 60 Hz the generator can supply 1200 Watts).

It is not just Kawasaki but all manufacturers who seem to adopt this type of exaggeration in their product nomenclature.

Unfortunately it seems that the story does not end there and many who have tried to run a generator at its apparent limit have found it wanting. The lesson here is really fourfold when selecting a generator:-

1. Be sure of the maximum power rating of the appliance to be run. (Allow for, surge requirements, efficiency, and power factor).
2. Be sure of the continuous load rating of the generator (at a frequency of 50 Hertz).
3. Select a generator with a continuous rating of at least thirty-five (and to be safe, one hundred) per cent more than the appliance power rating.
4. The only way to be sure the combination will work, is to test the generator with the appliance it is being bought to run, prior to purchase.

If a generator were to be selected to run a 15 Amps charger, the calculation would be: 15 A x 13.8 V = 207 W, so in a perfect world a 207 Watts generator would be required. As we know, the world is not perfect and neither are machines 100 % efficient. Chargers using older technology tend to have a low power factor and might appear only 60 % efficient to the generator, 207 / 0.6 = 345 Watts. If to this we add the 35 % safety margin, the power of the generator required is 345 x 1.35 = 466 Watts.

Even a 500 Watts generator running the charger could be close to its limit, with little or no additional capacity for other tasks.

A generator is a large piece of kit and must be found a home, preferably a permanent, soundproofed location from which it can be run safely and quietly. An electric start facility which can be operated from within the caravan would complete the convenience of the installation.

Some vans have enough room under the bonnet for mounting one of the smaller units. This is a very good solution as the environment is designed for an internal combustion engine, and the mounting is likely to require little more than a couple of brackets and some ingenuity. It will be necessary to ensure that the exhaust gases are cleared satisfactorily, perhaps to a wheel arch.

Without sufficient room in the engine compartment, the alternatives are bound to take up valuable storage space, and the option to run the generator from within a custom compartment will call for skill to provide adequate safeguards. Some motorcaravanners have found roof mounting to be the answer. Others have built a generator box on a platform at the back of the van.

As a last resort, the generator can simply be stowed wherever possible and set up beside the van when required.

Some of the smaller units run very quietly but even so could be deemed by a neighbour to be a nuisance. Soundproofing should therefore be given serious consideration. The noise pollution factor may be quite enough to put some people off generators (and their owners!).

VOLTAGE CONVERTERS

Black boxes exist which can provide a 24 Volts to 12 Volts conversion. These are useful in 24 Volts vehicles for running such devices as car radios which are invariably 12 Volts. (It is not good practice simply to tap off one of the series connected 12 Volts batteries.) It is possible to find a converter with a constant 13.8 Volts output which also will charge a 12 Volts battery from a 24 Volts one at a rate up to 15 Amperes.

I have found that such a device works well in my dual Voltage auxiliary power system. The 12 Volts auxiliary battery can be topped up by the 24 Volts auxiliary batteries as and when required.

MAINS HOOK-UPS (1)

Very few vans are built nowadays without an external connector for plugging the van into a local mains electricity supply. All except the more remote and basic campsites are equipped with a 220 to 240 Volts outlet on nearly every pitch. Virtually every campsite receptionist takes it as read, when you arrive, that you will want 'electricity' and expect to pay an extra pound or two a night for it.

The external van connector is wired (see Mains Hook-Ups (2) page 142) indirectly to mains chassis (wall) sockets inside the van. One internal socket may be sufficient, more can be installed if required. Into one will be plugged the battery charger.

The other uses will include any domestic consumers that the camper may care to take along, such as perhaps a television, a toaster, a hair dryer, a kettle, or a heater. Most campsites have limited power available through the hook-ups provided, as little as a two Amps or five hundred Watts supply being found, so this will control the appliances which may be used, or the sites at which one can stay. A caravanner might well select a site for a winter stay on the strength of the fact that it offers pitches with a 10 Amps supply, which can run a 2 kW electric fire.

Plugs and Sockets

The external connector fixed to the van, will probably be an international standard, CEE17 (BS4343), 16 Amps round blue, splash-proof, chassis mounting, 3 pin, male plug. It will be fixed to the van body and concealed behind a hatch. To plug the electric supply into this connector will require an adapter cable, on one end of which will be a cable mounting free socket also of the 16 A, CEE17 type. These 16 Amps round, blue, connectors are excellent, form good contact, and do the job well.

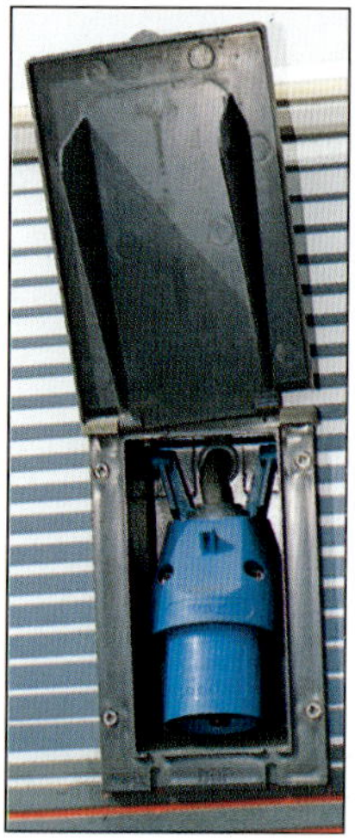

The industry standard round blue 16 Amps connector on the side of a van.

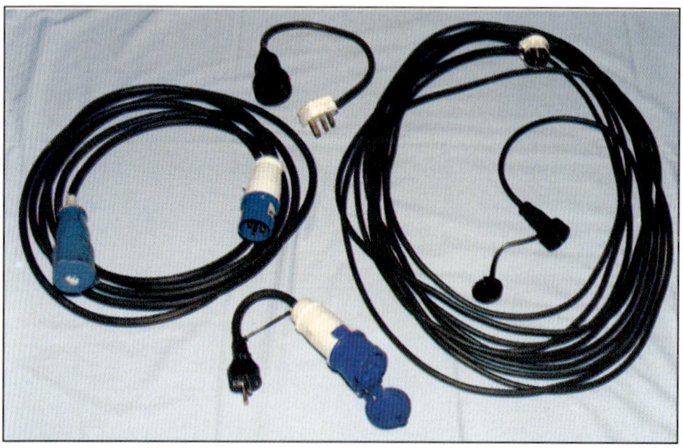

Cables and adapters.

10 Amps sealed round chassis mounting connector.

For those, like myself, who want to use a smaller alternative, there is a small glass-filled-nylon, sealed round connector as depicted. It is available with a 10 Amps rating, is compact, and small enough to be built onto the caravan almost anywhere. It is tough with good water and dust resistance (to IP68 standard). Providing the user does not need more than a 10 Amps (about 2.3 kW) rating, this range of connectors has much to offer the caravanner by way of a neat, elegant solution.

A Selection of Cables and Adapters.

Plug = standard blue CEE17, 16 A free plug. (Or sealed type 10 A plug)
Socket = standard blue CEE17, 16 A free socket. (Or sealed type 10 A socket)

1. **Mains Cable: 10 metres** (3 x 1.5 mm^2 or 3 x 2.5 mm^2 rubber shielded HO5 or the tougher HO7 type cable) with free socket on one end and free plug on the other end. (If preferred, cheaper PVC cable may be substituted for rubber. PVC cable can become stiff when cold, unless it is the special, low-temperature version.)
2. **Mains Cable: 25 metres** (Same specifications as 1.) (Normally only the 10 metres cable will need to be used, but sometimes the 25 metres will be needed. For the even longer run the two cables can be plugged together.
3. **Adapter: 1 metre** (Same cable as 1.) with free socket on one end and UK 13 Amps plug on the other.
4. **Adapter: 1 metre** (Same cable as 1.) with free socket on one end and 16 Amps French / German plug * on the other.
5. **Adapter: Polarity Reverser**: 1 metre cable (Same cable as 1.) Same spec. as 1. but with neutral and live wires swopped in one of the connectors.

(* Whilst the 16 Amps French and German (CEE7 Schuko type) plugs are slightly different, it is possible to buy an inexpensive version with euro-style combined earth, consisting of both a hole to accept the French earth pin and contacts for the German scraping earths. Such a plug will fit into either the French or the German sockets which are widely used in Europe.)

With the above cables, the nomadic caravanner should be able to plug-in directly to practically all mains supplies likely to be encountered in Europe at least. For those less inclined to carry adapters, appropriate plugs are normally available from reception offices at sites, so that a cable can be rewired on arrival.

(NB. When the supply is close to the van, and only a short length of a long cable is therefore required, it is safe practice not to leave the unused part coiled up, on a cable drum for example. This is because of an electrical phenomenon which can cause a coiled cable to heat up. The solution, although untidy, is to uncoil the cable and arrange it in an uneven bundle, perhaps under the van or wherever it is out of the way. Uncoiled cables heat up too, although this is minimised by using cables of sufficient cross sectional areas.)

MAINS HOOK-UPS (2) - USE OF AN RCD.

Having fixed an external chassis plug onto the van, it must be wired directly into a **residual current device** (RCD). All internal van mains sockets will be connected to this RCD, and benefit from the protection it affords.

In the UK, domestic switches are usually only single pole, disconnecting just the live line. This is not a problem in the UK because the neutral voltage should be close to zero, and plugs only fit one way. Across the channel, however, neutral voltages are often high, and some plugs can be plugged in either of two ways, swopping the live and neutral. Switches are therefore double pole, disconnecting both the live and the neutral lines.

The RCDs which we are obliged to install in our vans are two pole, (even triple pole in some cases, switching the earth as well), and usually have a test and reset button.

Depending on the type, an **RCD** can give protection against:

1) **Reversal of live and neutral connections.**
   If the RCD trips outside the UK, the plug should be plugged in the other way round. Failing this possibility, a polarity reverser adapter should be plugged in between the van and supply.
2) **Lost earth or earth leakage faults.**
3) **Lost neutral faults.**

RCDs may also have 13 Amps or 16 Amps fuses. However, **RCBOs**, (**residual current circuit breakers with over current protection**), are a more convenient form of RCD. They incorporate a thermal magnetic circuit breaker (MCB) instead of a fuse. If they trip due to a high current, they can simply be switched back on without having to replace a fuse, after the fault causing the trip has been resolved.

Faults in either a mains supply or the equipment plugged into it, are not unheard of. The now obligatory use of residual current devices will provide comforting, important protection whenever plugging the van into any external supply.

*An **RCBO**: an **RCD** linked to a thermal magnetic miniature circuit breaker, enclosed in a protective box.*

Wiring Regulations and Electric Shock

Work with mains electricity should be carried out by those qualified to do so, and according to appropriate wiring regulations. (At the time of writing, the IEE Wiring Regulations 16th edition applies in Britain .)

It should also be noted that working with 12 and 24 Volts, while not involving the same risk of electric shock as mains, does involve potentially very high currents which can start fires. It is therefore essential, always to avoid short circuits, and to incorporate fuses and breakers as necessary to protect against such dangers.

In Britain BS 6765 Part 3 applies.

INVERTERS

Mains power will from time to time, if not all the time, be useful to have in a caravan, and of course it is usually available from the site hook-up. If, however, like me there is a desire to be autonomous and not need a mains hook-up, yet still have a mains capability, the answer is either to use a generator or an inverter.

A modern inverter is a black box containing electronics (a switched mode rectifier) which converts 12 or 24 Volts DC battery power to AC mains power. They are compact and efficient devices but not 100% efficient and heat up in use.

It should be noted however that most units have certain limitations. The output differs from the usual household mains, and is not normally a pure sine wave. Under some circumstances these differences are not a problem, but it is important that such an inverter output is not connected to a distribution system in which neutral and earth are bonded. Also certain rechargeable items including torches and razors, which plug directly into sockets to recharge, can damage some inverters. Rechargeable equipment which uses a separate charger or transformer that is plugged into the mains should operate satisfactorily however.

The great advantage of an inverter is its convenience and silence. The great disadvantage is the enormous drain it can represent to the battery: for every 100 Watts drawn from an inverter by an appliance there is a corresponding drain of about 8 Amps drawn from the 12 Volts battery. (W = V x A; A = 100 / 12 = 8.33). In other words, to plug a 100 Watts light bulb into an inverter will draw about 8 Amps from a 12 Volts battery.

Clearly an inverter must be selected with caution, giving careful consideration to whether the battery and charging circuits are strong enough to accommodate it. With such high potential currents, large cross sectional area cables are essential.

A compact inverter with a continuous 200 Watts output capability. Its maximum output is 400 Watts for short periods.

MICROWAVE OVENS

A microwave oven is a power hungry appliance or consumer, and it represents a huge load to a battery, it is therefore useful to consider four ways in which it can be powered.

1. Standard 240 Volts Microwave Oven Fed by Campsite Mains Hook-Up

A typical domestic microwave oven has an output of about 650 Watts but absorbs twice this power from the mains supply. Such an oven would have an input specification of about 1400 Watts at 230 Volts, as can be read on the specification plate or sticker on the back of the oven.

Using the golden formula Watts = Volts x Amps, (as usual), allows us to calculate that the current consumption from a 230 Volts mains supply is about 6 Amps for such an oven (A = W/V = 1400/230 = 6.1 Amps). Whilst it is likely that the mains wiring and switching in the caravan will be sufficiently rated to cater for a 6.1 Amperes current flow, often the site pitch supply will not.

I once found myself in the rather embarrassing situation of having plunged a whole collection of campers on a site in Barcelona into a total mains blackout when I switched on my microwave oven with specifications as above. The breaker on the supply to my pitch, feeding my van, did not have time to trip before the main breaker feeding a number of pitches did. No doubt the distribution breaker was already 'busy' feeding everyone else and I was the last straw which broke the camel's back.

If a piece of equipment cannot be relied on to work every time it is required, there is a good argument that it is not worth having it installed. For that reason, I cannot recommend the use of a normal, domestic, mains powered microwave oven, by way of a direct campsite mains hook-up, unless the sites to be used are limited to those with sufficient power available, those having pitches with at least 6 Amps hook-ups.

2. Standard 240 Volts Microwave Oven Fed by Inverter

Using the same oven, with a 1400 Watts input specification, means of course that the inverter also would need to have at very least a 1400 Watts continuous rating, more to be safe, and preferably tested first to be sure that the combination will work.

1400 Watts connected to an inverter will draw in the order of 116 Amps from the poor old 12 Volts battery, assuming that the inverter is 100 % efficient which it will not be, (90 % is the highest probable efficiency, the 10 % or 140 Watts loss will heat up the unit, so it is important to mount an inverter in such a way as to allow a free air flow around it, preferably fan cooled).

As we have already seen, a rule of thumb maximum steady current which a battery should be asked to supply, in order to maximise its life, is ten per cent of its capacity. This means that to be able to provide the 116 Amps for the microwave oven, the 12 Volts battery ideally should have a capacity of 1160 Amp Hours!

An approximation to this could be achieved with the use of four 230 AH batteries in parallel, which together would provide a capacity of 920 Amp hours. Each of these batteries would weigh 63 kilos. This is clearly a large, heavy, expensive option.

On a more sensible level it would be necessary to accept that large currents would flow, so batteries should be selected for their specific ability to provide them. Full Traction Batteries can do this better, as can the Dryfit gel type batteries. Two 85 AH Dryfits in parallel could thus be used, each supplying 58 Amps.

An alternative approach is to run a 24 Volts system using a 24 Volts inverter, running off two 85 AH, 12 Volts batteries in series, each supplying again, 58 Amps. In both 12 and 24 Volts cases, more batteries would provide longer times between charges.

In either case the cable required to handle about 60 Amps is a minimum of 16 mm^2, and preferably 25 mm^2, to reduce the voltage drop.
This is unfortunately not the end of the story: we still need to have a sufficiently potent charging capability to put back what we take out of the batteries as a result of this heavy current consumption.

If we select a constant voltage battery charger with 15 Amps output, (for this type of high current battery, a higher charge current could be selected, perhaps 30 Amps), at 12 Volts, plugged into the site hook-up, we are then in business. What we take out of the batteries quickly with the oven, we can put back more slowly by way of the mains charger.

A modern, efficient 15 Amps, 12 Volts charger should run on a site 1 Amps supply: Amps x Volts = Watts. 15 Amperes x 13.8 Volts = 207 Watts. Allowing for a charger efficiency of about 90 %, this becomes 230 Watts battery charger power to be supplied by the mains. 230 Watts / 230 Volts = 1.0 Amps.

Another more elegant possibility, would be to keep the batteries charged with perhaps 8 fifty-five Watts solar panels which would be capable of charging the 12 Volts batteries at a rate of up to about 24 Amps during sunny hours, or 24 Volts batteries at half this rate. The actual size of the solar array required would depend on hours of sunshine and oven usage.

3. Standard 240 Volt Microwave Oven Fed Directly by a Generator

It is quite feasible to run the oven directly off a generator with an output of at very least 1400 Watts continuous.

I have tested a Kawasaki 1400 generator rated at a continuous 1050 Watts at 220 Volts 50 Hertz, and a maximum output of 1200 Watts limited to 15 minutes. It will not run my microwave oven which is rated at 1400 Watts input at 240 Volts and 50 Hertz, with an output of 650 Watts.

However, this generator can be set to 60 Hertz at 220 Volts, in which case the engine runs at 3600 RPM instead of 3000 RPM at 50 Hertz. The output at this higher frequency of 60 Hertz increases to 1200 Watts continuous, with 1400 Watts available for 15 minute periods. If I connect the oven at this higher setting it runs but only just, and at a lowered voltage. Clearly the generator is being taxed beyond its limit, and a model with a higher output of a true 1400 Watts continuous at 50 Hertz would be the absolute minimum required.

4. A 12 Volts or 24 Volts Microwave Oven Fed Directly from Batteries

There are both 12 Volts and 24 Volts ovens available which tend to be of a lower power rating than the usual mains types. I have seen such units with an input of 960 Watts and a 420 Watts output. This rating will draw about 80 Amps from a 12 Volts supply and 40 Amps from a 24 Volts supply.

As before, high current capable batteries could be used. Two 85 AH Dryfits would suffice.

For charging, again a 15 Amps or 30 Amps constant voltage charger would be ideal, and yet again between four and eight solar panels the most elegant solution.

The obvious advantage of the low voltage microwave oven is that it obviates the need for either a mains hook-up or an inverter, provided an alternative energy source is available.

In most cases, the lower the power of the microwave oven the better for the caravan application.

Microwave Oven Feed Cables

Whichever option were selected to run a microwave oven from 12 or 24 Volts batteries, high currents would always flow somewhere in the circuit, whether they be in the cables connected to a low voltage oven, or in those feeding an inverter supplying the oven.

Either way, as we have seen, it is unlikely that these currents will be less than 40 Amps, and possibly as high as 120 Amps. At these high currents and low voltages, the voltage drop in the cables can represent a significant proportion of the voltage itself.

It is therefore vital that cables of sufficient cross sectional area are used, and also that they are kept as short as possible. For currents of 40 Amps and 120 Amps at least 16 mm^2 and 35 mm^2 respectively should be used.

THE POWER SYSTEM - List of Components

Having decided on the nature of the built-in power system, consisting of auxiliary batteries, charging circuits, and mains capability, a list should be compiled of the power system components. It will then be possible to begin to draw a wiring diagram. The list will most likely contain items from the following:-

No. Item. Quantity. Type. Location. Fed From/To. Wire Gauge. Notes.

1. Batteries 12 V
2. Batteries 24 V
3. Mains charger
4. Charging relay
5. Solar panels
6. Solar regulators
7. Voltage converter
8. Inverter
9. Generator
10. Mains hook-up
11. Mains hook-up RCD
12. Mains sockets
13. Distribution system
14. 12 Volts Ring
15. 12 Volts sockets
16. Volts/Amps/Power Monitors

INSTALLATION COMPONENTS List

Before the wiring diagram can be completed it will be necessary to make a second list of every piece of electrical equipment to be installed in the van, either in the first phase of construction or at any phase envisaged in the future. The list will most likely contain some of the following:-

No. Item. Quantity. Type. Location. Fed From/To. Wire Gauge. Notes.

1. Water pump
2. Water heater
3. Water heater remote
4. Air heater
5. Air heater remote
6. Extractor fan
7. Cooling fan
8. Ice-Ex
9. Diesel heater
10. Gas gauge
11. Fresh water gauge
12. Waste water gauge
13. Diesel gauge
14. Radio
15. Lights
16. 12 Volts sockets
17. Inspection light
18. CO detector
19. CO_2 detector
20. Oven
21. Cooker/grill
22. Fridge
23. Fridge remote
24. Disc player
25. Loudspeakers
26. Rear view system
27. Thermometer
28. Electric gate valve.

LOOSE APPLIANCE List

It is also wise to create a third list of every piece, or type of equipment ever likely to be used in the van. Thought can then be given to how they will be powered, and where they will be situated when in use.

No. Item Quantity. Type. Location. Fed From/To. Wire Gauge. Notes

1. Television
2. Vacuum cleaner
3. Electric razor
4. Toaster
5. Electric Kettle
6. Electric Heater
7. Nicad battery chargers
8. Electric drill
9. Inspection light
10. Hair dryer
11. Anti mosquito machine
12. Fan
13. Iron
14. Food processor
15. Portable radio
16. Portable disc player
17. Portable telephone
18. Computer
19. Fax machine

The power system will have been largely based on the probable content of the second two lists as they are so closely linked. All the installed items listed will vary in terms of their required accessibility and controllability, and wherever possible the interconnecting wires should be as short as possible. Beside each item, on each list, should be added the actual location of the item inside the van, and the other relevant details.

POWER DISTRIBUTION SYSTEM

With the three lists together, some indication of the nature and complexity of the power distribution techniques should begin to become apparent. In its simplest form this may consist of a number of fuse holders wired to the auxiliary battery. For a more comprehensive and controllable system it could involve the use of a domestic consumer unit with a dozen or more circuit breakers. The latter is the system I chose to use.

Because my basic van had a 24 Volts electrical system, I decided to install a dual voltage auxiliary power system with both 12 and 24 Volts circuits. I would not necessarily recommend this option, but it does have advantages. These include being able to use appliances of both voltages, and being able to make the best of both worlds.

Isolator Switches

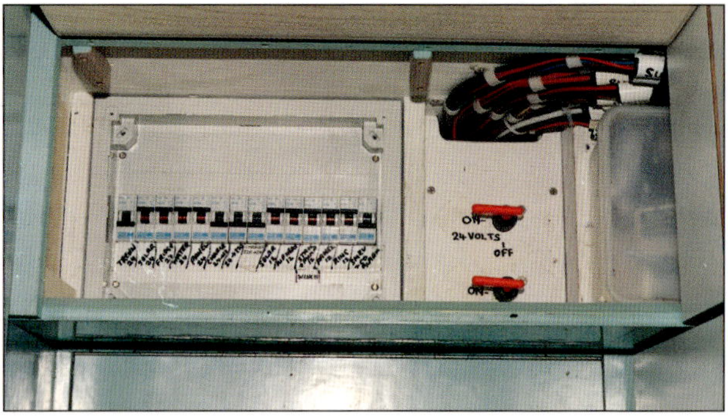

My auxiliary batteries are connected to the consumer unit through marine type single pole isolator switches. These provide a ready means of completely disconnecting the batteries from all circuits.

Consumer Unit

The isolator switches are wired to the respective split busbars of the consumer unit which contains fourteen thermal magnetic breakers mounted on a DIN rail. The busbar is split with eight breakers at 24 Volts, and six at 12 Volts. These 14 breakers have all the circuits in the van wired to them.

By opting for this type of distribution I was able to provide the circuits with both the necessary protection and easy individual isolation. This is a considerable aid for overall control, fault finding or maintenance.

It is not necessary for either the two main isolators or the consumer unit to be on display, as they are not used frequently. It is useful however, to have them easily accessible. In terms of cable runs, they should be as close as possible to the auxiliary batteries which supply them.

Control Panel

One of the breakers in the consumer unit supplies the display control panel, mounted on which are switches to operate those functions which may be required to be used several times each day, and are therefore deemed to be worthy of instant access and in full view.

This leads to yet another list, the switches and items to be included on the control panel. Illuminated switches or 'on' indicators are more informative (LED indicators use less power than incandescents).

Panels can be bought 'off the shelf' although this may not offer the exact layout required. Some suppliers will custom assemble panels. To home-construct a panel will require a sheet of hard grade aluminium alloy such as NS4, 3 mm thick, to be carefully drilled, filed, or hole punched, as the switches, indicators, and layout dictate. The alloy is not an easy material to paint and ideally the panel should be taken to the local anodiser for anodising black, (or any other colour if preferred), perhaps after sanding a slight parallel grain on it (linishing). For the professional finish an engraver will add the chosen legend. More cheaply and less permanently, Letraset type lettering can be used. For a one-off, silk screen printing is expensive and perhaps not as stylish as engraving. A hinged panel with a quick release catch would offer easy access for good serviceability.

12 Volts Ring

An advantage of running a 12 Volts ring is that by connecting both ends of the ring to the supply the current capacity of the cable is doubled. This is useful with low Voltages where a high percentage of the Voltage might be dropped along a cable run.

If the ring is run around the van at a high level it can be used to feed a series of short spurs at intervals, each of which can terminate in a 12 Volts socket. These can be used for plugging in lights and various appliances as required.

I also use a ring for radio power, and to supply all the compact fluorescent lamps off short spurs. The ring can be supplied by its own fuse or breaker in the consumer unit.

CABLES and SIZES

The most appropriate type of cable for the internal wiring is a flexible switchgear cable consisting of a plain copper multi-stranded conductor with a PVC sheath. The conductor size and overall cross sectional area will depend on the current that is to be carried, and the length of cable run. In low Voltage applications it is wise to err on the high side.

Voltage Drop

No cable is a perfect conductor, as every wire has an electrical resistance measurable in fractions of an ohm per metre. Whenever a cable carries an electrical current, there is therefore bound to be a voltage drop along it according to
Ohms Law: **Volts = Amps x Ohms (V = I x R)**.

The higher the current the higher the Voltage drop, or cable loss, in a given cable. Also the thicker the cable the lower its resistance and corresponding Voltage drop.

Any Volt drop becomes more significant with lower Voltage systems, quite simply because the drop represents a greater percentage of the system Voltage. To lose two Volts in a 230 Volts system is irrelevant, but in a 12 Volts system it could be a serious problem.

Furthermore, the product of the square of the current and the cable resistance is the lost power in Watts, which will heat up the cable. (V = I x R and W = V x I so W = I^2 x R.)

Short Runs and Bigger Cables

It is therefore sound practice, when selecting cable cross sectional areas for low Voltage applications, to err on the large side. Also, it is always desirable to keep cable runs as short as possible, an aspect to be considered early in the van design stage.

For most 12 Volts power wiring, the minimum cross-sectional area that should be used is 1.5 mm^2. Possibly 2.5 mm^2, 4 mm^2 or 6 mm^2 , even 16 mm^2, may be required for longer runs carrying steady currents of many Amps. Voltage measuring electronic controls rely on accurate readings and hence minimal voltage drops.

A 12 Volts microwave oven, or a 1000 Watts inverter, would draw about 80 Amps. For such high currents it would be desirable to use cable of at least 25 mm^2.

Attention should certainly be paid to the recommendations of the various manufacturers regarding suitable cable cross sectional areas for feeding their products. They will often specify varying sizes according to corresponding cable lengths. It is worth noting that their recommended sizes may be larger than one might otherwise have expected to use.

Conduits and Trunking

It will be enormously beneficial, as with electrical wiring in general, if as many of the cables as possible can be routed together and contained within a, preferably accessible, trunking system.

This will facilitate the van construction, including installing the wiring. If a trunking system with removable covers can be found an unobtrusive home, with future accessibility guaranteed, the whole wiring process will be simplified, with modification or upgrading in the future a simple matter.

Unfortunately for me, I did not use a trunking system which could easily be added to. I chose to use several runs of flexible plastic conduit which were built into the fabric of the van. With this system the wires need to be pulled through the tubes with the use of a wireman's tape. If the tubes are more than a couple of metres long with any bends in them, it is a two-man job to get them through. It can be quite a fiddly process and is one which definitely is best to get right first time. With this type of installation being difficult to add to, the safe option is to include a number of spare wires to allow for any oversight. I put in several and ended up using nearly all of them.

The advantage of using flexible tubes is that they can be easier to conceal. Also, as the wires are grouped in smaller tubes they can be easier to trace. Nevertheless, in the interest of general serviceability my recommendation would be to try to use the system that will be the most accessible when the van is finished.

THE CIRCUIT DIAGRAM

When the four lists are complete including that of the control panel functions, it should be possible to draw the van wiring diagram.

Only when the diagram exists and the location of all the equipment listed is known, should the actual caravan construction begin.

The diagram need not follow any particular convention, but it should be clear and unambiguous. Probably the original version will require updating and modifying several times before the definitive version is derived. This important diagram will prove invaluable for reference, troubleshooting and general electrical problem solving, and will be a vital part of the van 'User Manual'. ❍

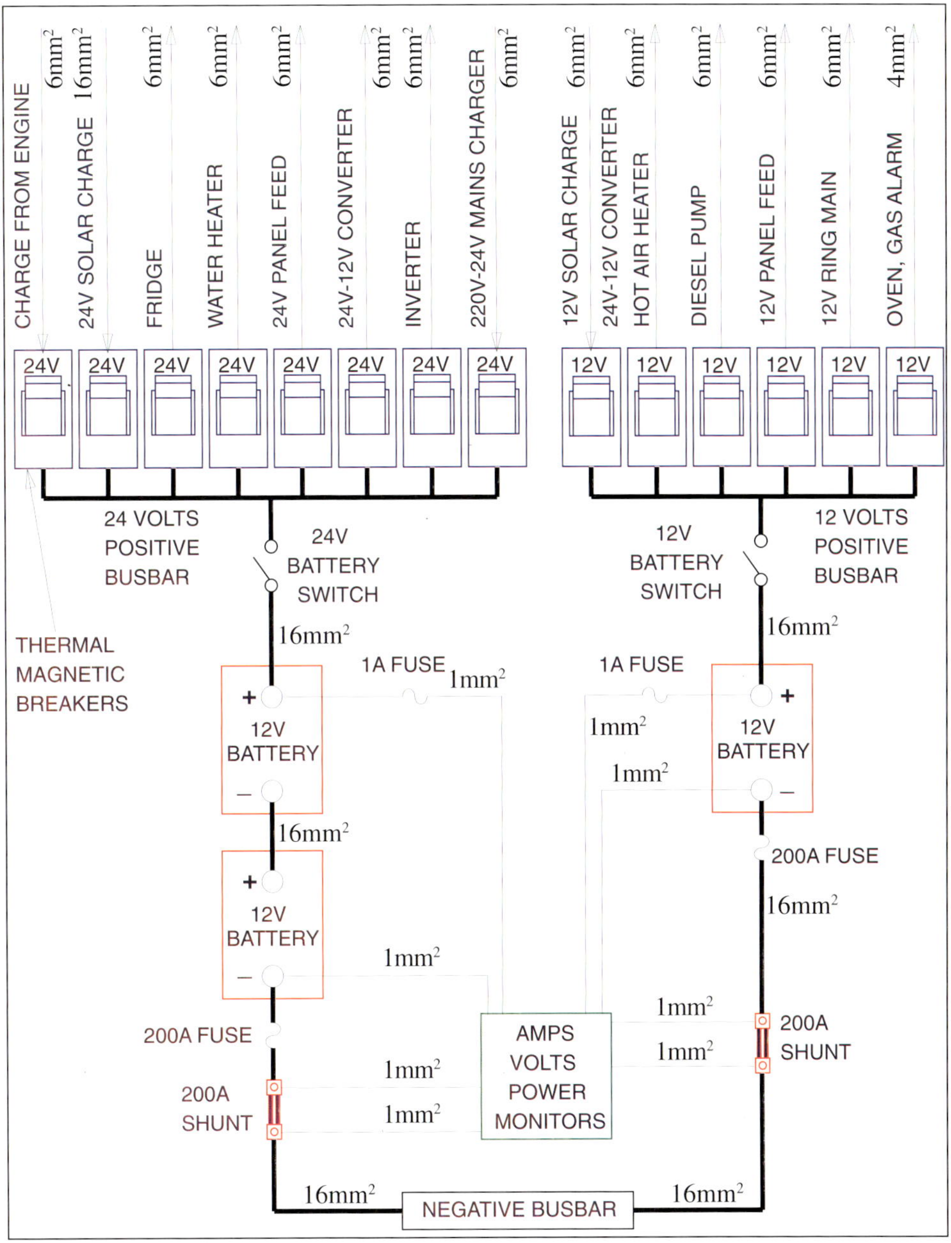

A wiring diagram showing cables and dimensions.

American motorhomes tend to have fixed installation gas tanks with typical capacities in excess of 100 litres. Gas (LPG) consumers can include furnaces (heaters), cookers, and generators. This classic 36 foot Airstream motorhome has a 4-Burner Cooktop and a 30,000 BTU (about 10KW) furnace. Such high powered consumers warrant large fuel capacities.

CHAPTER 10

GAS

Gas or liquid petroleum gas, (LPG), is a fuel without which the caravanner almost certainly will not be. There are ways its use can be completely avoided however, (See page 80 - Diesel Ceramic Cooker, page 122 - Extra Heater Boxes, page 123 - Auxiliary Water Heater, and page 162 - Petrol or Diesel Fired Air Heater).

Most caravanners use gas for cooking, air heating, water heating, and refrigeration. Unfortunately, to provide gas for all these four does consume a lot, and it is therefore advisable to consider incorporation of as large a gas container as possible.

Two Cylinder Types

1. Portable

The portable steel cylinder (also known as a 'bottle') is exchangeable. When empty, it is disconnected from the caravan connection, and taken to a shop or depot where it can be exchanged, (or sometimes refilled), for a full, same brand, same size cylinder.

That these cylinders can only be exchanged for the same brand, and that most brands operate only in one country, means that most types can only be exchanged in their country of origin. Sometimes it is possible to have them refilled in other countries, although this practice is normally discouraged. Portable cylinders must be used vertically.

2. Fixed installation

There are special steel cylinders or tanks designed for permanent installation in, or under, the caravan. They are refilled at fuel stations from a large LPG storage tank with a pump similar in appearance to a petrol pump. Many, but by no means all, European stations have an LPG filling facility. Fixed cylinders must be used horizontally exactly as specified.

Two Gas Types: Butane and Propane

For both types of cylinder, the gases are liquid petroleum gas (LPG). The most common is butane, but propane is also used. It is important to differentiate between the two, although LPG on sale at fuel stations is often a mixture of the two.

When stored under pressure (butane at about 2 bar and propane about 6 bar) in the steel cylinders, the gas is in liquid form, but when the tap is opened the pressure of the released gas drops (to atmospheric), and it boils or vaporises turning into its gaseous form.

When this vapour is mixed with the right proportion of air and ignited, it enables a smooth flame to be maintained.

Butane will not vaporise below zero degrees Centigrade.

Propane will vaporise well below zero.

A mixture of the two, sometimes available, offers improved cold weather and high altitude performance, compared with butane alone. (As an example: Camping Gaz offer versions of various cartridges with a butane and propane mix. The standard C206, as used in the little Bleuet stove, containing 190 gram of butane, will not operate below 0° C, the Super C206 however, which contains a 190 gram butane and propane mix, will operate at temperatures down to -10° C.)

High Pressure Burners

Some burners are high pressure (sometimes called high speed) and are designed to operate directly from a butane gas cylinder without a regulator or pressure reduction device. An example again is the little Camping Gaz Bleuet picnic stove referred to above. The loud, hissing, burning sound of this type of burner is a characteristic of high pressure burners.

Low Pressure Burners and Pressure Regulators

Some gas stoves, and in particular most gas appliances typically installed in caravans, are of the low pressure type. So that these stoves and appliances may safely be operated, it is necessary to connect them to the gas supply by way of a pressure regulator, a device which connects directly to the gas cylinder and drops the pressure to that required by the appliance.

All appliances and low pressure equipment have their operating pressure clearly marked on them. All regulators also have their outlet pressure clearly marked on them. It is important that the regulator outlet pressure and the appliance operating pressure both correspond.

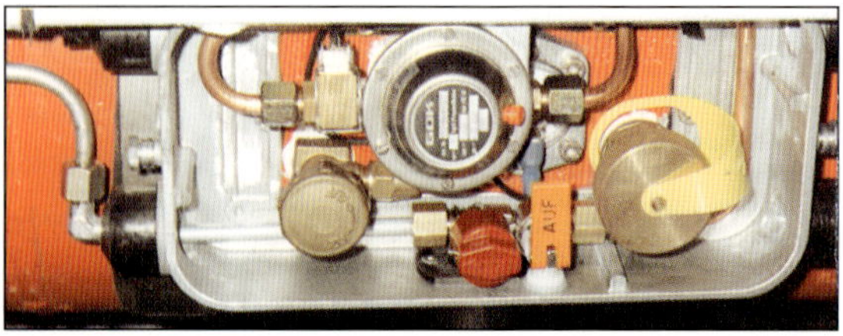

A red LPG tank regulator box containing filler on the right, on/off valve lower left, and regulator upper middle.

In the UK, low pressure butane apparatus is designed to operate at a pressure of 28 mb (millibars) and propane apparatus at 37 mb. Regulators with corresponding output pressures should be used.

I have installed a gas tank with a 30 mb output pressure regulator for the following reasons. This pressure regulator, according to the oven manufacturers, is correct for the oven, which they have tested at 28 mb and 37 mb for butane and propane respectively, and the gas normally available from filling stations is a mixture of butane and propane.

Appliance pressures can vary in different countries, in Germany, for example, the gas operating pressure used for both butane and propane appliances is more usually 50 mb.

Typical Cylinder Sizes

The most commonly used type of gas cylinder in Europe is the exchangeable version. They are available in various sizes up to about 30 kg (kilogram) although the largest size most likely to be used in a touring caravan is about 11 kg to 15 kg (depending on the make, and whether it is butane or the lighter propane) with a capacity of about 23 or 30 litres respectively.

Several countries use 11 kg to 15 kg cylinders widely, but unfortunately each country has its own type of fitting and sadly they are not interchangeable! Threaded adapter sets are available which can enable van fittings to be adapted to differing cylinders, but the problem then is that a new cylinder must be bought and storage found for the old one - this may be viable for those who frequently tour in a particular country.

Smaller cylinders are also in use, 5 kg and 7 kg being common.

Camping Gaz offer the refillable cylinders type 901 (0.45 kg butane), 904 (1.81 kg butane), and the 907 (2.72 kg butane) their largest, which they say is available in over 70 countries. Their connecting adapter enables all these three sizes to be connected to a standard UK regulator.

The Camping Gaz 907 holding 2.72 kg (6 Lbs) of butane is quite a compact cylinder with a capacity of about 5.5 litres.

By using the 907 cylinder exclusively, or alternatively by carrying a 907 and connecting tap, in conjunction with a larger local cylinder, you can be more or less guaranteed availability of gas throughout Europe. When the local cylinder runs out and cannot be exchanged or refilled, you can switch over to the readily exchangeable 907.

However, given the high rate at which heating equipment can consume gas, and if enough space is available, it makes sense to use the largest gas storage possible. If exchangeable cylinders are chosen, the largest likely limit will be two 15 kg cylinders.

If a refillable tank is permanently installed, it may be possible to find space for larger tanks, even those in excess of 100 litres, which are available.

Location of Cylinders

For exchangeable cylinders a compartment will need to be fabricated inside the van, but sealed from the inside, and usually with external access. A ventilation hole of about 4x4 cm should be provided in the floor of the compartment. As a result of the airtight seal and the ventilated floor, any gas (being heavier than air) leaking from the cylinders will not enter the caravan but drain away to the outside.

A red 60 litre refillable tank with attached regulator enclosure above the dog.

For refillable tanks, which more readily lend themselves to external location, particularly under the van close to the chassis, any leaks will escape outside. This type of cylinder is normally supplied with a gas level indicator mounted on it, although for greater convenience a remote contents gauge for installing inside the van is also available.

Installation

The gas installation is a job to be taken on only by the qualified technician and according to the relevant requirements. (In Britain the requirements of BS 5482 Part 2 apply.) All appliances are to be installed in accordance with the requirements of the manufacturers and as detailed in their installation instructions.

Except for the connection to an exchangeable cylinder, which will be a short flexible rubber gas tubing (marked as such with a pressure rating and expiry date, after which the hose should be replaced), all gas piping will be either copper or steel pipe.

Although available in various outside diameters, my preference is throughout to use the tough 8 mm zinc plated steel gas pipe. The appropriate compression fittings are used. Metal clips are fitted either side of every fitting and every 40 cm along the pipe run. Ideally a pipe bending tool is required to shape the pipe although a bending jig can be fashioned out of a circular piece and a straight piece of wood both fixed to a wooden board. A pipe cutting tool should be used to cut the pipe cleanly. Alternatively it may be cut with a hack saw. Any burrs should be removed with a file, taking care not to score the outside of the pipe. All the joints can be fitted with a smear of jointing grease on each compression gland ferrule before firm tightening with two spanners. All external pipework must be corrosion protected with an appropriate paint.

There must be a readily accessible control valve in the pipeline, inside the van, close to the point where the pipe enters the van (through a grommet), by which the gas can be isolated from within the van. All pipe branches must also have a control valve.

A final inspection and pressure test of the system are required using a manometer, and as described by BS 5482 Part 2. Inspection should be repeated regularly.

A correctly installed system should not have a smell of gas anywhere, and if any whiff is detected, or the pressure test is failed, the source of the leak must be found. Soapy water on each joint should produce tell tale bubbles around the bad joint. The joint must be undone, jointing grease smeared around the ferrule, and then the joint firmly re-tightened and re-checked.

A deformed pipe end may prove impossible to obtain a perfect seal with a compression fitting, in which case, if possible the deformed section must be cut off and de-burred before refitting, or the whole pipe replaced.

SAFETY IN USE AND VENTILATION

When using gas appliances inside the van it is necessary to allow fresh air to enter the van to aid the combustion process. In Britain, natural ventilation must be provided according to the requirements of BS.5601 Part 1.

Low Level Ventilation

A fixed free area of ventilation should be provided at low level also as specified in BS.5601 Part 1. (NB. It is expected that automatic ventilation will become a European Standard requirement. The basis is that the low level ventilation will close during motion, (to keep out exhaust fumes), but open automatically when the vehicle is stationary.)

The requirement of the fixed low level ventilation is to ensure that, under the specified test procedures, with all other windows and ventilators closed, a build-up of carbon dioxide (CO_2), which is heavier than air, will not occur when all the non room-sealed LPG appliances in the van are ignited and set to maximum setting.

High Level Ventilation

Whenever non room-sealed LPG appliances, including cooking equipment, are in use, a window should be open. Also a roof vent should be open to allow an exit for the rising, damp, combustion gases. They need not be open wide, although it should always be remembered that incomplete gas combustion produces the deadly **carbon monoxide**, an odourless gas which is lighter than air, that can, and sadly often does, kill.

Carbon monoxide (CO) can induce drowsiness and headaches, and soon renders the victim incapable of coherent speech or articulation, death can follow within ten or fifteen minutes; if the vaguest suggestion of any such symptoms are experienced as a result of CO poisoning the only hope of survival is to obtain fresh air quickly.

DANGER - YELLOW FLAME

Carbon monoxide is produced by incomplete gas combustion due to wrongly set up or incompatible appliances. A danger sign to look out for is a yellow flame, also a bad smelling flame, although it should be noted that carbon monoxide itself is odourless.

A correctly adjusted flame, when observed in dark, still surroundings, should be predominantly blue. It should be well formed with a fairly constant shape, without a gap between it and the burner, and with a quiet, low hissing sound.

If, on lighting a burner, it makes an unusually loud hissing or roaring noise, it has ignited wrongly and should be extinguished immediately, and after a few seconds re-lit.

Stories of carbon monoxide poisoning, typically in rented accommodation (mainly as a result of badly maintained gas appliances), are not uncommon. (About forty people a year die in Britain alone from this cause.)

The tragic consequences of incompatible equipment, or badly adjusted or maintained burners, and poor or no ventilation should alert us all to the need to be sure of proper gas installations and regular skilled check-ups and maintenance, and adequate ventilation.

Gas and Driving

When travelling, gas must be switched off at the cylinder. Gas may not be burned while driving on the road, or in the vicinity of fuel stations or any flammable vapours. Neither may it be burned whilst on board ferries. This restriction applies to all types of gas appliances.

The icing on the cake.

CHAPTER 11

HEATING

There are four sources of heater power that can be used in a caravan: gas, electricity, petrol and diesel.

Most medium sized insulated caravans can quickly be brought up to a reasonable temperature by a heater with an output of about 3 kilowatts. Then to maintain the temperature at a comfortable level, this heat output should be able to be reduced.

Given that heat rises, the heater should be situated close to floor level to reduce the cold feet and hot head syndrome.

All heaters must be installed in accordance with the manufacturers' instructions.

Some heaters are designed to generate warm air to be distributed through flexible ducts. Such equipment can be installed out of sight in cupboards or lockers.

Gas Heater Types

1. Sealed Combustion or Balanced Flue Heaters

This category covers the most commonly installed type of caravan heater. It is usually of the blown warm air type. Some are intended for visible wall mounting, others for concealed installation and ducted outlets.

Again it must be stressed that gas combustion can produce dangerous gases. The only type of gas heater that is safe to leave on during the night is the balanced flue, or sealed combustion type, which takes the air for combustion from outside and exhausts the combustion gas also to outside. This type ensures that no exhaust gases are emitted into the caravan and that no combustion ventilation is required from inside the van.

Several companies specialise in this type of heater specifically for caravan type applications.

Features to consider as worthwhile include:-

1. Balanced flue or sealed combustion
2. Piezo or electronic ignition.
3. Flame failure protection device.
4. Variable output control.
5. Built in thermostat.

2. Radiant and Convector Un-Flued Heaters

This group can be free standing or wall mounted, but does not have an external flue for either combustion air or exhaust gases. They should be treated with great care and observation due to both the fire risk and the danger of carbon monoxide poisoning. They must only be used with sufficient ventilation, both low and high level, as with a gas hob, and must not be left on while asleep.

3. Catalytic Heater

If an un-flued or portable heater is preferred, the catalytic type should be considered as a first choice due to its safer method of operation. Both the risks of fire and carbon monoxide poisoning are significantly reduced due to the catalytic element, which allows the gas to burn away at a relatively low temperature. Nevertheless low and high level ventilation must be adequate.

Electric Heaters

Although there is always a fire risk with any hot element, an electric heater poses no dangerous gas risk.

Electric heaters draw too much power to be run from the caravan batteries. Indeed, normal domestic electric heaters draw too much power for many campsite hook-ups. A 2 kW (2000 Watts) mains heater will require almost 9 Amps at 230 Volts, and a 3 kW unit 13 Amps.

Caravan shops sell lower power electric heaters which are suited to campsite low power hook-ups. Provided other mains equipment is not being used, a 2 Amp supply will be able to run a 460 Watts heater.

(Watts = Volts x Amps: Amps = W / V = 2000 / 230 = 8.7, and 3000 / 230 = 13 Amps. 230 Volt x 2 Amp = 460 Watts)

Petrol or Diesel Fired Air Heater

This type of heater is more commonly found in the boating world, and in the automotive industry, where additional vehicle heating is required. Truck drivers on cold overnight stops regularly rely on them. They are expensive to buy but cheap to run.

Either petrol or diesel fired units are available, drawing the fuel from the vehicle main tank by way of a standpipe, or from the fuel line, with their own small metering pump.

They have sealed combustion chambers taking their combustion air from, and exhausting to, the outside.

Every combustion process generates exhaust gas which has toxic constituents. The heaters therefore must not be used in confined spaces. Furthermore, due to the combustion flame, they may not be operated within the vicinity of fuel stations or any flammable vapours.

They may be mounted internally in which case they require an inlet and exhaust hole to outside.

They have a small heat exchanger chamber, the inside of which is heated by a flame. Air is blown over the outside of the heat exhanger and heated before being ducted wherever required. They are sophisticated little machines with many fail-safe features incorporated, however it is important to note that when they are switched on, for the first couple of minutes during the ignition stage, they consume about 20 Amps from the battery. Once fully ignited they draw a constant two or three amps depending on the power setting (2 kW or 3 kW units).

Several different ratings are available, and the output power perhaps most suited to caravan use is about 3 kW but with the option to switch to half power or less.

They tend to be quite noisy in operation, most of the sound coming from the air intake. A silencer should therefore be considered in the air-to-be-heated inlet, (not combustion air), particularly if it is drawing the air from inside the van for re-circulation.
Exhaust silencers are also advisable.

Clear Advantage

A clear advantage of this last type of heater is that they do not rely on an external power hook-up (providing the auxiliary batteries are in good condition and the charge facilities adequate), and do not consume any vital gas supplies. Their petrol or diesel consumption is less than half a litre per hour maximum, depending on output and settings. ⌘

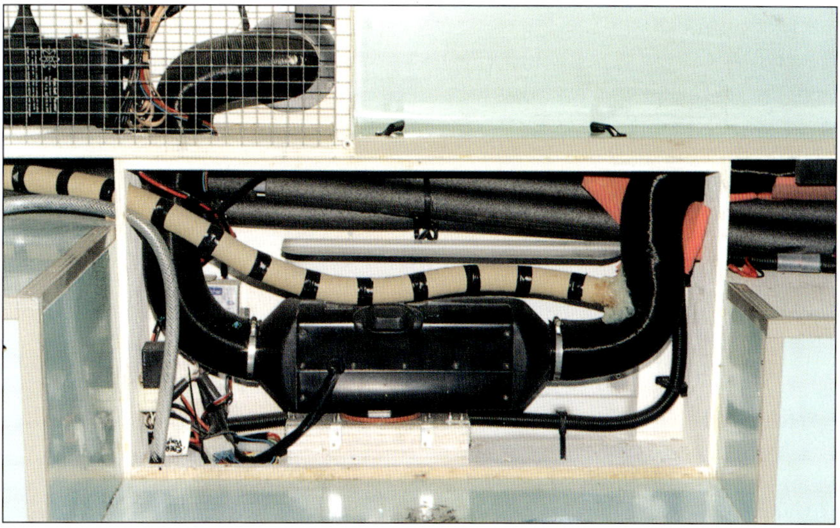

A diesel powered 3kW air heater. The unit's combustion air inlet and exhaust outlet are through the floor to the outside. This installation recirculates and heats the van air, the inlet is in the upper left wired-off box. The striped tube diverts a gentle flow of warm air towards the water filtration system, to avoid the risk of freezing in extremely cold conditions.

The luxurious interior of the 36 foot Airstream motorhome. Few American RVs would be supplied without at least one independent air conditioner. This Airstream is supplied as standard with a 13,500 BTU Air Conditioner and a 4kW Generator to power it. A second AC unit is available as an option.

CHAPTER 12

COOLING

Like heating, cooling systems consume large amounts of energy, which is probably the main reason for so few air conditioning systems being installed in European caravans. It is an entirely different state of affairs in America where many RVs are installed with one if not two potent AC units. To power these devices requires a hefty campsite hook up, although it is usual for American motorhomes to be equipped with powerful generators which are suitable to drive their AC units.

Just how effective much lower powered air conditioners are is arguable, and depends on the ambient humidity and temperature.

Of course sufficient power to run an air conditioner is readily available from the vehicle's engine and they are a normal option on many cars. The compressor for cooling is mounted under the bonnet and driven by the engine pulley-belt system. Such an installation, when in operation, can provide significant relief driving on a hot day. The price, apart from the capital cost, is higher fuel consumption. It is probable that an AC unit will add between five and ten per cent to fuel costs while it is switched on.

I have a factory installed system in the cab of my motorcaravan which I sometimes use when I am driving. It can be a relief in very high temperatures, in slow, congested traffic for example, when the air flow is low and an open window provides no refreshment.

When the van has been parked in the sun, switching on the system with the cool air directed towards the face for the first few minutes of driving can be a great help.

In very humid conditions when the windows steam up badly, the combination of heater and air conditioner, set on full, are most effective in rapid removal of window mist.

There are air conditioners available for installation in the roof of a caravan. Electrolux offer one which is mains powered, drawing 5.6 Amps at 220 Volts for a 1 kW cooling effect. It weighs about 50 kg. There are also units which operate on 12 Volts.

It should be born in mind that, in much the same way as a heater's effectiveness is proportional to its power consumption, the less power an AC unit consumes the less effectively will it cool. ◆

A Unimog 1300 expedition vehicle.

CHAPTER 13

REFRIGERATORS

Cooling by Evaporation

To keep milk and butter cool on a hot day without a refrigerator is not impossible: they can be kept in a container which is standing in shallow water in a bowl, a muslin type cloth draped over them with its skirt in the water, and the whole assembly placed in a draughty place in the shade; the air flow will cause evaporation which in turn will provide a cooling effect.

Cool Boxes

Insulated portable cool boxes without any cooling elements can keep food and drinks cool for a short time. Providing the box itself is cold it can keep butter cool for a few hours. On the other hand if the day is hot and the box already warm, it will not do so well.

A special re-freezable icepack, which some campsites will freeze on request in their freezer, can be placed on top of the food inside the box and will keep the contents colder, longer. In hotter countries, where ice is often readily available by the bag at sites or from service stations, the cool box becomes more useful still.

Peltier Effect Cool Boxes

Portable cool boxes with 12 Volts thermoelectric 'Peltier Effect' cooling elements are also available, although it should be noted that this type of cooler can only reduce the temperature in the box by about ten or fifteen degrees. This may not stop butter from melting. Furthermore they consume a lot of energy.

Compressor Cool Boxes

A portable cool box with a 12 Volts compressor unit is a more expensive piece of equipment, but it is a proper fridge that is very capable of freezing water. Due to its efficiency, it uses less electricity. Providing it is large enough, and a permanently installed fridge is not wanted, this is a good choice. They are available in capacities from 10 to 60 litres.

Refrigerators

Whilst one of the above techniques may be just the answer for some people, there is little doubt that if the de rigeur equipment supplied in almost any type of caravan is anything to go by, just like at home, nearly every caravanner is going to want a refrigerator installed in their van. We all know the advantages. They keep our food fresher for much longer. Importantly they also protect it from flies, wasps and other insects. The photographer knows that it is the best place to preserve film, (after removing the film from the fridge it should be allowed to reach room temperature before opening the packaging, to avoid the risk of moisture forming on the film surface). Some medicines are best kept in a fridge.

There are several companies manufacturing refrigerators and refrigeration equipment specifically for caravans and boats. Between them they offer a wide range of types and sizes. There are two types of refrigerators typically available for installation, which, although usually smaller than domestic refrigerators, are both much the same internally, with a freezer compartment at the top.

1. Absorption Refrigerators

This system continuously evaporates the refrigerant from an aqueous solution under pressure. It is condensed, allowed to evaporate, absorbing heat as it does, and then re-absorbed. The system is the most common in caravan use.

Absorption refrigerators are available with **three-way** powering options built especially for the caravan market. This means that they can be switched to operate from any of three supply options: **1.** Mains voltage. **2.** 12 Volts DC battery power. **3.** Gas.

These models do of course need the three separate energy supplies to be connected to them. For continuous safe operation on gas, the burner must be of the balanced flue type, which requires a sealed flue to be installed through the side of the van.

As usual, being a gas appliance, it may not be operated from gas whilst travelling, on board ferries, nor within the vicinity of fuel stations or any flammable vapours. It is normal to operate in 12 Volts mode during driving, when the heavy battery drain can be compensated by the vehicle alternator.

Gas would be used where a mains hook-up was not available.
Unfortunately absorption refrigerators are much less efficient than their compressor counterpart, consuming typically six times more power. They are therefore significantly more expensive to operate than their compressor refrigerator counterpart. This relative inefficiency also means that they generate more heat, and should be well ventilated all round to help keep the condenser cool and running as efficiently as possible.

An eighty litre absorption fridge will almost constantly draw about 10 Amps at 12 Volts. This is equivalent to a consumption of about 2300 Watts in 24 hours.

Their advantage is that they cost about half as much to buy as compressor fridges. Because of the three way operation, however, they are more expensive to install.

Absorption refrigerators are tilt sensitive and usually require to be operated within about two degrees of vertical. They are consequently inappropriate for installation in boats. Careful levelling of the van for any stop is therefore necessary for absorption refrigerators to operate correctly. Indeed humans too operate better when level! A van tilt greater than two degrees is not comfortable.

2. Compressor Refrigerators

This type of fridge uses a compressor with an oscillating piston or membrane to pressurise the refrigerant (usually Freon 12) into a condenser, through a throttle valve and on to the evaporator plate which cools the refrigerator cabinet. The freon then passes back to the compressor. This method of operation is the most reliable and consumes least energy.

Compressor refrigerators which are designed specifically for caravans and boats operate on 12 or 24 Volts DC and are able to operate at inclinations up to thirty degrees.

To run these low voltage units on 230 Volts requires a black-box rectifier to convert the mains to 12 Volts, although a constant voltage battery charger can keep a 12 Volts battery fully charged whilst it is powering such a fridge. So can enough solar panels.

It is worth noting that although fridge power consumption increases with a rise in ambient temperature, so too does the energy available from the sun. In other words compressor fridges and solar panels are a good combination.

When the compressor fridge is operating, the compressor only runs for between one and six minutes in every ten, just sufficient to maintain the preset internal cabinet temperature. An eighty litre compressor refrigerator will consume about 4.5 Amps at 12 Volts, but only while the compressor is running. The actual compressor 'on-time' depends on the ambient temperature, the fridge contents, the preset internal cabinet temperature, and the quality of the insulation .

As a very rough guide such a unit could consume about 30 Amp hours at 12 Volts or 360 Watts in a twenty-four hour period. This rate of power consumption is about one sixth of the power required to operate an absorption refrigerator under similar conditions.

Because heat is generated, an air flow, ideally fan assisted, should be created across the condenser, to assist cooling for maximum efficiency. This does not require a vent to the outside, merely enough space to let the air flow.

Models that use electronic control systems can be susceptible to low voltages, high cross-sectional area cable feeds should be used to avoid voltage drops.

Energy accumulators

Some compressor fridges can be bought with an 'energy accumulator' or eutectic plate option. This consists of a special evaporator containing a liquid which slowly solidifies when the compressor is running. It increases both the time that the compressor is running and the time that the compressor is off by a factor of up to ten for the same cabinet inside temperature. Such operation is not only more energy efficient, using up less vital battery power, but also, noise-wise, the reduced 'cycling', or switching on and off, is less noticeable to the van occupants.

With this option some models offer the possibility to stop the compressor running (for silence during the night for example) at the push of a button, during which time the 'energy accumulator' keeps the fridge cool, silently, for between five and twelve hours as the refrigerant slowly liquefies. The compressor then comes on again and the refrigerant is re-solidified. ☯

Autotrail Cheyenne

CHAPTER 14

COOKING

Preparing and cooking food in the van is an intimate affair. Everything is within arms reach. In this confined space the equipment should be compact, and oven mits to hand with places to put hot pans. A cutting board that can also receive hot pots and pans is useful and the table can be brought into play as an extra surface on which to put it.

Cooking Equipment

There are attractive cooking items designed specifically with the caravan in mind, such as a compact set of stainless steel nesting pans with small handles. The most cost effective solution, however, is to select various items from ones home kitchen. These will probably include the items which will comfortably fit on the hob, in the oven, and in the storage allocated to them.

Pressure Cooker

A small pressure cooker can be compact enough for van use, fast to cook with, and a good way to conserve gas. It also presents an opportunity to control the steam generated, particularly if the lid is taken off outside. There are a couple of Spanish brands available in stainless steel in various sizes at competitive prices. Eleven minutes for potatoes in a pressure cooker is quicker than any alternative.

Lids

A lid should be available for every pan in use. Not only does cooking with lids use less gas, but also reduces the steam put out into the van.

Handles

Pans with a small handle on each side are easier to store than those with a long handle on one side. They are also safer on a hob in a caravan environment.

Kettles

A stainless steel kettle is useful for boiling water for tea. A whistle ensures that it is not allowed to boil for longer than necessary, again filling the van with steam and wasting gas.

Electric Kettle

Some campers may prefer to use an electric kettle when 'hooked-up' on site. They should note, however, that most domestic kettles have an element rated at about 2.4 kW which will draw about 10 Amps from the supply. Since this size of feed is not always available, a low power kettle, designed for campsite applications and available from camping accessory shops, would be more appropriate, but slower.

Coffee Makers:

Cafétière

This is a recently introduced type of coffee making pot with a mesh plunger. It is perhaps the best technique for the van, particularly if a large volume of coffee is required. It does need the use of two vessels however. The water must be boiled in the kettle first, then added to the cafétière before the plunger is pressed down to hold the grains in place at the bottom of the pot.

Italian or Spanish Type Percolator

This is a tall pot which unscrews in the middle. Water is placed in the lower section, the perforated coffee holder is then dropped into the top of the lower section, coffee added to it, and a perforated lid placed over the coffee. The top section is tightly screwed onto the lower section, and the pot placed onto the burner. As the water in the lower section boils it is forced up, under pressure, through the coffee and into the top, ready to drink.

The advantage is that only one vessel is used and it is very easy to clean, not least because the coffee grounds come out nearly dry.

Filter Machines

Excellent and convenient though the latest models are, filter machines are perhaps bulky for vans and require about 4 Amps of mains electricity. They also require a filter paper. There are compact 12 Volts and 24 Volts units available, but they draw high currents and are quite slow. They are ideal for truckers who do not have gas, but less appropriate for caravanners.

Coffee Bags

These are as easy to use as tea bags, and probably therefore the easiest of all coffee making techniques for the caravanner.

Heating Milk

If like me you prefer hot milk with your coffee, you may find that heating it is a nuisance. It requires another vessel to be washed. I use a saucepan and watch it carefully to avoid boiling it. Once the milk has been poured out, if the pan is placed upside down in the sink, cleaning it later is significantly easier.

Two Three or Four Burners?

Whilst there is a tendency for caravan and boat cooking facilities to be restricted to as few as two burners, compact three and four burner cookers, grills, and ovens can usually fit in.

Combination Oven, Cooker and Grill

For the most efficient use of space and economy of installation, the easiest yet most comprehensive method is to install a combination unit which incorporates all the above features in one item. Because the grill is within the oven, the two cannot be used at the same time, but the oven provides heat shielding when the grill is in operation.

If a separate grill is installed, extra space must be provided beneath it for the grill pan, and heat protection must be provided under and around it. Both are jobs admirably performed by the oven in the combined unit.

The combination unit is not only very compact but also requires only one gas feed and one 12 Volts electric supply (for the very useful electronic spark ignition and oven light).

Combination Cooker and Sink

A compact. alternative approach, if an oven is not required, is to buy one of the elegant units which combines cooker, grill, sink, and ideally a drainer. This format is sold with 2, 3 or 4 burner cookers. Separate and matching units are available if preferred.

Flame Failure Devices

As a result of the low gas pressure and ventilation which may cause draughts, the flame can get blown out. The flame's virtual invisibility in bright light makes this hard to detect.

It is for this reason that ideally cookers (and in fact all gas burners) should be fitted with flame failure devices which automatically shut off the gas if a flame goes out. These take the form of small metal protrusions beside each burner which detect the heat from the flame. They control valves which stop the gas flowing in the absence of heat. To light a burner, the gas control knob must be held down long enough to override the flame failure device until it heats up enough for the valve to remain open.

Electronic Ignition

The other little device, often beside each burner, is the spark ignition which is usually fed by a 12 Volts supply and operated at the push of a button. It is so much more convenient than any other means of lighting a burner that it should never be omitted. Anyone who has ever wanted a cup of tea or coffee in a caravan equipped with tea, coffee, sugar, water and milk, but no matches, nor other lighting device, will immediately acknowledge one advantage of this particular feature. ❍

Island Plastics Hylo Romahome.

CHAPTER 15

SECURITY

One of the most important considerations in the caravan world is equally one of the most difficult to implement. When we take off with our vans we like to have all our equipment in tow, valuables of several varieties as well as a little cash. It seems that the hardest thing is to avoid having some or all of it stolen!

Never Leave the Van Unaccompanied

Probably the best way to avoid theft is never to leave the van unattended. This is based on the probability that the majority of thieves are not looking for a confrontation. It makes sense therefore to try to take it in turns van sitting. This of course is not much fun and not the answer we want to hear, but nevertheless on many occasions the best solution. Deciding which these occasions are is the problem, the wrong decision could be expensive.

Park in Safe Places

The next solution is to choose the parking place carefully.

Some places are likely to be safer than others. Some attended car parks are a good bet particularly if the attendant can be persuaded to keep on eye on the van. Campsites should be safe. It is hard to know where else is.

Leave Nothing on Display

It should never be forgotten, wherever the van is parked, however, that no small objects of desire should ever be left in sight through any window. The most obvious of these are a handbag, a radio, or a camera. Even safe parking becomes less so if it is obvious that a quick smash and grab will yield a guaranteed treasure.

It was at the Plaza de Catalunya, in the centre of Barcelona, that I experienced a break-in first hand. It could be argued that the whole event was educational, and there is no doubt that the consequences could have been far worse. Indeed, I look back on it all with gratitude not least for the very limited damage incurred.

I had parked the van in between the tourist buses, every one of which appeared to have its driver in attendance. (I have more recently noticed that parking there is now disallowed.) The location was thus concluded to be a safe bet and was certainly very central. The plan was to wander off down the famous Rambla and spend the afternoon looking at the sights.

Before we left the van however, I wanted to bide my time in the back with a cup of coffee. Whilst my companion was chomping at the bit to be on our way, for some uncertain reason I felt compelled to make the most of my coffee. Perhaps it was fate ... it was just as well whatever it was.

I felt the van rock slightly but paid no attention until we heard a noise: "What was that?" We queried. "It sounded a bit like breaking glass" but we were not sure, I remember thinking that I was even being silly and over cautious. Nevertheless, and more out of curiosity than anything, I looked through the curtain to the front and to my shock horror, (not to mention surprise having been so barely aware of anything being amiss), saw an emaciated looking youth, of perhaps twenty, with his arm through the smashed quarter light in the process of unlocking the door.

I am sure that what happened next was more the reaction of someone in a state of wild anger, having been confronted with the perpetrator in the act of a dastardly deed, than a cold and calculated response.

Screaming blue murder, I charged through to the front and out of the door after the miserable specimen who had broken it open. By this time he was moving very quickly, desperately even, and heading into the centre of the Plaza de Catalunya with me in hot pursuit.

He suddenly changed direction and shot out of another entrance, allowing me to outwit him, managing to head him off by leaping over a side wall.

By now I had moved into top gear and was really flying, bearing down on him rapidly. I then became aware that all eyes were on the chase, and I realised that I was going to catch him. I felt extremely swift and good about it, almost floating. Then, for the first moment since the start of the incident, I began to think about why I was chasing him, and what would be the consequences of catching him.

In a split second, as I was almost upon him, I decided that catching him was not going to get my window back and would probably lead to all kinds of subsequent grief which I could well do without.

I stopped running and let him go, and I am still not sure whether I made the right decision. Rumour has it, however, that assuming I would have been able to make a citizen's arrest, (without the possibility of an inadvertent or intentional needle spike, or some other injury to myself), and take him to a police station, I would have spent a great deal of unrewarding time there, not much would have happened to the youth, and my window would have remained broken. Such rumours do not augur well for our security problems.

Naturally enough, by the time my partner and I regrouped we were fairly depressed by the whole incident. We could not get out of Barcelona fast enough, forget the Rambla. We were homeward bound. During the drive, news on the radio announced the end of the Gulf war.

Dogs

A great disappointment was the total lack of any contribution by my potentially fierce dog who was with us in the back of the van at the time. She did not hear the break in, she did not bark once, and she did not assist in the chase! I might have hoped for more. Perhaps she would have done the business on her own in the van if we had gone off wandering. I would have left her in the cab and probably she would have made a great commotion on seeing the thief, and hopefully she would have scared him off, but I shall never know.

Of course, unfortunately it is not practical to take a dog out of Britain on holiday due to the quarantine regulations which would apply on the return journey.

For those living in most of the rest of Europe, however, crossing borders with a dog is quite viable and I imagine that many thieves, though certainly not all, would be deterred from breaking into a van containing a barking dog.

Many clouds do seem to have their silver linings though, and my experience in Barcelona taught me that the security on that van was just not good enough, and another fifteen minutes could have transformed the non-theft into a nightmare. The mere thought of that burglar (and rather unusually I met the wretched youth) helping himself to everything was bad enough to oblige me to improve the van's security.

As a result I fitted dead locks to all the doors so that they could not be opened, even from the inside, without a key. I will never know what my burglar would have done on finding the van so protected, crawled through the window?

I hope this story will not put off potential visitors heading for some of the wonders of Barcelona, rather that it will help them realise, if they do not already, that this is no place to treat without very careful thought to security. Indeed sadly almost no place is. I hasten to add that in my opinion Spain is probably no greater a risk that Britain.

However, it does prompt the suggestion that as long as thieves continue to get away with their crimes, they are unlikely to stop stealing.

On subsequent visits to Barcelona I have tried two alternative approaches. The first was to park the van in one of the several campsites just south of the city in Gava. Directly outside the camps are bus stops with low cost buses arriving at half hour intervals, and taking only thirty minutes to reach the centre of Barcelona. The second was to use a guarded car park in the city in which the van was left for a few hours.

The cost of either of these possibilities seems very small compared with both the direct cost and the heartache of dealing with a break-in. Such possibilities should be given serious consideration whenever contemplating leaving a van unattended.

Notwithstanding all the above there are several deterrents which can reduce the probability of a successful break-in, either by putting off the thief altogether (he may decide to look for an easier quarry), or by slowing him down.

In spite of the list of possible deterrents which follows, it is worth remembering always, that some professional thieves are well equipped. Those dressed in overalls and with a crane mounted on a flatbed truck, with the capability to lift the vehicle straight up off the road onto the back of the truck, are unlikely to be put off by alarm systems, wheel clamps, or almost any amount of immobilisation and anti-theft equipment.

The Alarm System

The alarm system is usually the first consideration for vehicle protection, although it has to be said that the mere sound of an alarm, however loud, is not likely to deter a thief who can carry out a smash and grab in probably not much more than five seconds. It also seems that few people go out of their way to investigate alarm sirens.

It is therefore appropriate not only to look for rather more from an alarm system than just a loud noise, but also to consider other protection that can be used in combination with it.

Given that thefts very often are of the vehicle itself, the most effective deterrents are likely to be those offering some means of engine immobilisation. Luckily, most thieves are not equipped to tow away an immobilised vehicle.

Comparison should be made between the various attributes and features of the many systems on offer, in particular their ability to fool the clever thief. It is said that some thieves are able to intercept, at a safe distance, the infrared signal from an alarm remote control, and copy them for later simple entry into the vehicle! Some manufacturers claim to have systems which combat this alarming development.

Numbers Etched on Windows

There are companies which specialise in etching a vehicle's registration number on all its windows. This will deter the thief who would rather steal a vehicle without this inconvenience. Before he can pass the vehicle on he will need to change the windows.

Steering Wheel Clamps

A very noticeable anti-theft device which requires no vehicle modification is one of the many versions of clamps that can quickly be attached to the steering wheel. Whilst fitted, the car cannot be manoeuvred. There are similar clamps which restrict the movement of the gear lever or the foot pedals. They are an effective means of deterring a theft of the vehicle itself, but are unlikely to prevent a smash and grab.

There is a type which incorporates the added deterrent of a siren and flashing lights which are activated by motion and shock sensors.

Wheel Clamps

Another high profile mechanism with similar attributes to the steering wheel, gear lever, or pedal clamps, is the wheel clamp.

Detachable Car Park Pole

A pole which locks into a socket cemented into the ground. This is clearly only suitable for installing in a private car park or drive. It is intended to be installed in front or behind the vehicle to prevent the vehicle being driven past it. Such an installation (with adequate lock) should prevent most of those disturbing stories of vans being stolen from outside the owner's house.

Battery, Ignition or Fuel Isolator

There are several ways that a hidden switch can be installed in a vehicle's circuitry. Without the switch in the 'on' position the engine can not be started.

A heavy duty switch may be installed in a battery cable to isolate the battery circuit. It must be capable of carrying the starter motor current of up to a couple of hundred amps. There is a nautical type switch with suitable contacts and a large red key which can be removed. A switch and valve, or a tap, can be used to cut off the fuel supply.

Alternatively, on a diesel vehicle, locate the fuel shut-off solenoid and install a switch in one of the feed cables from the ignition switch to the solenoid.

Dead Locks

The installation of a dead lock into each door, provided as always that the dead locks are reasonably un-pickable, is a means of reducing the probability of a smash and grab. The purpose of a dead lock is to prevent the door from being opened merely by smashing a side window and reaching in to unlock and open the door, a technique often employed by a thief. Alternatively he may use a 'thin jim', a piece of flat metal slid down the window opening, to spring the lock open. To open a door with a dead lock fitted, it is necessary to retract the lock with a key or some more devious means. If the door cannot readily be opened the thief may not be willing to enter through the broken window.

Window Grills

Perhaps the best way to prevent most smash and grab thefts is by the installation of some form of protective grills (probably steel mesh) on the van windows. This will not be an attractive option due to the difficulty of installing them, and their general inconvenience, both to store when not in use, and to fit before leaving the van and when returning.

There is no point in leaving a weak link, so all windows would need to be covered. Probably it would be easiest to fit the grills on the inside of the van.

Trackback Systems

Subscription to a company which offers this type of facility presents the chance for the police to catch a thief red-handed in possession of the vehicle. The company conceals a small signalling device somewhere in the vehicle. If the vehicle is stolen, once the police or company are informed, they are able to trace the vehicle by the signals which it emits. Apparently this system is effective but unfortunately it does not prevent the theft.

☼

In the Moroccan desert.
Finding diesel fuel in Morocco was never a problem, but the fuel filters became blocked with dirt, possibly drawn up from a dirty fuel tank. Filtering the fuel through a simple gauze or nylon filter would probably have avoided this time consuming problem.

CHAPTER 16

PETROL and DIESEL CAPACITY and STORAGE

The choice of fuel can be difficult to make, particularly with the changing pricing strategies. Stalwarts may be unwilling to consider diesel powered vehicles because the fuel is dirty and smelly and the engines tend to be relatively sluggish, more typically being associated with commercial vans.

Often petrol pumps are cleaner to use than diesel, although petrol fumes are known to be carcinogenic and breathing them at the pump can be harmful to our health. However, they do not have the same oily clinging stink of diesel, and a splash of diesel on the clothes or picked up on the soles of shoes is unpleasant.

Performance Characteristics

Petrol and diesel engine characteristics are different. For a given capacity, petrol engines tend to develop more power than diesels, and at higher revs. This is useful for sustained acceleration.

Diesel engines, on the other hand, usually develop more torque at lower revs, and are not revved so highly. They are better suited to pulling heavy loads up hills steadily at slow engine speeds. They are well suited to off-road applications, for example, where the vehicle is required to have good pulling power in arduous conditions at lower speeds.

Diesel engines are particularly suited to transport of heavy goods, where engines of ten to fourteen litres capacity, producing around four hundred brake horsepower, are typically common in trucks upwards of thirty tonnes. Such units tick over at about 1500 rpm at the European speed limit of 90 kph (56 mph), consuming about eight miles to the gallon (about 35 litres per 100 km). They are expected to run for hundreds of thousands of miles with minimal repairs necessary.

A smaller, modern, refined diesel engine can now offer a quite acceptable performance for the smaller vehicle.

Weight, Capacity, Power Output and Turbochargers

Because diesel engines operate at higher pressures (diesel compression ratios are typically twice that of petrol engines, a factor aiding efficiency) they need to be more substantially built. This, combined with the bigger diesel engine capacity required for similar power output, results in its being more solid and heavier than its petrol counterpart.

Turbochargers and intercoolers make the diesel engine run more smoothly, but turbochargers are noisy. They increase the engine's power output and torque, and can help to improve 'off the mark' acceleration to surprisingly nimble levels for the otherwise 'sluggish' diesel. Apart from the additional cost, regard must be paid to a possibly compromised engine structure, due to the higher cylinder pressures and heat flow caused by the turbocharger. This could result in a reduced engine life. It is to be hoped that this is fully taken into consideration at the engine design stage, and components appropriately strengthened. Therein lies a possible risk when adding a turbocharger to an engine not originally designed for one.

Noise

Petrol engines are quieter than diesel engines. The latter have a characteristic clanking type of sound, usually quite difficult to conceal. Manufacturers are working towards more effective ways of insulating the driver's compartment from this noise.

Running Costs

The diesel engine is inherently more efficient than the petrol engine, and consequently uses less fuel. This, added to the fact that in most countries, not Britain at the time of writing, diesel is much cheaper than petrol, means that significant savings can be made on diesel engine running costs, although this could change and also must be weighed against the higher initial capital cost.

Reliability

The characteristics of diesel engines, including their lower revving and of course the simple fact that they do not need electrics and spark plugs to ignite the fuel (the compression of the air in the cylinder creates sufficient heat to ignite the injected diesel fuel), all help to make them more reliable than petrol engines.

Pollution

All internal combustion engines pollute our environment and have adverse effects on our health. At the moment there is dispute whether petrol or diesel is worse. The pollutants, including nitrogen oxides, carbon monoxide, and unburnt hydrocarbons, lead to smog, acid rain, cancers, respiratory illnesses, lead poisoning, even death.

Availability

Regarding availability, there is probably little to choose between petrol and diesel, either being readily available. Some garages however, do not sell diesel.

Fuel Safety

Diesel fuel is an inherently safer liquid than petrol as it is does not readily burn or explode. In an accident, the fire risk from diesel fuel is significantly less than petrol.

Fuel Capacity

As the fuel tank empties, a fuel station will usually turn up within a reasonable distance. On longer journeys this forced stop can be an important safe break in concentration and driving fatigue.

There are occasions however, when additional fuel capacity would be welcome. At night on lonely roads for example, or in remote regions where garages are rare, when a four or five hundred kilometre fuel range may not be enough. The most obvious occasion when extra fuel capacity is worth having is when the next filling station is outside the remaining fuel range! There are also times when it is possible to stock up on fuel available at especially low prices.

At such times a large and full fuel tank, as well as a full auxiliary tank which provides some more hundreds of kilometres range, might just seem worth its weight in gold.

It is difficult to specify what could be considered an adequate total capacity, as the only meaningful answer would relate to a specific application. Perhaps the best approach would be to include as much additional capacity as could reasonably be accommodated.

The mere fact that a large fuel tank is available does not mean that it must be filled of course. If it is there it can be used when required.

Jerry Cans

The simplest way to carry extra fuel is to have it in spare cans such as the excellent Jerry cans. These will be limited to about 20 litres each. For emergencies a single such portable container, or even smaller, can be a boon. For the more demanding situations mentioned above, a number of Jerry cans may provide a solution, although full, they are heavy and their stowage could present a problem. Petrol is highly flammable and should be stowed with great care.

Loose fuel tanks carrying more than a small emergency amount may prove of interest to a customs officer, who could insist on charging duty on any fuel they contain.

Auxiliary Fuel Tanks

An auxiliary fuel tank is sometimes an option available from the base vehicle manufacturer, when buying new. This will probably be the most cost effective way of increasing the vehicle's range. It will be the tidiest solution and should be taken, as later addition would be more costly.

It is likely that this extra tank will be linked into the main tank in such a way that once filled they form effectively one tank, although each will need to be separately filled. During running, the engine will draw from them both as required.

Some systems utilise a change-over lever which must be shifted from tank one to tank two. An alternative is by way of an additional fuel pump which is used to transfer fuel from the auxiliary to the main tank. The best choice will depend on the application.

Custom Built Fuel Tanks

If an 'off-the-shelf' auxiliary tank is not available, the solution is to locate a company specialising in their manufacture. Such companies can often be found advertising in truck magazines. The most commonly used material is welded aluminium alloy which results in a strong but light tank which can withstand reasonable flexing.

It is unlikely that they will want to design the tank, so you must work out exactly where it will go and draw it with all details and dimensions shown. Whilst its capacity can be maximised by working out a complex shape which fits exactly into any space available, the simpler the shape the easier and cheaper it will be.
DANGER: It is important, particularly if the fuel is petrol, to position the tank where any collision damage is least likely to affect the tank and its contents.

Cardboard model

Once the drawing or sketch is complete, it is sound practice to make a full size model out of cardboard and sticky tape. When made, this should be offered up to the van body to be quite sure that it will fit in the space allocated, and not impede any suspension or other van components.

Tank Fixings

An integral part of the tank design will be the fixing technique. This may use separate brackets or straps, or brackets welded directly to the tank, or some combination of these.

The securest support will be the chassis. Many vans and trucks have their fuel tanks supported on cantilever brackets fixed to their chassis.

I found enough space, under my van floor behind the back axle, to incorporate a custom built aluminium alloy diesel tank of about 230 litres capacity. It is suspended from the chassis by two stainless steel straps supplied by the tank manufacturer. Empty its weight is negligible, full it weighs about 250 kilograms.

Having decided the shape of the tank, it will be necessary to finalise the systems for filling, breathing, fuel pick up, and contents display.

Tank Filling

Petrol or diesel filler pipes should have a diameter of no less than 40 mm. If, once fitted, the tank will be visibly accessible, the best place for the filler may be welded directly to it, preferably with a neck to raise the filler opening above the level of the tank, to avoid spillage through the cap.

More probably, as with the usual arrangement of the main fuel tank in many vans, a second tank will not be accessible, and will require a flexible pipe from the tank, passing up through the van floor to a filler fitting, fixed through the van wall.

Only proprietary fuel pipe should be used for diesel or petrol. The rubber pipes will be slid over tubes welded to the tank and fixed with jubilee clips (worm drive hose fixings). For tight fits the pipes may be eased on with the aid of grease.

Filler Breather

As fuel enters the tank it displaces air. This displaced air must be able to pass from the highest point of the tank, out through a breather fitting, through a rubber breather tube, and on to an outlet hole (at atmospheric pressure) which is usually provided beside the filler cap. The principle, as with a water tank filler and breather pipe, is to prevent a pressure build up and blow-back, up the filler pipe, when the tank is filled. A suitable breather tube diameter would be about 8 mm external or more.

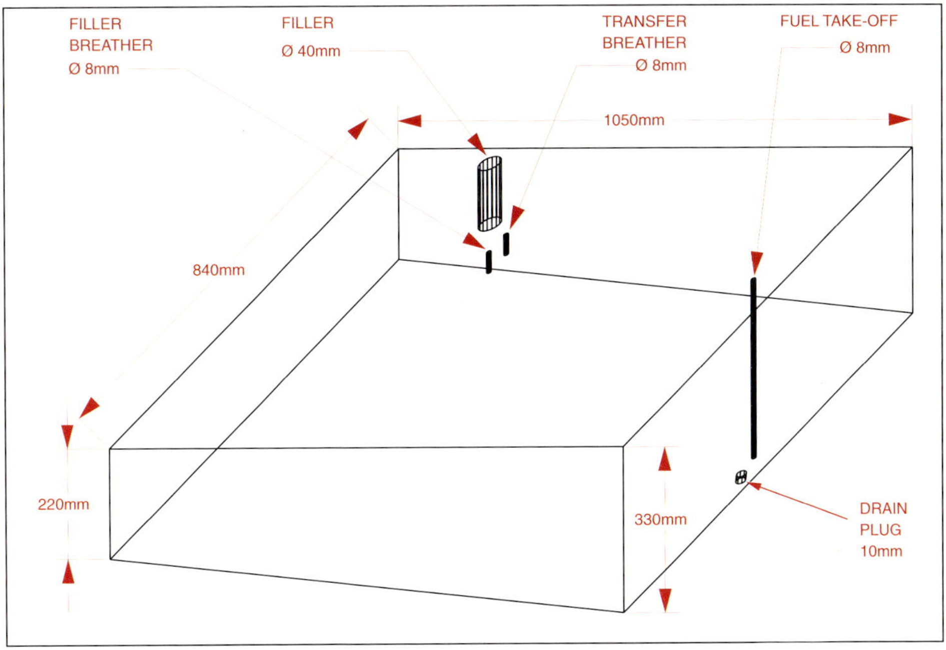

An example of a drawing of an auxiliary diesel tank.

Fuel Transfer

If both tanks are close, and have their lowest points at the same level, by far the simplest means of transferring the fuel from the auxiliary to the main, is via a pipe connecting the lowest points of each tank. The fuel will simply flow into the main tank automatically as gravity equalises the two fuel levels. In this case the tanks act as one, but consideration should be given to the possibility, on a long steady climb, of fuel flowing back into the rear auxiliary tank.

If this technique is not possible it will probably be necessary to transfer the fuel by a pump as required. A method is to draw the fuel from the bottom of the auxiliary, up through a fuel take-off stand pipe, fixed in the top of the tank. It then passes through a flexible tube to a readily cleanable filter, through the pump, and through a flexible tube to the main tank. This technique will require a transfer breather.

High pump flow rates are desirable to speed the fuel transfer. The transfer tube diameter must suit the pump specifications, but might be an external 8 mm or more.

Fuel Transfer Breather

As the fuel is transferred, the pressure reduces in the auxiliary and increases in the main tank. This pressure difference relates to the volume of the fuel transferred, and can be equalised by introducing an additional pipe, to allow the displaced air from the main tank to flow into the auxiliary. This breather needs to be installed between the top of each tank, and if convenient may be linked into existing breather pipes. Such a breather could be of similar diameter to the transfer tube.

Drain Plug

A drain plug of perhaps 10 mm should be installed at the lowest point in the tank.

Auxiliary Fuel Take-Offs

If the intention is to use the auxiliary tank for supplying fuel for an auxiliary air or water heater, an appropriate additional fuel pick-up pipe should be installed. Webasto, Mikuni, and Eberspächer offer such pipes for installation through the top of a tank. They must be cut to suit the depth of the tank.

Contents Gauges

A reliable fuel contents gauge is an almost essential feature of a built-in auxiliary tank. There are primarily two types available. Both are fixed in a hole in the top of the tank.

1. The traditional version has a float on the end of a lever. This moves up and down inside the tank with the change in fuel level.
2. The other, with no moving parts, has fixed probes of differing lengths which are immersed at varying depths into the fuel.
3. A variation of this latter system has sensors fixed at varying heights through the side of the tank. (This requires more holes to be drilled in the tank which have to be sealed.)

All types are wired to a remote gauge which may be installed inside the van to display the tank contents.

Although some principles of water and fuel tank gauges are the same, the two are sometimes not interchangeable and care must be taken to ensure that a particular gauge is suitable for its intended use. ⌘

A substantial motorcaravan and trailer with sufficient ground clearance for auxiliary tank installation beneath,

A Hymer 690E

CHAPTER 17

THE MUSIC SYSTEM RADIOS and TELEVISIONS

Few people consider a car complete without a radio installed, and the market is so well catered for that every caravanner could benefit from the impressive array of in-car sound equipment now available.

Some motorcaravanners might well think that any radio installed in the cab will be sufficient for the living quarters as well. I would like to suggest to those of such persuasion that they should perhaps stop to consider for a moment some lost opportunities by settling for this compromise. After all, speakers best set up for sound while driving, probably will not be ideal for listeners in the van.

The very nature of the caravan and motorcaravan is such that with not too much effort exciting sound reproduction can be built into its structure. The prime requirement to indulge in this possibility, is the careful selection and installation of a pair of stereo loudspeakers. The combination of the very immediacy of the speakers and the soft furnishings, can contribute to the production of an excellent, clear, rich sound.

The existing cab or car radio can be used to drive the speakers and possibly, if the radio is of the plug-in type, a separate chassis could be acquired and installed in the living quarters so that the radio could be plugged either into the caravan or the cab or car as required, thus driving only the required speakers.

Loudspeakers

There are two choices of loudspeaker types that may be considered for the van. Before buying the self-contained type, it would be desirable to hear them operating, to be reasonably satisfied that their sound is an acceptable reproduction, ideally of a known piece of music, preferably supplied by oneself in tape or disc form. To evaluate a pair of unenclosed speaker chassis is harder to do, because their sound is dependent on the way they are installed. The solution is to be guided by their specifications, their reputation or a recommendation.

Self-Contained Speakers in Boxes

The advantage of a pair of self contained enclosed speaker boxes is that they are fairly easy to mount, usually only requiring screwing or bolting to a wall or cupboard. They often incorporate two or three speakers and their sound quality is predetermined.

There are many small versions available of varying sound qualities and like many things, you tend to get what you pay for. The cheapest will not provide the clearest range of frequencies and may have a boxy sound. The more expensive may be better! The relatively small sized enclosures likely to be accommodated in the van, compared with at home, will have a limited bass or low frequency response. This bass can be boosted by the addition of a sub-woofer.

Unenclosed Loudspeakers

The alternative approach is to use basic loudspeaker chassis which are designed for installing into a box, a hole in a wall, cupboard, or car door. The idea is that the cupboard or car door forms the speaker cabinet.

Since the depth of bass frequency that a speaker can reproduce is linked to the volume of the cabinet in which it is mounted, this type of arrangement, given a large cabinet, can produce a much lower bass frequency response than is likely to be obtainable from a small enclosure.

It may be productive to experiment with speaker installations: the more rigid the fixing for the speaker the better, the use of special absorbent materials inside the 'cabinet' can help to reduce any 'boxy' sounds which may otherwise be present.

The choice of loudspeakers available is vast and need not be limited to those specifically aimed at the automotive market. 'Full Range' speaker chassis are available covering the full sound spectrum from the lower to the highest frequencies. If such speakers are used, only one for each of the two stereo channels is required.

More expensive systems usually include two or three loudspeakers for each of the two stereo channels. With a three speaker per channel system, the sound is split between low, medium, and high frequencies by a crossover. The crossover is usually supplied as part of the system and consists of a black box, usually one per channel, with two input connections which connect to the car radio or amplifier output, and output connections which connect to the loudspeakers.

The bass or low frequency speakers are often referred to as 'woofers', the medium frequency speakers as 'mids', and the treble or high frequency speakers as 'tweeters'.

Speaker Positioning

Where appropriate, the speaker systems should be positioned in accordance with the manufacturer's instructions. However, in the absence of recommendations which can be applied to this out-of-the-ordinary application, it is important at least to make every effort to point the speakers towards the listeners' heads without intermediate obstructions.

This orientation consideration is particularly important for the higher frequencies which are very directional and readily absorbed by soft furnishings. In other words, tweeters should always point towards the listeners' heads, although in some cases it is convenient, and effective, to reflect high frequencies off smooth, hard surfaces back towards the listener (off a car windscreen for example).

Lower frequencies are less directional and it is therefore less important to be able to see bass speakers. They can be mounted lower down, or even pointing in other directions if necessary. If the speakers are full range however, the higher frequencies should take precedence and the speakers pointed towards the listeners.

Notwithstanding any of the above, the best stereo image will be created if the stereo speakers are equidistant from the listeners' heads.

When looking for a suitable cupboard in which to mount the unenclosed loudspeaker chassis, it should be borne in mind that in the interest of bass response the larger cupboards might be the best solution, for bass speakers at least.

Sub-Woofers

These are speakers, usually available as single units, designed, (when mounted in a large enough enclosure), to reproduce the deep bass lower frequencies. This usually central bass unit, (often with twin coils), when supplied with its own crossover and wiring (as is normally the case), is straightforward to connect to an existing stereo system. Since the low frequencies are fairly non-directional, the speaker can be situated anywhere convenient. If it is mounted in a large enclosure, such as a wardrobe or car boot, the extra musical depth can impressively increase the range of sound.

This presents an opportunity for a useful compromise available to the caravanning music aficionado. A pair of small, self-contained mid and higher frequency units can easily be mounted, almost anywhere, pointing in the chosen direction. These can be driven by one stereo pair of amps within a 4 channel stereo cassette or CD car radio. Add a sub-woofer (with twin coils and crossover) mounted, as convenient, in the largest available van enclosure for the lower frequencies, powered by the other stereo pair of amps. Result: Exciting sound!

Sound Quality

Sound is very subjective and it is unlikely that two people, particularly sound engineers, would agree whether one sound is better than another. Just what quality of sound needs to be reproduced in a caravan is a matter of personal taste, and to an extent how much money is invested. Rather more important is the ingenuity employed. Although it is possible to spend a great deal of money on the system and install unbelievably powerful equipment, (there are some fanatics driving small cars around with amplification in excess of 1000 Watts, and with speakers that can take it, although I am not so sure about the ears or the neighbours!), the caravan compartment is so small, and ambient noise when stationary relatively low, that high amplifier powers really are not necessary for all but a very few.

It is always useful to have some system 'headroom' however, so that loud transients do not distort, but in my opinion most people will be satisfied with an amplifier output of twenty to thirty Watts per channel in a car or caravan. This level of power is readily available from many car radio models without additional amplifiers. Most of the time the system will be operating well below these potential levels.

Car radios are available with four channel outputs each of twenty or so Watts. This increases the scope for those who wish to have two pairs of stereo speakers without the need for extra amplifiers, although the trend in car audio is towards more than four channels.

If there is a desire to boost a car radio output, either with numbers of channels or Watts per channel, the answer lies in a separate amplifier, or number of amplifiers. It is not good practice to take the auxiliary amplifier input from the radio speaker output: a low level car radio preamplifier output should be used when available. Unfortunately not all radios offer this facility but a helpful electronics engineer may be willing and able to add one.

The Signal Source

The Radio

Most listeners will require a radio. Most radios offer FM (Frequency Modulation, formerly called VHF for Very High Frequency), MW (Medium wave), and LW (Long Wave). As we all know, FM offers the best quality of signal, but unfortunately its nature is such that its range is limited. The consequence is the traveller's frequent need to re-tune to stronger local signals as he passes overland. There is therefore a strong case for selecting a radio with automatic tuning.

Auto Tune

Pioneer call it BSM (Best Station Memory) and Sony call it BTM (Best Tuning Memory). Other manufacturers use other names for it, but for all practical purposes they function reasonably similarly. A button on the radio is held down for a couple of seconds and the radio begins to search for, and tune to, the strongest signals available. Usually six stations are tuned and allocated to six push buttons. For any listener, and the traveller in particular, this capability really is a boon and can save much distracting, even dangerous, knob twiddling and button pushing.

RDS

RDS stands for Radio Data System; it is a European standard. An RDS radio receives an inaudible signal from transmitters telling it the best frequency for each station. It is intended to ensure that listeners can quickly and easily find the radio station to which they want to listen. The most noticeable RDS feature is that the radio automatically displays the name of the station rather than the frequency. It can also re-tune automatically to the best frequency available for the required station, a feature very useful for a vehicle on the move. To benefit from RDS, the listener must have an RDS equipped radio and the broadcaster an RDS equipped transmitter.

Some additional features are currently offered by RDS and others are likely to be added in the future. These include local time and date display, local travel bulletins, selection of program by type, radio text message display, and download of data into microcomputers.

RDS is a standard developed by the BBC with its European Broadcasting Union partners; RDS radios therefore work equally well in most countries, although features may vary between them. At the time of writing, many stations throughout Europe broadcast at least their names under the Radio Data System which is certainly more informative to the traveller than a frequency read-out. As time passes, more radio sets will offer the RDS facility, and it is a feature I would require from any new car radio, portable radio, or Home Hi-Fi tuner.

How to Select a Radio with RDS

When selecting a new radio the sign to look for is the RDS logo on the front panel. The latest versions should also have the three letters EON (Enhanced Other Networks) included in the logo: it is an additional capability enabling the radio to respond to further features broadcast by the transmitter.

Cassettes and Discs

Cassettes have been around for a long time and need no introduction. They offer the obvious advantage of being recordable, but it is doubtful if the dynamic range, background noise, and general sound quality can equal the now common Compact Disc or CD. As far as track access is concerned the CD is excellent and without equal, offering almost instant access to any track.

For those who have committed to CD, it is likely that ideally they would want both CD and cassette in the van. Possibly the best way to achieve this is with a car type RDS cassette radio incorporating a CD multi-changer control facility.

The attractive, newer mini disc is beginning to appear in the shops and offers the clear advantages of being both recordable and more compact, but we might be best advised to wait and see if prerecorded music becomes widely available in this format.

Short Wave Radio Signals

The traveller abroad, in particular, may want to be able to tune to certain radio stations which often can only be received on a Short Wave or worldband radio receiver. When in distant lands, such lifelines as BBC World Service, Deutsche Welle, Radio France International, and Voice of America are stations for which a short wave receiver is essential. Unfortunately there are few car radios that offer short wave reception and they are all expensive. At the time of writing, no short wave receiver is available with a CD facility.

The alternative for those who need to keep in touch abroad is to take a portable digital, or analogue, shortwave radio. Some of the latest offerings also include a stereo FM band and RDS circuitry.

Satellite Radio and TV Reception

Vans equipped with satellite reception equipment for TV are also able to tune into the many radio stations that are transmitted with hi-fi quality stereo sound radio. This type of equipment can offer far better reception than the 'old technology' of short wave. Naturally it is a little more cumbersome to carry around a satellite dish, but a growing number of caravanners are now doing just that (not wanting to take their holidays without the omnipresent TV available as usual).

These systems offer the unprecedented opportunity to watch programs from 'home' almost irrespective of the van's location (provided the dish has a clear view in the direction of the satellite and there is no very bad weather about).

Satellite Receivers and Decoders

For satellite reception, apart from the dish on the roof, a satellite receiver is required, as is a decoder. These items are in addition to the television, which can be the same as a normal terrestrial unit.

The decoder is for those satellite TV programs which are not free (most) and are scrambled. On payment of a subscription, the decoder de-scrambles the program to make it viewable on the television. More than one type of decoder will be required to receive most of the channels broadcast. Twelve Volts units are available.

Tuning In and Picture Quality

At each new van location it is necessary to point the dish towards the appropriate geo-stationary satellite to tune-in the satellite receiver. As with a good TV yagi directional aerial one soon learns how to do it quickly and easily, the similarity ends there though.

When travelling away from home, (unlike the often excellent terrestrial radio reception), normal terrestrial TV picture quality, with either an omnidirectional aerial or the more effective yagi type, is hit and miss. With satellite equipment, reception tends to be superb. The quality of satellite program material, however, is a rather different issue and very much a matter of personal taste. Some love it and some do not. For sports fans cover can be excellent.

The real benefit of satellite reception for motorcaravanning TV fans, is that the same satellite channels as at home, are available throughout much of Europe, with the same excellent picture quality, and in English. Other languages are often available if preferred.

Unfortunately, at the time of writing, the four UK terrestrial TV channels are not available on satellite. There is however BBC Prime, a mixture of material from BBC 1 and 2.

Automatic Satellite Dishes

For the real icing on the cake, one could splash out on a fully automatic motorcaravan satellite TV and radio reception system. They are not cheap but they are impressive. The dish lies almost flat on the van roof, hardly noticeable. On parking, one merely switches on the system, nothing more. After a short time the usual satellite channels are available with the usual excellent reception.

The method by which this is achieved is by way of servomotors connected to the dish. When switched on, the motors lift the dish, and scan it across the sky looking for satellite signals. The position of each satellite located is memorised. When a station is selected, the dish turns towards the correct satellite and the program appears. On switching the system to 'park', the dish returns to its flat roof position for driving. What could be simpler?

Televisions

The television set can be the same whether it is to be used for terrestrial or satellite viewing. If both types of reception are required, both a terrestrial aerial and a satellite dish will be necessary.

There are small televisions available for use at both 12 Volts DC and 230 Volts AC. With such a set, the caravanner is not dependent on a mains hook-up to be able to view, provided he or she keeps a close watch on the battery capacity. For really compact viewing there are pocket sized, low current drain, battery powered colour televisions with small LCD screens.

Regarding terrestrial broadcasts, it must be noted that television broadcast standards differ between countries: in the UK and Germany the standard is PAL, whilst France and Spain use the SECAM standard. (America and Japan use the NTSC standard.) Consequently a television normally used in the UK cannot be expected to receive terrestrial broadcasts in France or Spain. For international viewing, the surest solution is to look out for a multi-standard set, built to receive broadcasts of all three types.

Radio and TV Interference and Fluorescent Lights.

Unfiltered fluorescent lamps radiate an intolerable amount of AM radio and TV interference. Unless adequate filters are used, halogen bulbs are the best choice during AM radio and TV reception.

Swift Kon-tiki.

CHAPTER 18

THINGS TO TAKE

Vehicle Checks

Fuel Level	Power Steering Level	All Lights
Oil Level	A/C Refrigerant Level	Tyre Pressures
Water Level	Windscreen Washer Level	Wheel Nuts
Brake Fluid Levels	Battery Fluid	Service Interval
Clutch Fluid Level	Air Tanks	

Spare Bulbs	Tow Rope	Wheel-brace
Warning Triangle	Shackles	Wheel Chock
Van Tool-kit	Torch	Jump Leads
Jack	Spare Fuses	

Foot Pump / Compressor	User's Handbook	Windscreen Scourer
Pressure Gauge	Maintenance Booklet	Squeegee
Air Line	List of Service Stations	Bucket
Spare Wheel		
Snow Chains	Sand Ladders	

Caravan Checks

Drinking Water	Water Filter	LPG Cylinders
Water Disinfectant	Waste Tanks	

Tools

Tool-box 1	Driver Bits	Glue
Tool-box 2	Electrical Tape	Torch
Drill/Driver	Gaffer's Tape	Xtrem Pad
Drill Bits	WD 40	Scissors

Outdoor

Table	Folding Spade	Shovel
Chairs		Floor-mats
Loungers	Light	Charcoal
Sun Umbrella	Extension cable	BBQ

Kitchen

Washing Up Liquid	Drip Stand	Washing Bowl
Scourers	Floor Cloths	Soap
Washing Up Brush	Washing Machine	Waste Bags
Dish Cloths	Dust Pan + Brush	Tablecloth
Tea Cloths	Clothes Line + Pegs	Duster
Cutting Board		Hot Mits

Pots and Pans

Kettle	Frying Pan + Lid	Strainer
Saucepans + Lids	Casserole Dish	Colander
Pressure Cooker	Oven Dish	Chopping Board
Steamer	Teapot	Baking Tray
Grill Pan	Coffee Jug	Plastic Containers

Dishes

Plates	Cups	Glasses
Bowls	Mugs	Egg Cups

Cutlery

Knives	Bottle Stoppers	Can Opener
Forks	Can Stoppers	Bottle Opener
Spoons	Bread Knife	Peeler
Tea Spoons	Sharp Knives	Grater

Food

Butter
Tea
Sugar
Coffee
Milk
Bread
Potatoes
Spaghetti
Pasta
Couscous
Rice
Cheese
Ham
Bacon
Eggs
Beans
Tuna
Sardines
Corn Flakes
Muesli
Bran
Fruit
Vegetables
Biscuits
Jams
Marmalade
Salt
Pepper
Vinegar
Oil

Drinks

White Wine
Red Wine
Lemonade
Whisky
Vodka
Gin
Fruit Juice
Tonic
Water

Bathroom

Towels
Soap
Face Cloths
Nail Brush
Swarfega
Tooth Brush
Tooth Paste
Razor
Mosquito Repellents
Oil of Citronella
Talcum Powder
Hair Brush + Comb
Hair Shampoo
Toilet Paper
Toilet Fluid
Toilet
Scouring Cleaner
Sun Tan Creams
Perfumes
After Sun Creams
Cosmetics
Toilet Bags
Flip Flops

Bedding

Duvets
Sleeping Bags
Blankets
Sheets
Pillows
Pillow Cases

Clothes-His

Socks
Underpants
T-Shirts
Shirts
Ties
Shorts
Trousers

Belts
Jeans
Pullovers
Jumpers
Cardigans
Coats
Jackets

Pumps
Shoes
Boots
Wellingtons
Hats

Clothes-Hers

Stockings
Panties
Bras
T-Shirts
Blouses
Shorts
Trousers

Belts
Jeans
Skirts
Dresses
Jumpers
Coats
Jackets

Pumps
Shoes
Boots
Wellingtons
Hats

Medical

First Aid Kit
Plasters
Bandages
Pure Alcohol
Cotton Wool

Lint
Sticky Plaster
Scissors
Panadol
Aspirin

Ointments
Pills
Thermometer

Literature

Maps
Books
Magazines
Guide Books

Bird Book
Tree Book
English Dictionary

Italian Dictionary
French Dictionary
Spanish Dictionary
German Dictionary

Useful

Umbrella
Mosquito Machine
Mosquito Tablets
Blue Tack
Alarm Clock
Clothes Brush

Iron
Paper Towels
Paper Tissues
Sewing Kit
Sellotape
Ratchet Straps

Fixing Straps
Candles
Mirror
Shoe Polish + Brushes
Matches
Lighter

Music, TV. and Video

Video Tapes
Cassettes
CDs
Short Wave Radio
Television
TV Equipment

Documents

Passport
Driving Licence
Insurance Certificate
Green Card
Credit Cards
Cash-Notes
Cash-Coins
Foreign Currency
Cheque Books
Traveller's Cheques
Caravan User's Manual
Gas Test Certificate

Vehicle Registration (Matriculation) Document (Log Book)
Vehicle Test Certificate (MOT)
Customs Carnet

Personal

Diary
Cameras
Tripod
Films
Binoculars
Computer
Calculator
Paper
Envelopes
Stamps
Pencils
Pens
Spectacles
Spare Specs
Sunglasses
Lighter
Penknife

Sports

Bicycles
Motor Bike
Boat
Outboard Motor
Lilo
Bats
Balls
Swimming Trunks
Swimming Costumes
Swimming Hats
Swimming Shoes
Skiing Kit
Diving Kit
Fishing Kit
Walking Boots
Walking Socks
Rucksacks
Compass
Altimeter
Water Bottle

Amusements

Playing Cards
Games

☺

Winnebago Rialta 21 feet.

CHAPTER 19

PAPERS DOCUMENTATION MONEY and BANKS

There are five documents to be carried always whilst driving a vehicle throughout Europe. In most countries it is an offence not to be in possession of these, and produce them on demand by a police or customs officer, whilst in charge of a vehicle. (In Britain it is acceptable to produce the documents at a Police Station within seven days.)

FIVE OFFICIAL and VEHICLE DOCUMENTS

1. Vehicle Registration Document

The main document to be carried at all times whilst driving any vehicle is the official document which states: Owner's Name (In Britain the 'Holder'), Country of Registration, Registration Number, Chassis and Engine Numbers, Other Vehicle Details, Dates of Validity.
In Britain this document is called the 'Log Book'.
In Germany it is the 'Fahrzeugbrief'. In France it is the 'Cart Gris'.
In Spain the 'Certificado de Matriculación'.

If the vehicle is borrowed or hired it is also recommended to have from the owner, a convincing letter of authorisation to use it.

2. Certificate of Insurance

A current certificate of insurance is essential. For travel outside the country of issue, this is a 'Green Card'. It must state the vehicle registration number, the name and address of the insured, the countries in which the insurance is valid, and dates of validity.

3. Driver's Licence

A current driver's licence is required, showing details of the holder's name and address, date of birth, categories of vehicle, and dates for which the permit is valid. For international driving a European Communities version is recommended.

4. Test Certificate

A current test certificate, as required in the country of origin, detailing the vehicle and dates of validity, should be carried.

5. Passport

An up to date passport is essential for crossing any border. It is also almost invariably requested in all countries from any foreigner at any roadside check, routine or otherwise, by police or customs officials.

Customs Carnet

Certain countries, mainly outside Europe, may require this cumbersome and possibly expensive document for the temporary importation of a motorcaravan, a boat or equipment. To ensure correct discharge on return to the country of issue, the carnet must have been stamped by customs at all specified borders in a precise manner. These documents can be organised through the AA or the RAC.

Car or Van User's Manual

The car's, or van's, User's Manual should be close at hand. It contains details of the controls, the bulbs, the lubricants and many other things one hopes not to need to refer to when travelling, but may well.

Maintenance Booklet and List of Service Stations

It may just be that the vehicle will need a service whilst on tour. An oil change for example, or perhaps something unexpected. It is therefore wise to take along both the Maintenance Booklet, and the Manufacturer's List of Official Service Stations for countries to be entered.

Caravan User's Manual

This too should be close at hand. In the case of the home constructor in particular, this manual will be the van Bible, comprising the whole collection of instruction books, installation instructions, brochures, manuals, constructional details, wiring diagrams, looming charts, gas certificates, sketches, and all manner of relevant information compiled during the construction process.

This printed and hand written material will, as much as possible, detail aspects and specifications, particularly operational, of the van and its installed equipment. A suitable robust, alphabetically compartmentalized file could be used to keep it all together.

Medical Insurance

Falling ill overseas can be very expensive. As can injuries from motor accidents. Medical insurance should therefore be considered a wise precaution if only for the peace of mind it will engender.

Keep proof of insurance close to hand and be ready to show it to the doctor or hospital. This ought to include a card with the insured's name, dates of insurance, and phone numbers for clarification.

On sight of valid insurance, the doctor should be willing to bill the insurance company directly, for the treatment. However, some may provide treatment only after phoning the company for clearance. Others may require payment by the patient. Some will even withhold treatment until after they have received cash settlement. In such cases it will be essential to obtain from the doctor appropriate, official bills, with which it should subsequently be possible to reclaim the costs from the insurance company.

When buying the insurance, one should try to establish the procedures that would be involved if medical treatment were to be required, and the nature and limits of the benefits provided. Studying of the terms and conditions in the small print on the certificate, *before* any unfortunate incidence of an accident or illness, should help to avoid unpleasant surprises.

Cockburn Holdsworth Tempo.

MONEY and BANKS

Cash

Most convenient for the traveller is to have access to local currency, but large amounts of cash are a liability and should definitely be avoided. Credit cards should be used wherever possible, both for direct transactions and also to obtain small amounts of cash on a regular basis for incidental payments. Cash, however, is the most immediately acceptable method of payment in many shops, restaurants and service stations. Almost no-one refuses it. For convenience and emergencies, a selection of **small amounts** of widely used currencies is useful when several countries will be entered.

French Francs, Deutsch Marks, Pounds Sterling, and US Dollars can be used widely. Francs and Marks will be exchangeable almost anywhere.

A further word of warning about cash: I have had several experiences, particularly at motorway service stations in some countries, of opportunistic (thieving is probably the right word) cashiers at fuel pumps. They attempt to prey on innocent travellers, especially, no doubt, those who are not too familiar with either the language or the local currency. The trick, quite simply, is to short-change the customer, who may be fatigued from driving and not notice. He may also be too shy, or confused, or unwilling, or unable, to make a fuss. Ways to minimise this high probability of occurrence are:-

1. Be *sure* of the value of the paper money before handing it over.
2. Know the value of the fuel used and the change expected.
3. Look at the assistant when handing over the note and loudly declare its value.
4. If caught out, make a fuss, ask to see the manager.
5. The **safest method** is, at the outset, to avoid using cash. Use a **credit card** instead and check the amount written on the slip.

Traveller's Cheques

Rather than carrying much cash, a safer option would be to buy traveller's cheques, because if lost or stolen they can be reported to the issuing body, which will then replace them. They are not as negotiable as cash as they must be signed in front of the recipient, and the corresponding passport also produced. Often, only banks will cash them.

Credit Cards and Banks

Mastercard, Access, and Visa cards, and, to a lesser extent in Europe, American Express cards, are very widely accepted and the safest payment options. They can eliminate the need to carry large amounts of cash or traveller's cheques and could prove invaluable for an unexpected cost.

It must be remembered that although they can be used throughout Europe, credit cards are not accepted equally widely in all countries.

The very useful aspect of the credit card for the traveller, is the facility to draw cash from automatic cash dispensers and overseas banks which have reciprocal arrangements with the card issuing bank. In banks abroad, it is essential to produce one's passport for such transactions.

Very careful attention should be paid to the conditions of use pertaining to each card, in particular the conditions relating to the loss or theft of any card. It is certainly most important to keep cards safe, and to know at all times that they are safe, and to report any loss or theft without delay. Time is of the essence, for in many cases, any use after a card is lost (or stolen), will be at the card-holder's expense until the time that the loss (or theft) is reported. ⌘

Autosleeper Trooper

Swift Royale

CHAPTER 20

CROSSING BORDERS

The words inside the front cover of a British passport make interesting reading and I quote: "Her Britannic Majesty's Secretary of State Requests *sic* and requires in the Name of Her Majesty all those whom it may concern to allow the bearer to pass freely without let or hindrance, and to afford the bearer such assistance and protection as may be necessary."

Generally speaking, and particularly within the EEC, most customs checks are now quite routine and efficient, and at many borders the customs officer is so out of sight he might just as well not be there. It is no more than a question of looking through the driver's window to try to spot him to catch his eye. If he sees you he gives you the nod to drive on, and if you cannot see him you drive on anyway. Naturally, if you have any documents that need processing, such as a carnet or import documents, you must stop and find him to get the necessary stamps.

With border checks however, there are always going to be exceptions, and when you are next negotiating a difficult customs post, it is certainly worth thinking of the high-faluting words inside the UK passport. They are a Request, in the Name of no less a person than the Queen, to allow *you*, the holder, free passage across the border!

Whether an over zealous customs officer, in the process insistently of searching your van, would be overly impressed by your drawing his attention to Her Majesty's Request, is doubtful.

This is in no way to advise you to adopt a high and mighty stance when it comes to dealing with **any** passport or customs officer. It is to remind you that these servants of their country, provided your baggage and papers appear in order, are obliged to allow you to pass freely across the borders they are employed to control. But it can not pay to treat these officers with anything less than the utmost respect.

For, notwithstanding the Request in the Name of Her Majesty, and in spite of your complete innocence and right of free passage, they, the officers, are only human. As such, they are quite capable of adopting a most unreasonable attitude, which quite probably they will not have to justify to anyone. Even if they were called on to account for themselves it takes time, your time, when all you really want to do is to press on with your journey.

Furthermore, I do not advocate that any traveller adopts a grovelling stance, but I do suggest that it would be unwise to attempt to get ‘one-up’ on the officer or try to be clever or impudent with him. Merely respond to his every request regarding, production of documents or presentation of baggage and contents, or provision of a guided tour, and explanation, of the caravan and some of its features. I would suggest a pleasant, polite attitude, giving him as much information as requested but no more.

In the unlikely event he asks you to give him something from your possessions, a polite no, with the excuse that you need it, is certainly in order.

It is wise to have a well rehearsed story of your travel plans on the tip of your tongue. It need not be completely true (particularly if you consider your real plans your own business, and what is more you are always entitled to change your mind), but it must be credible. Any apparent uncertainty on your part, regarding your intended destination, just may be the chink in your armour that informs your interrogator that he has an international smuggler in front of him. At such a point the search may really start.

On a recent trip overland to Greece I had the interesting experience of crossing a border from Hungary to Romania. It was about six o’clock on a scorching hot afternoon and I had just filled up with diesel in anticipation of the border, and with no knowledge of where I might encounter the next service station. I was cruising south in a pleasant rural setting, dawdling along in the bright sunshine, through fields of sugar beet, chuckling away at the frequent sight of large Herons sitting in nests precariously perched on the top of telegraph poles. As I was the only vehicle on the road I assumed the customs post would be uncongested.

I was not expecting to reach the border for another ten kilometres or so when a lone policeman, standing rather dangerously in the middle of the road, indicated that I should pull over to the left hand side. At first it was not at all clear what he meant because I could see an empty road ahead. I felt distinctly unsafe proceeding down the ‘wrong’ side of the road expecting an on-coming vehicle to come charging around the next bend toward me at any moment.

It was not long however, before I cautiously rounded a bend only to find a queue of traffic ahead, to the back of which I was obliged to attach myself. The ‘right’ side of the road was kept empty by policemen. I assumed there was an accident ahead but it was not until a truck was ushered past on the ‘right’ side of the road that it dawned on me that perhaps this was the queue for the border which must be closer than the map indicated.

As time went by, the truck column gradually filled up. Eventually the road was full of traffic as far as the eye could see in front and behind. There was no sign of any border.

Sometimes it was the turn of the trucks and sometimes the cars to move a few metres each, with breaks of perhaps twenty minutes in between. My plan was soon hatched.

It struck me that an easier solution would be to let the cars in front make two or three moves forward before I would catch them up. Thus I would gain a longer break in the back of the van before moving up into the control room, starting the engine, and proceeding one hundred yards instead of twenty.

Excitedly I waited for the opportunity to continue not moving. After all, some truckers, who always know best, were doing it. I could see the wave of movement gradually approaching down the queue of cars in front, as progressively closer cars appeared to be creeping forward.

Very often it was difficult to see whether there was movement or not, until the moment when one was sure, when the wave was close enough to be certain "Yes! They are off again".

And then suddenly it was upon me, the four Bulgarians in front all piled out as usual to push their car. I never did conclude whether they were saving their Lada's battery (assuming it had one), or just enjoying the exercise.

Lots of drivers and passengers seemed to prefer this method of shunting their cars forward, after all it was usually barely twenty metres and there was no rush.

It seemed like only a few tense moments after the Bulgarians set about their exercise before there was a loud knocking on my driver's door, accompanied with the cry of "Comrade! Comrade!..." and many more words which I could not possibly repeat.

Apparently, the Romanian in the surprisingly modern looking VW van behind could not bear to be kept waiting any longer, and was insistent that I catch up without further delay. Who was I, a foreigner, to argue with a rumbustious Romanian apparently in a hurry to get home?

I started my engine as slowly as I dared, and crept forward even slower still only too aware that the Romanian had rumbled my ruse. I was not going to give him the pleasure of any more than half a kilometre an hour.

It is not since the now distant days of crossing the East German corridor into Berlin more than twenty years ago, that I have experienced such customs delays, and for sheer longevity and entertainment this one compares favourably, although I have yet to be caught at some of the notorious African borders.

As the evening wore on, there was a driver several cars in front of me who kept falling asleep. This really was the last straw for the ranting Romanian whose mind became almost totally diverted away from my existence, as the sleeping challenge was a far greater threat.

I am sure that he was well aware of the continued risk that I posed, and there is little doubt that he was keeping an eye on me, but by now he really had his work cut out, because even at a brisk trot it took him quite a few seconds to reach the sleeper, and having got there, waking him was not easy, let alone persuading him to get a move on. Then there was the run back to his own van to be sure to keep close ranks and not keep those behind him waiting.

I was truly impressed by the sleeper's persistence and ability to fall asleep time and again in spite of the certain knowledge that he was going to be rudely awoken by the ranting Romanian. But sleep he did time and again, and wake him up the Romanian did time and again.

Meanwhile the truckers were making their cups of tea, drinking beer, strolling about chatting, and watching television. The hedge beside the road became a toilet and the once rural scene an instant community.

At times I felt sorry for the Bulgarians in front, four big men in their little Lada. One of them was so tall that he should not really have been in that car. It was best when he sat in the front but they seemed to swop about and it was not just a question of his head pressing into the roof causing him to crouch, but also the way their shoulders were so close and they were sharing their seats with so much stuff, bags and things. The tall one went for a walk down the road and eventually came back with some fruit and bottled water which they were all very pleased about and it made me feel much better.

As night descended, the community fluctuated between darkness and then light, as distant headlamps and rear lights flickered back to life way up the line, and slight movement once again started up and ever so slowly approached.

I was comfortable and with careful timing cooked, relaxed, read, wrote my diary, did my toilet, opened windows, closed windows, changed clothes, listened to music, tuned in to the World Service, and generally got on with my show.

Every now and then my ranting neighbour reminded me that I was late but by midnight I had sight of distant tall lights which might possibly have something to do with the border. As we very slowly got closer things started to hot up and other bright glows which by now I had been aware of for quite some time turned into makeshift kiosks at the side of the road. Perhaps this was where the Bulgarian had acquired his provisions.

It seemed that ahead but before the tall lights, there was some sort of cross-roads. Every now and then, with my binoculars, I could make out a bus coming towards our queue, and then going off along a road ahead and to my left in the distance, alongside the sugar beet field. As I got closer it was clear that this was very disruptive, keeping several uniformed men quite busy trying to ensure the buses got through, and there was often much horn blowing.

It was round about this area, and just beside the largest, brightest kiosk, that I became aware of the shifty looking leather-jacketed smoker and his sidekicks who, when he was not discussing secret matters with the young kiosk keeper and his attractive female assistant, was engaging in conversation with quite a number of my fellow motorists, and offering them cigarettes which they smoked while they chatted. He seemed quite friendly with the Bulgarians in front but he did not offer me a cigarette and I felt left out. It seemed strange to me for these characters to be 'hanging out' in this way, particularly since it was after midnight by now. I concluded that they were plain clothes customs men surreptitiously vetting questionable travellers and their motives for being on the move.

Shortly after as I approached the first of the smaller buildings, by now very brightly lit, I was approached by a young, pretty and petite, gypsy girl, very colourfully and characteristically dressed, and with head scarf. She was the unmistakable archetypical Romanian gypsy. She had a whole entourage of people, apparently her family, and some small suitcases. The group included the oldest of grandmothers and the youngest of children and babies, perhaps eight or ten people in all whom she was herding about. They all looked very tidy and well turned out. In between, she was approaching car after car asking, I assumed, for a lift across the border.

When it was my turn she made eye contact and fixed me long and hard in the most appealing stare imaginable. It was difficult to resist, but of course I knew I must and she finally moved on. There were several travellers on foot hanging around the customs post, some with bags some not, one looking distinctly mad and sadly decrepit. They came and went and several more appealed to me for assistance. The uniformed officers, now becoming more apparent, seemed not to notice them.

By the time I actually drove into the Hungarian customs shed it was one o'clock in the morning and I was fairly tired: unlike the sleeper I had remained awake throughout the evening. I think that, had all this have taken place during the heat of the day, it might well have been more trying, and quite possibly have taken even longer.

But now I was here at last. A group of uniformed Hungarian officers swarmed around my van. At long last it was my turn, and if one thing was clear, the Hungarians do not let people leave their country without very careful consideration, and keeping people waiting did not seem to be their prime concern. It had taken me seven hours to get this far.

One of the officers with a few key words in German requested my passport and then asked me where I was going. My mind went blank and for the life of me I could not remember a single Romanian city which I had seen on the map. Of course it would have been quite acceptable to have said "Greece", but I was tired and at that moment my mind ran amok and I deliberated. Suddenly the officer's routine attitude changed and, without waiting a moment longer for my reply, he became very animated and let out the shrill staccato words "Zoll Controle! Zoll Controle!". ("Customs Control" in German).

He immediately sent off one his sidekicks to bring the customs chief and indicated to me that he wanted me to open the back of my van.

For a few fleeting moments I really thought I must be the international smuggler that the customs officer had been trained so carefully to wheedle out from the innocent. There is little doubt that he did, and it was only a question of minutes before all would be revealed and his boss would be commending him. Surely now promotion was close.

I was just about to open the back doors when the 'big man' and his entourage approached.

The chief's visage was different, he was clearly the boss and had a big moustache, tell-tale rosy cheeks, and a friendly face. He was in good humour and did not seem to mind having been disturbed at all and grinned at me. Of course the conversations went over my head but his arrival seemed to defuse what I had felt had become an uncomfortable volatile situation (not that I had anything to hide). I think the boss more or less told his keen student of the mind of the criminal, that it was just possible that I was not the one for whom he was looking.

The search subsided into a rather cursory look inside the van and an enquiry as to whether I had a video or magnetron (?). This customs officer also felt the similar strong urge that consumed others on the trip, manicly to press nearly every button on my CD player before giving up unsuccessfully. He then returned my passport and waved me, an innocent man, on my way.

The queue sadly did not end there, and I was barely out of the main customs shed before I rejoined it on my way into no man's land between Hungary and Romania. It was at this point that I made contact with the hyperactive Hungarian in the over-revving Skoda, whose antics had become increasingly noticeable during my sojourn in the customs shed. I had already observed his unusual mannerisms in the distance, earlier in the evening. He was the nervous rapid strutter who marched around his car and often rapidly changed direction for no apparent reason, perhaps because he obviously had a far weaker bladder than most, as he used the community toilet regularly. Each time he restarted his struggling Skoda it burst into an appallingly, uncontrollable, screaming revving.

He was the one who, contrary to the book recommendations, angrily argued with the customs officials every step of the way, and, not surprisingly, they insisted on a complete search to his clear disgust, which is why I caught him up and he replaced the Bulgarians in front of me.

I had already, much earlier in the evening, decided that he was 'off-his-tree'. Now he approached me to tell me in painfully slow broken English to switch off my headlights, I could see him searching his memory banks to find the words:
"...........LIGHTS!...........OUT" were what he came up with.

I was delighted with his efforts, and burst out laughing which pleased him, and we struck up an extremely slow but nevertheless meaningful conversation.

For the next two hour's crawl through 'no-mans-land' to the Romanian customs shed he and I found much to talk about, although it could probably have been said in two minutes had our ability to communicate been more efficient.

On arrival at the shed, I handed over my passport. Having paid fifty-two Deutsch Marks to a heavily perfumed woman in a small wooden shed, who typed my data into her computer for my Romanian visa, the subsequent passage through the Romanian customs area involved a search by the customs officer. Eventually my passport was returned from the passport control office further ahead.

It was a busy area with many comings and goings. It later transpired that the customs officer earlier, had grilled my new Hungarian friend as to what he knew about me and my plans.

I finally drew out into Romania at four o'clock in the morning not knowing what to expect but feeling over ready to sleep, so pulled into a narrow lay-by opposite a brightly lit fuel station. There was an almost immediate knock on my door and there was my Hungarian friend who said he too would stop here until sunrise at six o'clock. Although pleased to have a friendly vehicle parked beside me I explained that I would not be getting up at sunrise, quickly excused myself saying goodbye and crawled into bed, my brain scrambled.

I awoke in pain out of a deep sleep unsure why, until I realised there was knocking at my door, which would not stop even though I tried to ignore it. It was 6 a.m. and I felt terrible.

The next thing I knew the van began to rock violently so I crawled out of bed to peep discretely through the window. There on the step to my driver's door, hanging on to the door handle and jumping up and down wildly, was my Hungarian friend...Awful though I felt, I made myself slightly decent, went forward, and opened the window as little as possible.

"Give me your address and I will write to you all the time" he said. In my daze I did not want to give him my address but I did not want to offend him, so I asked him to give me his, and he rushed off, and came back with a slip of paper with some scrawl on it.
I gingerly made my way back to bed and fell into a long, deep, well-earned sleep.

Ocean Blue on the way to Ennistymon.

TRAVELLER'S DRESS

The prime requirements for free passage across borders are the passport and the vehicle documents, and of course the requirement to keep within the customs allowance.

There are still some countries, and some individual officers, who are suspicious of certain types of appearance and for this reason it should be remembered that the quickest border crossing is most likely for those turned out tidily.

ROAD CHECKS

Never think that once the border has been successfully negotiated, the story is over. Customs officers normally are associated with customs posts, but this is not the only place where they may turn up. France is a good example where spot road checks by both customs officers and police seem to be on the increase. A favourite opportunity for the peripatetic police or customs officer is the lay-by, or autoroute 'Aire', as the service areas are known, where they pull over moving vehicles or approach stationary ones, to go about their business. This can range from a question or two, and probably a passport check, to a full document and vehicle search. These chaps are often dressed in plain clothes and are quite capable of asking the most personal questions. In the best interests of getting on with ones journey, as usual there is little point in doing anything but co-operating fully, however tempting it may be to let one's emotions get the better of one, a situation which could lead to time consuming consequences. ☯

An Eriba Touring Caravan.

Patras to Brindisi ferry.
On this ferry, motorcaravans on the upper, open deck can be occupied overnight.

CHAPTER 21

FERRIES

Ferries are an integral part of a traveller's routine and it is unlikely to be long before the caravanner will need to drive his shell up (or down) the ramp of a ferry of one form or another. Leaving Great Britain by the usual routes through the busy ports of Dover or Harwich for example, is naturally enough very straightforward. The purchase of tickets could not be simpler and the subsequent passport and customs checks quite routine.

From then on the ferries are so big that going aboard is hardly any different from a normal continuation of the journey with barely an awareness of the transition from terra firma to arrival on deck. The large sticker, provided with the ticket, is stuck to the windscreen and informs all the stewards and officials exactly which ferry is required. The consequent flow through the port is quite efficient.

Once on the ferry it is of course necessary to park closely to the vehicle in front and without much space on each side, as directed, but this is routine, driving into one end of the ferry in England, and then once across the English Channel, La Manche, as it is called by The French, out of the other end at disembarkation.

With the construction of the Channel Tunnel, both the approach to Dover and those of Calais and Boulogne have improved out of all recognition. No doubt when motorcaravans are allowed to travel through the Tunnel, the process of travelling to or from the UK will become even more efficient.

Boarding ferries is not always as simple. Some ships to the Greek Isles, for example, are only stern entry, with access often requiring reversing the van onto the ferry. After bright sunshine this can be like driving backwards into a black hole.

Reaching the point from which one is signalled to board the ship however, can be an even more challenging experience at an unknown port, where large windscreen stickers may not be in use, and one is not sure which queue to join, and none of the many apparent officials offers to show the way. Unfortunately the one who really can help may not be in uniform, and it may be impossible to know which one he is until he makes himself known, which he may never do, particularly if the van is not in the right place!

The relief of finally being directed on board may be tempered by having to enter the black hole under the instructions of one of the stewards, whose undisputed skill is being able to drive the van by hand signals. He knows that most drivers cannot reverse into his boat as quickly and precisely as his regular truckers, and consequently he tries to do your steering remotely, by waving his arms about, and yelling sometimes unintelligibly.

Without much of his interference, embarkation would probably be rather easier. One should not allow oneself to be rushed or intimidated, even though those truckers manage to reverse their leviathans, into the same black hole, with more ease, speed, and accuracy, than most drivers could a car (many of them probably do it nearly every day of their lives). There is little doubt that any accident would certainly be a much bigger problem for a driver than the steward. If in any doubt, getting out for a look behind would be far more helpful than those stewards, who can appear to be directing left when they mean right.

At the risk of stating the obvious, a few things should be remembered about buying tickets and using ferries.

Usually it is quite clear where to buy the tickets, which boat they are for, and from where and when the boat departs. At some ports however, this is not the case, particularly if there are several shipping lines involved, and if there are different docking stations which may be on opposite sides of the harbour, or in different harbours.

The first thing to make sure of is that the ticket is for the right destination. This also may seem too obvious to mention, but in the heat of the moment, at a crowded ticket office where not even the ticket sales person is willing or able to speak any of your languages, and what is more the alphabet is unintelligible, it may just be possible to end up buying the wrong ticket.

The second is to make sure of the exact point of departure. When, for example, a return ticket has been purchased, it is not safe to assume that the dock used for arriving will be the same as that for departing for the return journey. Probably the safest way to be sure is to search the area for a ticket office, (it is often to be found in the port area rather than at the dock entrance), where an assistant can confirm the exact point of departure and is able to answer all other questions. Some may be more helpful than others.

When finally on the ferry, it is useful to make a conscious effort to note exactly where the van is parked, the deck number for example, its location, and the best way to return to it at the end of the voyage.

Notwithstanding these potential pitfalls, ports and ferries can be fun and an interesting part of the journey.

Leaving Patras for Brindisi, an overnight trip arriving early in the morning. Sleeping in the van was allowed.

The Camping and Caravanning Club's beautiful Ardgartan site.

CHAPTER 22

CONVERSION TABLES

Length

1 metre	=	39.3701 inches		
1 metre	=	3.28084 feet		
1 metre	=	1000 mm		
1 metre	=	100 cm		
25.4 mm	=	1 inch		
1 km	=	1000 metres		
1 km	=	0.621371 miles		
100 km	=	62.1371 miles		
1 mile	=	1760 yds	=	1.609 km
1 yd	=	3 feet	=	0.9144 m
1 in	=	25.4 mm		
1 UK nautical mile	=	1.15 mile	=	1.85 km

Area

1 m^2	=	10.764 ft^2		
1 km^2	=	247.105 acres		
1 $mile^2$	=	640 acres	=	259 ha
1 hectare (ha)	=	2.471 acres		
1 acre	=	4046.86 m^2		

Volume

1 litre	=	1 dm^3		
1 m^3	=	1000 dm	=	1000 litres
1 litre	=	0.219969 gallons (UK gal)		
1 UK gal	=	4.5461 litres	=	1.2 US gal
1 UK gal	=	8 pints		
1 litre	=	1.76 pints		
200 litre	=	44 UK gal	=	1 standard oil drum

Weight and Mass

1 kg	=	2.2 lb		
1 oz	=	28.35 g		
1 lb	=	16 oz		
1 tonne	=	1000 kg	=0.984207 ton	=2205 lb
1 ton	=	2240 lb	=1016 kg	=1.016 tonne (t)
1 cwt	=	112 lb	=50.8 kg	

Atmospheric Pressure = 1 atm = 1 bar = 1000 mbar

1 bar = 760 mm Hg = 29.92 in Hg

Power

1 hp	=	0.7457 kW		
1 PS	=	1 CV	=	0.7355 kW

Tyre Pressures

bar	psi	bar	psi	bar	psi	bar	psi
0.5	7.3	1.5	21.8	2.5	36.3	3.5	50.8
0.6	8.7	1.6	23.2	2.6	37.7	3.6	52.2
0.7	10.2	1.7	24.7	2.7	39.2	3.7	53.7
0.8	11.6	1.8	26.1	2.8	40.6	3.8	55.1
0.9	13	1.9	27.6	2.9	42.1	3.9	56.6
1.0	14.5	2.0	29	3.0	43.5	4.0	58
1.1	16	2.1	30.5	3.1	45	4.1	59.5
1.2	17.4	2.2	31.9	3.2	46.4	4.2	60.9
1.3	18.9	2.3	33.4	3.3	47.9	4.3	62.4
1.4	20.3	2.4	34.8	3.4	49.3	4.4	63.8

Temperature

Celcius	Fahrenheit	Celcius	Fahrenheit
100	212	20	68
60	140	15	59
50	122	10	50
45	113	5	41
40	104	0	32
35	95	-5	23
30	86	-10	14
25	77	-20	-4
		-40	-40

Celcius = 5/9 (F-32)
Fahrenheit = 9/5 C + 32

Fuel Consumption

litres / 100 km	mpg	litres / 100 km	mpg
5	56.5	15	18.8
6	47.1	16	17.7
7	40.4	17	16.6
8	35.3	18	15.7
9	31.4	19	14.9
10	28.3	20	14.1
11	25.7	21	13.5
12	23.5	22	12.8
13	21.7	23	12.3
14	20.2	24	11.8

mpg	km / litre	mpg	km / litre	mpg	km / litre
10	3.5	20	7.1	30	10.6
11	3.9	21	7.4	31	11
12	4.2	22	7.8	32	11.3
13	4.6	23	8.1	33	11.7
14	5	24	8.5	34	12
15	5.3	25	8.9	35	12.4
16	5.7	26	9.2	36	12.7
17	6	27	9.6	37	13.1
18	6.4	28	9.9	38	13.5
19	6.7	29	10.3	39	13.8

On the front line of a Greek campsite, just a few metres from the warm sea.

SOME SUPPLIERS

General

Addresses from motorcaravan magazines. Local camping, caravan, boating and hardware stores, electrical wholesalers.

Adhesives

CMC Reimo, Unit 4, Lympne Ind Pk, Lympne, Hythe, Kent, CT21 4LR Tel. 01 303 261 062
Cruisermart, 36 Eastern Esplanade, Southend-on-Sea, Essex, SS1 2ES Tel 01702 460055
Pumpkin Marine, 100 The Highway, London, E1 9BX Tel 0171 480 6630

Batteries

Chloride, Unit 8B, Cosgrove Way Ind Est. Luton, Beds, LU1 1XL Tel 01582 405073
Delco Remy, Blackfriars House, 399 South Row, Witan Gate, Central Milton Keynes, Bucks MK9 2PU. Tel 01908 678000
Pumpkin (see Adhesives)
Varta, Unit 9 Grand Union Ind Est. Abbey Road, London NW10. Tel 0181 9657991

Battery chargers, controllers, monitors. Inverters and Dividers

Cetrek, 1 Factory Road, Upton, Poole, Dorset, BH16 5SJ. Tel 01202 632116
Cruisermart (see Adhesives)
Mastervolt, 6A Lawrence Sheriff Street, Rugby, Warwickshire, CV22 5EJ Tel 01788 567123
Merlin Equipment, Colebrook House, High Street, Goring-on-Thames, Oxon, RG8 9AR Tel 01491 875599
Pumpkin (see Adhesives)
Sowester, Stinsford Road, Nuffield, Poole, Dorset, BH17 7SW Tel 01202 667700
Telesonic Marine, 60 Brunswick Centre, Marchmont St, London, WC1N 8AE Tel 0171 837 4106
Waeco, (see Calorifiers - Aqua Marine)

Calorifiers

Aqua-Marine MFG, 216 Fair Oak Road, Bishopstoke, Eastleigh, Hants, SO5 6NJ Tel 01703 694949
Cleghorn Waring, Icknield Way, Letchworth, Herts, SG6 1EZ Tel 01462 480380

Connectors - 10A Sealed Round

RS Components, PO Box 99, Corby, Northants, NN17 9RS Tel 01536 201234
Simpson Lawrence, 218 Edmiston Drive, Glasgow, G51 2YT Tel 0141 4275331

Cookers

Simpson Lawrence (see Connectors).
Ceramic Hob (Diesel or Paraffin) from:-
Cruisermart (see Adhesives)
Telesonic Marine (see Adhesives)

Cruise controls

Mardi Gras Motorsport, Unit 9, Silverstone Circuit, Towcester, Northamptonshire, NN12 8TL Tel 01327 858006
Ultimate Design, 37 Pytchley Road, Kettering, NN15 6ND Tel 01536 514400

Fridges

Aqua-Marine (see Calorifier)
CMC Reimo (see Adhesives)
Cruisermart (see Adhesives)
Electrolux, Oakley Raod, Luton, LU49QQ
Waeco (see Calorifiers - Aqua Marine)

Fuel tanks - auxiliary

The Tank Company, 10 Chantry Park, 2 Cowley Road, Nuffield Ind Est, Poole, Dorset, BH17 0UJ Tel 01202 682830

Gauges

CMC Reimo, (see Adhesives)
Cruisermart (see Adhesives)
Telesonic Marine (see Adhesives)

Heat exchangers

Aurora, Schulz, D-6933 Mudau (Odenwald), Südring, Germany.
Peck, Campion House, Lincoln Road, Leadenham, Lincoln, LN5 0PE Tel 01400 72100

Heaters - Air and Water

Eberspächer, Headlands Business Park, Salisbury Road, Ringwood, Hampshire, BH24 3PB Tel 01425 480151
Mikuni, Unit 2, Goodwood Road, Boyatt Wood, Eastleigh, Southampton, Hants, SO5 4NT Tel 01703 653777
Webasto, Centigrade Controls, Unit 1, Wick 1 Ind Est, Gore Road, New Milton, Hants, BH 25 6SJ Tel 01425 620602

Insulation - Xtrem

CMC Reimo, (see Adhesives)

Lamps

Aqua-Marine (see Calorifier)
CMC Reimo, (see Adhesives)
Cruisermart (see Adhesives)
Pumpkin (see Adhesives)
Simpson Lawrence (see Connectors).
Sowester (see Adhesives)
Telesonic Marine (see Adhesives)

LPG Tanks

CMC Reimo, (see Adhesives)
Tartarini, Carlton Miniott,Thirsk, North Yorks, YO7 4NJ Tel 01845 523213

Rear View Systems

Mitsubishi, Sony.

Reversing Aids

Datalink Projects (PDM), 24 Lady Leys, Cosby, Leicester, LE9 1RJ Tel 0116 2752131

Roof Hatches

Cruisermart (see Adhesives)
Pumpkin (see Adhesives)
Telesonic Marine (see Adhesives)

Sand ladders

Brownchurch, 308 Hare Row, Cambridge Heath Road, London,E2 Tel 0181 7293606

Sinks and Taps

Simpson Lawrence (see Connectors).

Snow and Mud Traction

Challenger Commission, **Tracmats**, PO Box 104, Hereford, HR1 2PW Tel 01432 354599
Euro-Trac, Flockton House, Audby Lane, Wetherby, LS22 4FD Tel 01937 64548
Snowchains, Bourne Ind est, Borough Green, Nr. Sevenoaks, Kent, TN15 8DG Tel 01732 884408

Tanfield , Blatchford Road, Horsham, West Sussex, RH13 5QR Tel 01403251199

Solar Panels and Regulators

Ampair, PO Box 416, Poole, Dorset, BH12 3LZ Tel 01202 749994
Sporti, The Haven, Arrowsmith Road, Wimborne, Dorset, BH21 3BG Tel 01202 692414
Wind and Sun, The Howe, Watlington, Oxford, OX9 5EX Tel 01491 613859

Water Filters

Hydrotech, 24844 Anza Drive, Valencia, California 91355 Tel 805 2571777
Katadyn, S. Norman-Lüthy, 37 Town End, Wilsford nr. Grantham, Lincs. NG32 3NX Tel 01400 30285
Safari, **Fospur**, Alfreton Trading Est, Somercotes, Derby, DE55 4LR

Water Pipes and Fittings

Cleghorn Waring, (see Calorifiers)
Whale, Old Belfast Road, Bangor, BT19 1LT, N. Ireland, 01247 270531

Water Pumps

see Lamps and Water Pipes

Water Tanks

Amber Plastics, Broombank Road, Chesterfield Ind Est, Sheepbridge, Chesterfield S41 9QJ Tel 01246 453544
CAK, 10 Princes Drive, Kenilworth, Warwickshire, CV8 2FD Tel 01926 54271
Plastic Fabrications 2000, Unit 18 Carcroft Enterprise Park, Station Road, Carcroft, Doncaster, DN6 8DD Tel 01302 727788

Windows

CMC Reimo, (see Adhesives)
CAK (see Water Tanks)

Other Specialist Suppliers

Därr's Travel Shop, Theresienstrasse 66, 8000 München 2, Germany. Tel 089 282032
Bernd Woick, Gutenbergstr.14, 73760 Ostfildern, Germany. Tel 0711 455038

An awning is a most attractive feature offering the comfort of outdoor shade.

The awning at full extension.

INDEX

D

Q